Advertising in Modern and Postmodern Times

Theory, Culture & Society

Theory, Culture & Society caters for the resurgence of interest in culture within contemporary social science and the humanities. Building on the heritage of classical social theory, the book series examines ways in which this tradition has been reshaped by a new generation of theorists. It also publishes theoretically informed analyses of everyday life, popular culture, and new intellectual movements.

EDITOR: Mike Featherstone, *Nottingham Trent University*

THE TCS CENTRE
The Theory, Culture & Society book series, the journals *Theory, Culture & Society* and *Body & Society*, and related conference, seminar and postgraduate programmes operate from the TCS Centre at Nottingham Trent University. For further details of the TCS Centre's activities please contact:

Centre Administrator
The TCS Centre, Room 175
Faculty of Humanities
Nottingham Trent University
Clifton Lane, Nottingham, NG11 8NS, UK
e-mail: tcs@ntu.ac.uk
web: http://tcs.ntu.ac.uk

Recent volumes include:

The Body and Social Theory
Chris Shilling

Religion, Realism and Social Theory
Phillip A. Mellor

The Body in Culture, Technology and Society
Chris Shilling

Globalization and Belonging
Savage, Bagnall and Longhurst

Advertising in Modern and Postmodern Times

Pamela Odih

SAGE Publications
Los Angeles ▪ London ▪ New Delhi ▪ Singapore

First published 2007

 SAGE Publications Ltd
1 Oliver's Yard
55 City Road
London EC1Y 1SP

SAGE Publications Inc.
2455 Teller Road
Thousand Oaks, California 91320

SAGE Publications India Pvt Ltd
B 1/I 1 Mohan Cooperative Industrial Area
Mathura Road, New Delhi 110 044
India

SAGE Publications Asia-Pacific Pte Ltd
33 Pekin Street #02-01
Far East Square
Singapore 048763

British Library Cataloguing in Publication data

A catalogue record for this book is available
from the British Library

ISBN 978-0-7619-4190-3

Library of Congress control number available

Typeset by C&M Digital (P) Ltd., Chennai, India
Printed on paper from sustainable resources

This book is dedicated to my mother Mary, with love.

Contents

Acknowledgements   ix

Introduction: The Cultural Economy of Time in Modern
and Postmodern Advertising   1

Part I   Marking Time in the Making of Modern Advertising   **21**

1   Selling Space in Advertising History   23

2   Selling Time in Advertising History   50

Part II   Dialectics of Advertising in Modern Times   **75**

3   Advertising, Time and the Commodity-Form   77

4   Time and the Commodity-Sign   105

Part III   Advertising in Postmodern Time(s)   **143**

5   'The Times, They Are A-Changin'': Transformations of Work
and Leisure in the Time/Space Economies of Modern
and Postmodern Advertising   145

6   Mapping the Subject of Postmodern Advertising Technology   171

7   Sign of the Times: Postmodern Disruptions in
Advertising Times   187

Conclusion: Globalization and the Future
of Advertising   207

Bibliography   212

Index   223

Acknowledgements

I would like to express a heartfelt thank you to Professor David Knights who supervised my doctorate and has continued to inspire and mentor my academic development. Professor Barbara Adam's prolific contribution to the study of time and society has been inspirational and I would like to pay tribute to her work.

My colleagues at Goldsmiths University, Professor Celia Lury, Professor Bev Skeggs, Dr Brian Alleyne, and Doreen Norman have been particularly supportive. I would like to thank Professor Chris Rojek for encouraging my initial book proposal. Susan Dunsmore's editorial assistance is much appreciated. And big thank you to my close companions, Simon Meats, Andrea Salmon and Senol Ali.

Figure acknowledgements

Cover: O2 Happy Hour. Reproduced by permission of O2, Ashton Keiditsch (photographer) and with the assistance of Matthew Bundy (Account Executive, VCCP ad agency)

Figure I.1 'Time present and time past': Rover advertisement, 1949. The Rover Company Ltd, Solihull, Birminsham House, London, 1949. Reproduced by permission of Nanjing Automobile (Group) Corporation Limited and Rover Library Club. www.rovercarclubaust.asn.au/photos5.htm

Figure I.2 'Time flies. It also drives', Ford GT, 2003. Reproduced by permission of the Ford Motor Company Limited

Part I: Commodity culture of Victorian England, 1880. Reproduced by permission of The Edinburgh Room, Central Library, George IV Bridge, Edinburgh © and reproduced with acknowledgement to Peter Stubbs, www.edinphoto.org.uk

Figure 1.1 A man pasting up a poster. William Henry Pyne, London, 1808. Reproduced by permission of the British Library, shelf mark 143.g.2

Figure 1.2 'Modern advertising': a railway station in 1874, Ocean Railway and General Accident Assurance Co. Limited. Reproduced by permission of the British Library, shelf mark 2350.a.9

Figure 1.3 'Taken in and done for', 1865. Spellman Collection of Victorian Music Covers. Reproduced by kind permission of Reading University Library.

Figure 1.4 Royal Agricultural Hall World's Fair. Henry Evanion, 1880. Reproduced by permission of the British Library, Shelf mark c4214-01.

Figure 1.5 Victorian imperialist advertising aesthetic. Reproduced by permission of British Empire. (www.britishempire.co.uk/images)

Figure 1.6 Farini's Earthmen. Henry Evanion, London, 1885. Reproduced by permission of The British Library, shelf mark EVAN.265.

Figure 1.7 Empire Marketing Board Poster, 'Highways of Empire', 1927. Artist: MacDonald Gill. Reproduced by permission of the National Archive. Image reference CO 956/537 A.

Figure 1.8 Empire Marketing Board Poster, 'Tobacco plantation in S. Rhodesia' Artist: Frank E. Page. Reproduced by permission of the National Archive. Image reference CO 956/90

Figure 1.9 Empire Marketing Board Poster, 'Our trade with the East'. Artist: Kenneth D. Shoesmith. Reproduced by permission of The National Archive. Image reference CO 956/13

Figure 2.1 Prudential Insurance advertisement, 1960s. Reproduced by permission of Prudential PLC

Figure 2.2 Lottery dividends. H. Sampson (1857) *History of Advertising*, p. 455. London: Chatto and Windus

Figure 2.3 Lottery insurance advertising post-1778 Regulatory Act. H. Sampson (1857) *History of Advertising*, pp. 460–61. London: Chatto and Windus

Figure 2.4 Lottery insurance advertising puffery. H. Sampson (1857) *History of Advertising*, p. 463. London: Chatto and Windus

Figure 2.5 Image used for the Prudential Mutual Assurance Company seal in 1848. Reproduced by permission of Prudential PLC

Figure 2.6 Re-branding insurance in the Gilded Age, North British and Mercantile Insurance Company LTD, 1809–1959. Reproduced with acknowledgement to Peter Stubbs, www.edinphoto.org.uk

Part II: Utility, style and the commodity-sign. Reproduced by courtesy of Whirlpool and Tessa Traeger (photographer)

Figure 3.1 Reason-why advertising and the utility of time, AGA Cooker advert, 1932. Reproduced by permission of AGA. Image courtesy of the Advertising Archives

Figure 3.2 'Welcome to a new world! of driving!' US magazine advertisement, 1950s. Image courtesy of the Advertising Archives

Figure 4.1 Ideal Motherhood and the sign-value of a spotless wash, Surf advert, 1950s. Reproduced by permission of Unilever. Image courtesy of the Advertising Archive

Figure 4.2 The return of the present moment, Canon advert, 2005. Reproduced by permission of Canon (UK) Ltd

Figure 4.3 'You never actually own a Patek Philippe. You merely look after it for the next generation', Patek Philippe, 2006. Reproduced by permission of Patek Philippe

Figure 4.4 'It's your watch that says most about who you are', SEIKO, 2005. Reproduced by permission of SEIKO UK Ltd

Figure 4.5 Capture every moment', Olympus, 2005. Advert owned and produced for Olympus Europa GmbH. Reproduced by permission of Olympus.

Figure 4.6 Engendering time and domestic labour, Addis advert, 1950s. Reproduced by kind permission of Addis Housewares Ltd. Image courtesy of the Advertising Archive

Part III Advertising and time (space) disruptions in postmodern virtual worlds, Toshiba, 2005. Reproduced by permission of Toshiba

Figure 5.1 Utility and leisure in car advertising, Chrysler, 1960. Copyright DaimlerChrysler Corporation. Reproduced with permission

Figure 5.2 Reproduced *The Ford Times*, August 1926. Ford Motor Company Limited. Peter Roberts, *Any Colour as Long as it's Black*, David & Charles, 1976, by kind permission of the publishers, London: Reproduced with kind permission of Ford Motor Company Limited

Figure 5.3 Armstrong-Siddeley Sapphire, 1955 © The British Motor Industry Heritage Trust

Figure 5.4 'Work hard. Be successful. Go Someplace where none of that matters', Range Rover, 2001. Courtesy of Land Rover

Figure 6.1 Advertising and modern technologies of power, Business Insights, 2005. Reproduced by permission of Business Insights Inc.

Figure 6.2 SMART 2005 Segmentation. Reproduced by permission of Strategic Marketing and Research Techniques®, www.S-M-A-R-T.com

Figure 6.3 TargetPro GIS, MapInfo, 2005. Reproduced by permission of MapInfo Ltd

Figure 6.4 Women's Plan 1997. Reproduced by permission of AXA PPP Healthcare

Figure 7.1 'Like time, I wait pour non homme', FCUK, 2006. Reproduced by permission of FCUK

Figure 7.2 Pastiche in postmodern advertisements, Sheila's Wheels, 2005. Reproduced under licence © 2005 Esure Services Limited.

Figure 7.3 Multiphrenic intensity of postmodern signs, Harvey Nichols, 2005. Reproduced by permission of Harvey Nichols

Figure 7.4 'Waste time, faster', Siemens S45, 2006 (C). Reproduced by permission of BenQ Mobile UK.

Introduction

The cultural economy of time in modern and postmodern advertising

Time present and time past
Are both perhaps present in time future,
And time future contained in time past.

T.S. Eliot's poetic contemplation provides an apposite beginning to a chronicle of advertising in modern and postmodern time. Eliot's poetry evokes simultaneity as the aesthetic form of time. To this extent, Eliot was concerned with the intersections between moments and the complexity of an instant. Advertising imagery also excites liminal moments, which intersect private and public with the immediacy of experience. The event epitomized in Figure I.1 is neither static nor derived from a historical imagination. Rather, we are encouraged to observe a fractured moment, a shifting dialogue between class and status. The hallmark of the motor car is its exclusivity as an expensive and novel commodity. The effect of juxtaposing quintessential rural aristocracy with urban commercialism captures the symbolic dimension of the motor car as a prestigious aspirational object. Indeed, the text of the advertisement is replete with narrational devices intent on generating a seamless blend of mass-produced functionality with the refined quintessence of style. The first line of the advertisement's text states, 'No one who drives the Rover Sixty or Seventy-Five for the first time can easily forget the experience'. This desire to integrate the streamline functionality of the mass-produced motor car with the imaginative aspiration of prestige effects a triumph of advertising's capacity to transform time into an object of economic exchange. Indeed, an integral feature of capitalist accumulation is the ability of advertising to constitute a cultural economy of time.

Modern advertising emanated from a systemic conjuncture in Western capitalism (Goldman, 1994: 190). Of specific relevance is the dialectical transition from industrial capitalism to oligopoly and monopoly capitalism at the end of the nineteenth century. Industrial capitalism is a mode of production based on the expropriation of relative surplus value, which in turn is made possible by the technical concentration of capital. The progressive accumulation of value had historically fostered the rising technical composition of capital, which generated labour-saving technology. But the diffusion of industrial technology was increasing 'constant capital at the expense of variable' (Graham, 2000: 135). By the end of the nineteenth century, capital investment was perilously

No one who drives the Rover Sixty or Seventy Five for the first time can easily forget the experience. Here are all the traditional smoothness and refinements so long associated with Rover cars, plus a new responsiveness which gives a fresh meaning to the words "One of Britain's Fine Cars." Yet despite their brilliant performance and remarkable flexibility these new Rover engines demand less fuel than their predecessors. Such is the result of high quality design.

ROVER

One of Britain's Fine Cars

THE ROVER COMPANY LTD., SOLIHULL, BIRMINGHAM AND DEVONSHIRE HOUSE, LONDON

Figure I.1 *'Time present and time past': Rover advertisement, 1949*

Source: The Rover Company Ltd, Solihull, Birmingham, House, London. Reproduced by permission of Nanjing Automobile (group) Corporation Limited and Rover Library Club. www.rovercarclubaust.asn.au/photos5.htm

concentrated in the sphere of production (Pope, 1983). This meant that indus-trialists were investing much of their resources in machinery and in finished products in anticipation of consumer demand. However, fixed capital has an inert materiality as it is the result of a 'past poiesis' involving the expropriation of surplus labour time (Gorz, 1989: 52). Karl Marx stated, that the magnitude of value possessed by each commodity is determined by the quantity of socially necessary labour time required to produce it. Consequently, an increased investment in fixed capital, relative to 'living labour', precipitated the transition towards a disaccumulation stage of capitalist formation (Goldman, 1995). To maintain capitalist expansion, the circulation rates of capital had to be controlled at levels that maximized the realization of commodity value. Thus, capital-intensive and maturing industries faced a formidable challenge in their endeavours to abate the declining rate of profit. It is these broader economic and social trends that partly explain the large-scale reorganization of industrial ownership after the Great Depression (1875–1890s) and the heightened commercial concern to 'control the market' (Williams, 1980: 176). The disjuncture between the productive capacities of capital and market demand threatened the key variable of time, and the expropriation of surplus labour time as a source of profit. The value of labour is represented by time, and commodity relations between people are themselves an expression of time (Heydebrand, 2003). The operation of the capitalist mode of production inevitably objectifies commodities so that we misrecognize labour time as a source of value. By the end of the nineteenth century, the penetration of the commodity-form into the labour force meant that workers had neither the skill nor the time for domestic production (Goldman, 1994). Time has become a commodity and the worker is obliged to pay for the retrieval of leisure time (Wearing and Wearing, 1992: 5). These observations on time and production locate the emergence of modern advertising within the context of capitalist exploitation. Advertising materialized as a specialized vehicle for extending the commodity-form and, in so doing, reproducing the expropriation of surplus labour time at the level of consumption. This book examines how advertising's past continues to shape its present. Advertising is an intrinsic dialectical link between capitalism's economic rationalization of time and the production of consumer subjectivity. Consequently, an analysis of advertising and modernity goes a long way towards tracing the mobile systems of relationships, which have been effective in disciplining our relation to the temporal rhythms of the productive economy.

Modernity pronounced a universal history that would be all-inclusive. The past was a historical artefact constituted by a system of delineated, homogeneous relations, which exhibit predictable patterns of transformation. Each present has a discrete presence and it is presumed that it can be represented as such. Modernity is about managing both time and space 'at a distance' through a process of representation. That is to say, an uncertain future is represented as a concrete set of probabilities to which monetary values can be attributed. Time and space are then represented as objects of remote control where future possible events are displaced or (re)presented in an abbreviated and thereby managerial form (Cooper and Law, 1995). Fordist production epitomized the ordering of bodies in time and space, according to expertly designed managerial systems. In this mode of capitalist production, time is a unit for regulating daily activities in accordance with the clockwork rhythms of standardized assembly line production. Fordism pioneered the introduction of time and motion studies into the wholesale rationalization of labour. It fostered national aspirations to regulate the economy by embedding mass production and mass demand into national frames (Fraser, 2003: 161). These imperatives required a level of technical, organizational and cultural restructuring defined as a regime of accumulation. The Fordist regime of accumulation was premised on large-scale mass production carried out by vertically integrated organizations geared towards meeting the 'needs' of mass consumer markets. Axiomatic to this regime of accumulation is the existence of non-economic processes operating to synchronize and co-ordinate social, cultural and political relations. Advertising operates here as a mechanism for standardizing the rhythms of consumer demand. The vast size of Fordist production created a new kind of organizational complexity, which forced businesses into the limited role of anticipating and creating mass consumer markets. Needless to say, Fordist production required long lead times to research and develop new products, given the rigidity of its production systems and the confined specialization of the labour force (Gorz, 1999: 28). Consumer demand, adumbrated through mass advertising, countenanced the long time scales of mass production. But advertising was also a source of in-built rigidity as experts linked advancing prosperity with the production of 'a homogeneous society of loyal steady buyers' (Pope, 1983: 258). Nevertheless, advertising constitutes an important area of continuity between the end of Fordist growth in the 1970s and the transition to flexible specialization and post-Fordism. Towards the end of Fordist mass production, most companies were attempting to abate stagnation either by diversification or by accelerating product turnover and thereby increasing built-in obsolescence (Gorz, 1999: 27). Developments in advertising research responded to both these crucial changes in the needs of modern corporations. Advertising had become an integral feature of the marketing mix. And as a core component of marketing orthodoxy, advertising was committed to the use of market research as the basis of design and media decisions. This partly explains the perfusion of lifestyle market segmentation during the 1980s, the demassification of consumer markets and the timely proliferation of advertising channels.

Post-Fordist capitalist production is insidiously distinct from its historical predecessors. Unlike 'organized capitalism' with its synchronous flows of capital and labour circulating on a national scale, contemporary capitalism is 'disorganized' (Lash and Urry, 1994). Fragmented, flexible production and networks of financial flows now circulate on an international scale. Harvey (1990) defines post-Fordism as involving a transition from Fordism to 'flexible accumulation', which accelerated the rise of flexible labour markets and flexible geographies of production. Piore and Sabel (1984) identify rapidly fragmenting consumer markets, coupled with advances in flexible technologies (e.g., Computer Aided Manufacturing), as enabling the spread of low-cost, semi-customized commodities. Piore and Sabel argue these transformations in production are evidence of a new post-Fordist technological paradigm defined as 'flexible specialization', whereby, flexible technologies and economies of scale enable firms to 'respond to the growth of flexible markets' (Amin, 1995: 15).

Under Fordist production, labour is considered to be a factor in the production of material commodities, which are themselves recognized as embodying specific use-value. Indeed, 'all commodities are only definite masses of congealed labour time' (*Capital*, vol. 1, 2003: 47). Advertising operates in Fordist production to reproduce the incorporation of labour time into capital. Conversely, in post-Fordist production, an accelerated circulation of objects is 'the stuff of consumer capitalism' (Lash and Urry, 1994: 2–3), whereby, a depletion of meaning precipitated by rapid turnover rates ensures a 'homogenization, abstraction, anomie and the destruction of the subject' (ibid.: 3). The Fordist separation of economy and culture invited consumers to constitute their identities through the purchase of products whose stories and images echo historically specific grand narratives (Firat, 1994). By contrast, the consumers of postmodernity transcend these narratives of self and subjectivity. For we are now entering an era 'in which the production of objects has been replaced by the production and proliferation of signs' (Sarup, 1998: 110). Our attention is drawn here to an inter-subjective movement away from regarding goods merely as utilities having a use and exchange-value. Postmodern consumer culture is a rich and complex signifying system in which cultural objects acquire new levels of fascination. Rather than being related to some fixed system of human needs, exchange involves the consumption of signs (Baudrillard, 1975, 1981) that are 'free floating' – not tied to an object of signification but simply circulating in a space of signifiers. For Baudrillard (1975), a central feature of commodity culture is that the object is no longer determined by the existence of an 'essential' use-value. The pervasion of exchange-value in capitalist society has resulted in the commodity becoming a sign. In line with Saussurean semiotics, this understanding of representation exceeds the reductive notion of the sign as indexed to a real and independent reality. 'The object-become-sign no longer gathers its meaning in the concrete relationship between two people' (1981: 66). Rather the relations between sign and referent are completely arbitrary. The sign obtains its meaning through its 'differential relation to other signs' (ibid.: 66). Think of the trademark 'swoosh' insignia of Nike. The logo is prominent as a self-referential sign. It has little direct reference to the material world. Indeed, Nike creatives employ 'concept-based' advertising, which entails generating an atmosphere and associating the brand with that mood (Proctor et al., 2002: 33). In this process of 'image transfer', non-linguistic meanings and the rapid succession of images replace the more traditional use of narrative dialogues, placing the 'commodity in the consumer's everyday life' (ibid.: 33). Instead the aesthetic appeal of the postmodern sign is 'determined by its position in a self-referential system of [floating] signifiers' (Featherstone, 1991: 85). In postmodern consumer culture, signs are entirely self-referential, making no attempt at signification or classification, their only point being to make a temporary impact on our consciousness. This detached status of the code obviates any relation to the 'real' and opens up what Baudrillard has famously designated as 'hyper-reality', i.e., 'the generation of models of the real without origin or reality' (1983: 2).

Advertising in the current era lives on the playful and self-reflexive nature of postmodern culture. Advertisers are constantly involved in complex processes of meaning transfer, whereby commodities come to be imbued with cultural meanings only arbitrarily linked to the referent that they originally signified (Firat, 1994). Advertisers attach signifiers to disparate objects and just as rapidly detach them, in the mischievous pursuit of novelty and difference. In the hyper-real world of postmodern advertising, everything mutates into everything else, all is image, appearance and simulation. Axiomatic to these transformations in the temporality of advertising aesthetics is the 'convergence' of advertising channels and their proliferation into the diaphanous streams of new electronic media.

What is emerging in postmodern advertising is a new type of capitalist accumulation involving multi-layered temporalities, as opposed to the continuous linear tempo-spatial frames of previous regimes of capitalist accumulation. Liberated from the linear rationalist boundaries of 'organized capitalism', flows of capital, information, images and symbols are overwhelming linear rationalities by 'disordering the sequence of events and making them simultaneous, thus installing society in eternal ephemerality' (Castells, 2000: 467). There is little doubt that advances in global electronic communications involve a more intense compression of time and space than we have ever previously experienced. In the micro-electronic world of virtual communication, time has to be seen much more as tied to the social context of its use rather than as an unproblematic medium whose neutrality permits comparison and communication across diverse boundaries. For these very boundaries are in disarray as we begin to realize that every communication is a prosthesis or projection of a unique identity (Burrill, 2005). Instantaneous communication and consumption mean that we no longer experience a common time 'in' which we all live in more or less mutual relevance, but, on the contrary, events in convergent electronic media are simultaneously global and local, representing a unique and unrepeatable period of time (Adam, 1990; Ermarth, 1992). Indeed, Baudrillard identifies hyper-reality as ensuing dramatic discontinuities in the contextual link between the subject and its specific world. In the 'third order of representation', technologies gain their own momentum, providing a simulacrum of actual events effacing any access to a 'real', which itself is an effect of the code system (Sarup, 1998: 111).

Time in postmodern advertising is a function of position, as a dimension of particular self-referential events, time is fractured, multiple and discontinuous. Moreover, the search for an authentic, integrated self through identification is displaced, disrupted and fragmented by the 'pure' sign that resides within a self-referential tempo-spatial context and almost coincidentally collides with 'products' (which are themselves mere signs). This book argues that advertising in the postmodern times is productive of radically new forms of consumer subjectivity only tangentially recognised in the texts of leading cultural theorists. The three parts, which constitute this book, collectively present a historical overview of the way in which advertising has developed and the cultural economies of time that have informed changes in the nature of advertising.

Part I Marking time in the making of modern advertising

Part I of this book provides a historical account of the dialectical link between industrial capitalism and the economies of time and space which led to the emergence of large-scale advertising in the nineteenth century. Chapter 1, 'Selling space in Advertising History' critically examines legislative measures geared towards the regulation of commercial spaces in the nineteenth century. Familiar examples of these processes are described; these include legal regulations deployed to control street advertising, legislative controls on the selling of advertising space in the printed press, and editorial controls on display advertising. The chapter also critically examines the selling of the British Empire in Victorian commodity culture. The chapter argues that the selling of the Empire responded to a crisis in capitalist accumulation and industrial capitalism's subsequent need to extend the commodity-form. Post-colonial analyses of Victorian commodity culture reveal a distinct colonial sentimentality evident in nineteenth-century advertisements, of the Empire and its 'Others'. This chapter argues that the rationalization of commercial space in the selling of the Empire was an integral development in the formation of monopoly capitalism.

Chapter 2, 'Selling Time in Advertising History' continues with a historical theme, as it focuses on advertising with respect to the emergence of insurance as a morally accepted commercial enterprise. The mid-nineteenth century is generally recognised as constituting the Golden Era of insurance. It was the time when the selling of insurance transformed itself from a practice of ill repute with unsavoury links with gambling, into a reputable moral enterprise. Advertising ingenuity played a crucial role in the fortuitous transformation of the insurance industry in the nineteenth century. Insuring oneself from future hazard was transformed from mere speculative folly into a morally responsible task. Advertising promotion is largely accredited with having engineered a turnaround in the image of the insurance industry. In so doing, advertising represented a vital component of disciplinary technologies keen to make links between the buying of insurance and the adoption, by individual subjects, of a responsible attitude to the future. Insurance was transformed into a moral imperative and advertising was a key instrument in the creation of subjects disciplined in the moral efficacy of financially managing their future. Chapters 1 and 2 provide the reader with a historical introduction to the crucial links between advertising, early capitalism and the establishment of time-disciplined consumer subjectivity.

Part II Dialectics of advertising in modern times

Chapter 3, 'Advertising, Time and the Commodity-form', examines the work of Marxist theorists who have identified modern advertising as having emerged as a response to specific historical crises in the reproduction of exchange-value (Ewen, 1977; Lee, 1993; Goldman, 1994). These authors observe how advertising was used by capitalist industrialists, as a means of establishing time-disciplined social relations and control over the labour process.

Ever since the emergence of institutionalized advertising in the late nineteenth century, advertising practitioners have been concerned to establish an orthodox rational discipline (Leiss et al., 1990). In the early part of the twentieth century, the attempt to achieve rational orthodoxy in advertising knowledge was largely a consequence of market saturation, and the need to formulate theories of consumer behaviour, so as to guarantee the efficient application of advertising practice. The persuasive possibilities of advertising soon became a site of expertise and this in turn coincided with the emergence of psychology as a scientific discipline (Ewen, 1977; Leiss et al., 1990). One of the earliest attempts to formulate a systematic scientific examination of advertising was made by Professor Walter Dill Scott in his ground-breaking œuvre, *The Psychology of Advertising* (1908). Walter Dill Scott's discourse epitomized the 'reason-why' approach which pervaded advertising practice in the early part of the twentieth century. The reason-why approach attempted to motivate consumer behaviour by constructing a reasoned argument to justify the purchase of a commodity. The pervasive appeal of reason-why advertising, was largely a consequence of the imperatives of national advertisers to generate demands for a burgeoning array of new commodities (Leiss et al., 1990). In both Britain and the United States, advances in the productive capacities of factories had precipitated the introduction of a wide range of newly available products. The greater quantity and variety of commodities resulted in the need for manufacturers to distinguish their products through brand differentiation. In this marketing model, manufacturers of branded products sought not only to attract consumers but also to communicate the firm's label. In response, advertisements assumed a persuasive educational style designed to inform consumers of the merits of the product (ibid.).

Advertising copy in reason-why advertising focuses on the written text and the use of images as part of the process of conveying practical information about the product. The operative model of consumer subjectivity evident in this approach is fundamentally rationalistic, in the sense that the advertiser endeavours to provide the utility-maximizing consumer with a clear motivation for using a product. To achieve this, advertising phenomena within the social world must be amenable to causal analysis involving their reduction to a set of quantifiable variables similar to those of the natural sciences. The social world is assumed to exist independently of the observer, although made knowable only through sense perception of social action and events. It is axiomatic to rationalistic consumer behaviour models that time and space should be ascribed the characteristics of abstract, quantifiable, singular units.

In time–space relations, reason-why advertising stimuli take the form of a trajectory within which the future arises out of the present context, and preceding conditions form a history relative to the advertising event. The basis of this determination can only be reckoned by a conception of time which reduces the present to a negligible element in the teleological ordering of the passage of time. Resonances between this conception of time and the mechanistic rhythms of the productive economy efficaciously coincided with the need to sell standardized products to mass markets. The manufacturing quest, to accurately time production operations, had been largely realized in the 'scientific management' techniques of Fordist production but the ultimate breakthrough in the manufacturing dream of productive efficiency was contingent on matching the productive process with consumer demand. Accelerated rates of production had speeded up the circulation of goods to consumers, and existing distribution channels struggled to contend with increased rates of production. Access to mass markets was an advertising imperative and there was no room for complex differences in the location of individuals in time and space. Advertisers had to attract the attention of consumers, arouse desire and transform these into buying instances. Moreover, they had to perfectly perform these grandiose tasks wholesale, so as to appeal to a mass market of hundreds of thousands (Pope, 1983: 249). In order to achieve this inordinate task, advertisers needed to become familiar with the behaviour of consumers. Consequently, the minutia of daily experience necessitated delineation into calculable terrains for the application of advertising technology. Even in the privacy of the home, consumers had to be conceived of as operating according to determinable factors within a predictable and calculable flow of time. Reason-why advertising provided a means of mapping consumer subjectivity in accordance with the clockwork precision of the productive machine.

The rise of oligopolistic industries, producing differentiated goods, increased the popularity of an advertising model predicated on identifying the distinctive characteristics of a product and promoting its superiority. Reason-why advertising provided a clockwork operational technique for stimulating desire and this was particularly evident in the sale of mass-produced household appliances. Pope (1983: 36) provides an account of how home appliances such as vacuum cleaners, modern cookers and washing machines tended to substitute capital for household labour. Advances in domestic equipment were indeed labour-saving as they reduced the amount of time required to complete a domestic task. In the early twentieth century, the home had become a privileged site for the individual consumption of mass-produced commodities (Lee, 1993). As Andrejevic observes, 'Each household served as the repository for a private set of appliances that displaced or replaced forms of collective consumption: The automobile displaced the trolley, the radio the concert hall, the TV set the downtown movie theatre and so on' (2003: 133). The physical demarcation of private space, provided by the small family unit, enabled the translation of mass-produced domestic appliances into devices which promised to increase an individual's discretionary use of time. In this rational utility model, consumption is designated to occur within a given tempo-spatial context. It is only in this sense that predicative correlations can be made between time-saving and consumer behaviour. Rational advertising knowledges fasten upon that necessary conditioning of a determinant space and determinable time, as a basis from which to claim the certainty of deduction. Indeed, the standardized features and unitary scale of the family unit provided an effective context in which an increase in the discretionary use of domestic labour time could be communicated to consumer markets (Lee, 1993). In the early twentieth century, reason-why advertising campaigns drew heavily on the labour-saving themes of new consumer durables in their efforts to offer mass-produced products to an increasingly urbanized consumer market.

Changing the subject: psychodynamic times and the mobilization of consumer subjectivity (1950s–1960s)

During the 1950s there continued to be an intimate connection, both institutionally and intellectually, between advertising and psychology. Psychologists at that time were raising intellectual questions which mirrored advertising's concern to gain scientific knowledge of decision-making in order to predict buyer behaviour. The psychological disposition of the consumer became an integral feature of commercial discourse. And advertising was keen to adopt psychology's accrescent constructions of human behaviour. With the advent of Freudian analysis, the intellectual field of psychology increasingly began to articulate challenges to the rational psychic operator (a *homo economicus*) and this would have a profound effect on the legitimacy of reason-why advertising.

Advertising practices in the early twentieth century were designed to attract the attention of an undifferentiated consumer market. The cost advantage of mass Fordist production yielded high dividends for companies, but profits were predicated on the use of inexpensive distribution systems (Pope, 1983). This was a key reason why products were advertised in accordance with their broad utility appeal to a mass consumer market. Since production technology dictated a standardized output, appeals to a homogeneous consumer market appeared apposite (ibid.: 260). Paradigmatic transformations in advertising psychology radically challenged the discursive assumption of mass advertising and the notion of an undifferentiated consumer market. Psychological theories of personality claimed the existence of systematic and stable patterns, which categorized groupings of individuals according to determinative personality traits. Trait factor theory propounded the existence of enduring and distinguishable attributes, which, while common to many individuals, vary in absolute amounts, as and between individuals (Gunter and Furnham, 1992: 45). It follows from this assumption that humans are highly distinguishable. Consequently, psychological enquiries at this time were dispelling the notion of a 'single type' of consumer and the existence of an undifferentiated audience for advertising communication (Leiss et al., 1990).

The concept of personality traits combined with the widespread belief that behaviour was the outcome of motives and instinctive drives. Freud's highly influential theories concerning the ego (the basis of consciousness) and the id (the basis of the subconscious) emphasized the significance of symbolic and unconscious motivations to the formation of subjectivity. The human psyche involves a constant struggle to balance the desire for immediate gratification with the need to apprehend social convention and adhere to the normative order. This Freudian model was further developed by behavioural scientists, so as to formulate links between the human psyche and observed behaviour. Human behaviour was seen as a result of unconscious efforts to control inner drives and instincts motivated by petty emotions, sexual desire and anxiety. Advertising readily embraced this development in psychodynamic discourse and eagerly placed irrationality at the heart of consumer behaviour. Individuals were conceived of as differentiating from one another on the basis of the unconscious nature of personality and motivation. And 'buyers are motivated by symbolic as well as economic-functional product concerns' (Michman, 1991: 22). Armed with an exciting array of psychodynamic apparatus (e.g., projective techniques), advertising practitioners attempted to penetrate the consumer's inner world of fantasy and dynamic processes.

Rather than manipulating consumers, as was the fear of government officials, advertisers 'mobilized' consumers (Miller and Rose, 1997) to explore connections between commodities and the structuring of experience in time. Advertising experts were aware of the criticism of brainwashing and countenanced these accusations by preaching that 'consumer choices' were dictating economic activity (Pope, 1983: 251). They claimed to persuade rather than compel consumers and proclaimed this to be 'the democratic alternative to authoritarianism' (ibid.: 251). Consumers were viewed as a complex ensemble of impulsive and irrational traits; less inclined to manipulation than persuasion. The use of dream sequences and appeals to the suppressed or repressed desire were indicative features of psychodynamic advertising aesthetics. In this era of advertising practice, the consumer is enticed 'to focus less on rational product information and more on the feelings evoked by their recollected memories' (Braun et al., 2002: 2). Because consumers use advertising as cues to recollect their past experience, it follows that 'autobiographical memories may be spontaneously activated within the context of an advertising message' (ibid.: 2). This psychodynamic account of advertising practice is particularly significant as it is indicative of how the technologies of advertising are productive of 'new kinds of relations that human beings can have with themselves and with others through the medium of goods' (Miller and Rose, 1997: 3). Advertising is indeed a major site of ideological influence in the dynamic production of consumer subjectivity. Psychodynamic discourse is productive in its endeavours to know the human psyche. The intervention of psychodynamic technologies into the depths of human consciousness is constitutive of knowledge. In the absence of projective tests, advertisers would struggle to support the claim that consumers differ from each other, according to determinative psychological traits. However, knowledge produces both regimes of truth and subjugation (Foucault, 1982a). Advertising's knowledge of the consumer psyche has a powerful constitutive effect that is realized in the micro-practices of daily life. Psychodynamic knowledge mobilizes consumers to identify with consumption as a potential means of gaining self-understanding. Consequently, the intrusion of advertising technology into the realm of human psyche, and the appropriation of memory as a constituent feature of buying, function to link subjectivity ever more closely to commercial objectives.

Chapter 3 argues that advertising's preoccupation with use-value and then psychodynamic discourse in the early twentieth century operated to connect consumer subjectivity to the clockwork rhythms of the productive economy. The Marxist analysis of time and commodity culture identifies advertising as directly implicated in capitalist accumulation (Ewen, 1977; Lee, 1993; Frow, 1997; Williamson, 2000). Marx established the value of a commodity to be defined in its magnitude by the amount of socially necessary labour time invested in its production. It is labour time which produces value. Embodied in the commodity is the abstract unit of socially necessary labour required to produce it. This represents a source of profit in addition to any that may be made from the 'exploitation' of labour. But labour, in its identification with advertising communication, misrecognizes its basis as a source of value. Consequently, advertising operates to reproduce the expropriation of surplus labour time at the level of consumption.

Marxist analysis provides a valuable means of theoretically engaging with the peculiar mix of rationalism and psychodynamics that characterized advertising discourse in the early twentieth century. If a commodity can be shown to yield a utility, then the labour time invested in its production and time required for its consumption can clearly be communicated to the consumer. In reason-why advertising, time is transformed into objects that exist external to the individual, in fixed immutable units (hours/minutes/seconds). These units in turn yield an implicit utility to the consumer (e.g., being able to save time). The implicit utility facilitates the transformation of time and spaces into other entities such as money or products. It is therefore of no surprise that the clockwork precision of this commodification of time encouraged its application to a wide variety of buying instances. Time is a controllable scarce resource: a 'pressure' in decision-making; an exchangeable commodity; and of course a principle component of 'risk'. Similar translations of time into money are in effect in psychodynamic advertising discourse. Chapter 3 identifies how time was axiomatic to the development of advertising psychology, especially with respect to the use of psychodynamic models of consumers and the endorsement of 'pecuniary emulation' (Veblen, [1899] 1994).

Lifestyle segmentation and the timely proliferation of advertising discourse (1960s–1980s)

During the 1960s, advertising practice expanded rapidly alongside the multi-media conditions of consumer culture. Electronic media brought into

Figure I.2 *'Time flies. It also drives', Ford GT, 2003*

Source: Reproduced by permission of the Ford Motor Company Limited

being new powers of persuasion far exceeding the static images of the printed text. Sound and motion dramatically enhanced the display aspects of advertising. And creative enterprise increasingly revolved around the production of commodity aesthetics. Display rather than utility became the all-important Unique Selling Point (USP), as advertisers endeavoured to associate commodities with a wealth of symbolic meanings expropriated from the cultural knowledge of consumers. This transition in advertising discourse signalled a second wave of advertising which regarded the focus on functional utility as a 'crude form of consumer propaganda' (Lee, 1993: 151). This second generation of advertising expertise emphasized the symbolic properties of products. Advertisers were increasingly less inclined to promote commodities as embodying fixed meanings determined by a recognizable use-value (Goldman, 1995: 18). Nor were commodities merely defined by their financial value. This era of advertising expertise witnessed the genius of a new level of meaning defined as the 'commodity-sign' (ibid.: 18). The advertisement in Figure I.2 exemplifies advertising's ingenuity in the production of commodities as signs.

Encouraged by the growth of visual culture, advertisers introduced storyline dialogues into their campaigns. Television permits the advertising of commodities to be woven into vignettes of everyday life. Dramatized commercial vignettes provide an accessible way of staging the demonstration of products, as well as enabling advertisers to draw upon a wide range of cultural reference systems (Leiss et al., 1990). David Ogilvy's now famous exposition, *Confessions of an Advertising Man* (1965), provides additional historical insights into the rise of commodity aesthetic in advertising culture. In a chapter dedicated to television commercials, he states: 'In the early days of television, I made the mistake of relying on words to do the selling ... I now know that in television you must make your pictures tell the story; what you show is more important than what you say' (1965: 130). Suffice to say, the growth of electronic media has been a crucial factor in contemporary advertising's spectacular progress in the attribution of symbolic value to commodities.

Chapter 4 historically examines the progression from use-value to sign-value in modem advertising discourse and practice. The transition to monopoly capitalism in 1900 witnessed a systemic transformation in capitalist accumulation from a strategy of 'absolute surplus value' to relative surplus value. Relative surplus value extraction entails reducing working hours through an increased productivity of labour and the development of technology in the mechanization and rationalization of the labour process (Goldman, 1995: 16). The more advanced the capital, the more predicated it is upon the continuous expansion of market relations and the more it strives for the accelerated appropriation of surplus value through 'greater annihilation of space by time' (Marx, 1973: 539). But in relative surplus value production, the accelerated pace of surplus value creation requires both a quantitative and qualitative expansion of existing consumer markets. This is because the creation, by capital, of absolute surplus value involves making deductions from 'a given quantity of [value-creating] labour' (1973: 554). In these circumstances capital is continually maximizing the expropriation of objectified labour through extended working hours and this enables 'capital to renew this profitable bargain,....on a more enlarged scale' (1973: 550). Conversely in relative surplus value an increase in the productivity of work is accompanied by a decrease in the number of hours worked. This leads to an accumulation of undifferentiated commodities and the need for the 'creation of new use values' (1973: 408). This suggests the creation of values which exceed the notion of useful values and encompass a spectrum of qualitative differences. To this extent 'the surplus labour gained does not remain a merely quantitative surplus, but rather constantly increases the circle of qualitative differences within labour' (1973: 408). It is, therefore, apparent that the production of relative surplus value must be augmented by the expropriation of a 'non-capitalist social strata as a market for its surplus value' (Luxemburg, 1971: 368). And this non-capital reservoir does not refer to the quantitative time of the productive economy. Instead it refers to the need for the commodity form, to extend into the realm of subjectively meaningful social times. Marx provides some indication of this when he states that:

> This creation of new branches of production, i.e., of qualitatively new surplus time, is not merely the division of labour, but is rather the creation, separate from a given production, of labour with a new use value; the development of a constantly expanding and more comprehensive system of different kinds of

labour, different kinds of production, to which a constantly expanding and constantly enriched system of needs corresponds'. (Marx, 1973: 409)

It is evident that capital accumulation requires a reservoir of non-economic times as a basis for the production of relative surplus value. In contemporary regimes of capitalist accumulation this translates as 'the universal appropriation of nature as well as of the social bond itself by the members of society' (Marx, 1973: 409). Just as production founded on absolute surplus value expropriates the objectified time of 'value-creating labour', so the production of relative surplus value entails 'the exploitation and exchange of natural and mental forces' (1973: 410). Consequently the qualitative times of social reproduction are an integral resource of capital accumulation. In the late modern era advertising operates to advance capitalist accumulation through its unique abilities to create a cultural economy of time.

Advances in advertising aesthetics witnessed the emergence of the 'commodity-sign' and this precipitated a revolution in advertising promotions. The chapter ascribes particular attention to the dynamics of the 'commodity-sign' with respect to the logic of capitalist production. Sign-values do not circulate freely and indiscriminately, rather, critical theorists identify the 'commodity-sign' as defined by the logic of the commodity-form. Goldman (1994) identifies the commodity-form in capitalist societies to effect an univerzalization of social relations. This process manifests according to a specific logic which imposes 'formalized standards and rules of the market ... upon social relations to effect a quantitative, standardized process of exchange' (ibid.: 20). Time penetrates the inner workings of the 'commodity-sign' and materializes in the narrative semiotics of modern advertisements. Advertising, with its focus on allegory, symbol and narrative, is therefore central to the marketing of modern consumer subjectivity. But what becomes of narrativity when, as is evident in contemporary times, epistemic struggles transform cultural texts into polysemic spaces 'where the paths of several possible meanings intersect'? (Barthes, 1977: 37)? Writers identify postmodernity to be both a condition and the consequence of a decline in 'narrative realism' (Lash and Urry, 1987).

Part III Advertising in postmodern times

The postmodern condition suggests that we are experiencing an intense phase of time/space compression and a fragmentation of time at both the global and local levels. Moreover, the postmodern condition entails the treatment of time as a finite event (i.e., time as tied to the social context of its use) no longer an unproblematic medium whose neutrality permits comparison and communication across temporal and spatial distances, no longer a common time 'in' which we all live in more or less mutual relevance, but, on the contrary, a local definition, a dimension of an event, a unique and unrepeatable period.

Modernity involved a rational ordering and delineation of time and space where no such conceptualizations had existed under premodern forms of life. Conversely, the instantaneity and simultaneity characteristic of the postmodern condition mitigate against the delineation of time and space into rationally co-ordinated spheres. One might suggest this intense time/space compression is simply an intensification of the dilemmas that have occasionally be set capitalist procedures of a constant revolution of the forces of production in the past. While the economic, cultural and political responses may not be exactly new, the range of these responses differs in certain important respects from those which have occurred before. The intensity of time/space compression in Western capitalism since the 1960s with all its emergent features of excessive ephemerality and fragmentation in the political and private as well as in the social realm does seem to indicate an experiential context that makes the condition of postmodernity somewhat distinctive. This is not to argue that all that went before has been displaced but only to suggest that tenses in the sense of past, present and future and distance or what is remote, comparatively close and intimate are blurred. There is clearly intensity and tension (Cooper and Law, 1995) around temporal spatial relations that was perhaps not so evident in modern regimes of control. For example, radical advances in information and communication technologies have given rise to processes of growing global inter-dependency. Adam (1992) identifies how, with global communication and air travel, day and night have lost their fixed social meaning, and have become thoroughly relativized. While linear time continues to be a valuable resource, its centrality to the productive economy has been displaced by a contextual relativity 'to the temporality of other firms, networks, processes or products' (Castells, 2000: 439). Space, it seems, is no longer an obstacle to global capitalism. Adam argues that when conditions arise in which 'virtual simultaneity of communication and instantaneity of feedback are not only the accepted but an expected norm, then the speed of light appears to be the only absolute limiting factor to the transmission of information' (1992: 177). In the writings of Castells, capital accumulation proceeds and profit is generated, 'increasingly in the global financial markets enacted by information networks in the timeless space of financial flows' (2000: 472). Castells identifies a revolution in information technology and a dramatic restructuring of world capitalism to have brought into being a new social structure, the network society. In the 'network society', capital operates globally as a unit 'in real time' (ibid.: 471). As networks progressively constitute the new social morphology of our societies, distances between networks contract, enabling light-speed operations. Castells describes the 'space of flows' as inducing 'systemic perturbation in the sequential order of phenomena' which may assume the form of 'instantaneity' or else 'random discontinuity in the sequence' (2000: 464).

The notion of a historical disjuncture in modernist economies of time and space is also evident in Bauman's most recent writings. In *Liquid Modernity*, Bauman (2001: 145) describes early modernity as characterized by a mutual dependency of capital and labour, which serves to fix their pursuits in bounded spatial locations. The routinized linear time of Fordist production is described as having immobilized labour, while expansive economies of scale and permanently fixed labour 'bonded the capital' (ibid.: 116). Bauman argues that with the advent of 'software capitalism and light modernity' (ibid.), capital became unshackled from its previous immobility. Similarly, Castells describes how global capital has become less reliant on specific labour, 'capital and labour increasingly tend to exist in different spaces and times; the space of flows and the space of places, instant time of computerized networks versus clock time of everyday life' (2000: 475). Capital is now 'free-floating capitalism' distinguished by the 'disengagement and loosening of ties linking capital and labour' (Bauman, 2001: 149).

Industrialization brought linear synchronicity to the assembly lines of Fordist factories. It heralded clock-time as the main organizing principle of modernist production. The mechanistic epistemology of Fordism fully embraced a perspective of time which posits metaphysical essences such as stable self-identity, transcendental laws, scientific analysis, objectivity and the existence of an objective reality. Time represents a taken-for-granted concept that remains largely unexplored and unquestioned even when it is the focus of social attention. Where the issue of time is explored, all too often, analysis is guided by an operational definition of time which relates to its measurement (e.g., time and motion study). Time is presupposed as an objective, quantifiable phenomenon divisible into discrete units, an invariant quantity unaffected by the transformations it charts, a parameter in which actions are organized and structured. Linear time and its mechanistic manifestation, the clock, inform the philosophical ideals of Fordist production. And its hegemony to the modernist episteme is such that linear time is represented as if it were time *per se*.

Post-Fordist economies subvert modernist metaphysics that posits essences like rational linear time as a basis against which productivity can be measured and controlled. The emerging world of flexibility and 'just-in-time labour' has invoked dramatic transformations in the ordering of time and production. The mechanical predictability of linear time is struggling to contain radical challenges to its Cartesian subject–object dualism, its rational ordering of space and its 'common media of exchange', which guaranteed Fordist productive systems (Ermarth, 1992: 6). Twentieth-century science has long since interrogated the determinacy of time. Newton's scientific laws lead physicists to argue that the universe was completely deterministic. This doctrine of scientific determinism was radically challenged by the great revolutions in the physical sciences. Einstein established that time and space are relative to observers and their frames of reference, thus eliminating the Newtonian vision of absolute time and space. Quantum theory revealed a model of the universe defined by indeterminacy as opposed to Newton's dream of controllable measurable processes. Indeed, the uncertainty principle informs us that our attempts to predict the future position and velocity of a particle will 'change its velocity in a way that cannot be predicted' (Hawking, with Mlodinow, 2005: 90). And the revolution in chaos theory has irrevocably undermined Laplace's world of deterministic predictability (Gleick, 1998). The revelation that is indeterminate time transcends disciplinary boundaries because it poses problems that defy accepted ways of theorizing reality.

Part III of this book argues that technological advances in advertising systems map on to the complexity of capitalist accumulation in postmodernity. Part III contains three chapters each intent on tracing the time/space paths followed by consumers within the individuating matrix of post-Fordist production and the digitalized revolution in advertising media. The signifier time/space represents a paradigmatic shift, intended to emphasize the intense compression of time and space in the postmodern era.

Chapter 5 links changing patterns of work and leisure with transformations in advertising practices. Advertising in the modern era reproduced the segmentation of culture and the separation of life into distinct value spheres; culture differentiated from economy, work from leisure, and public from private, and so on. Conversely, advertising in the postmodern era encourages an intense time/space compression and the conflation of work and leisure times. This chapter identifies how advertising's use of commodity-signs operates to extend the logic of the commodity-form into work and leisure time. But the encoding and decoding of socio-symbolic meaning arise through social interaction. And social relationships are mediated by our lived experiences of time. Consequently, the subjective possibilities of daily experience are capable of producing a theoretically infinite range of social definitions of leisure and work times. In the modern era, indeterminacy in the socio-symbolic decoding of leisure time is abated by the hegemony of linear time to the productive economy. Consequently, work time is clearly differentiated from the socio-symbolic meanings attributed to 'free time'.

Conversely, post-Fordism involves a transition from the clockwork mechanistic determinacy of Fordist production and the rise of a subjectivization of workplace time and space (Lash and Urry, 1994). Organizational flexibility is axiomatic to the new post-Fordist technological paradigm of flexible specialization. And the application of flexibility to the organization of work inculcates what the Japanese call *kaizen*, which means constant improvement. In post-Fordist production there is a relentless attempt to find ways of speeding up and improving processes. Within the discourse of lean production, workers are expected to envision the workplace as a sphere for self-actualization, creativity and autonomy. Thus, the management of work assumes a 'new paternalism' directed at cultivating enterprising subjects through the development of self-improvement schemes articulated in the quotidian of organizational practices (Du Gay, 1996: 61). Direct parallels exist between these transformations in the governing of organizational life and recent innovations in the creation of corporate brands. A substantial number of prominent marketing academics have been keen to convince modern capitalistic organizations of the need to harness the corporate brand to a social realm that is mobilized around corporate culture. A widely acclaimed contributor to this new intervention in corporate hegemony is Jesper Kunde. Chapter 5 provides a discourse analysis of his book, *Corporate Religion* (2000). Although Kunde's discourse has humanistic roots, its clarion call for a new subjectivity created through self-actualized corporate life attends to wider processes in post-Fordist production intent on inculcating subjectivity into capital. Axiomatic to the new religiosity of corporate branding is consumer-centric advertising. And it is at this interface that the time/space de-differentiation of self, subjectivity and the sphere of capitalist work reaches its zenith. In advertising circles, recent innovations in data-driven, customized marketing present unparalleled possibilities for real-time advertising communications. The chapter provides a critical examination of 'value-for-time' marketing as part of this new generation of 'mobile commerce'. Mobile commerce refers to the marketing applications of wireless communication technologies. The ability of mobile commerce to customize the delivery of goods and services by tracking the time/space paths of consumers is evidence of advertising's intrinsic role in the de-differentiation of work and leisure in post-Fordist times. This has disconcerting consequences for the continued incorporation of leisure time into the realm of consumer culture.

Chapter 6 continues to examine the theme of advertising and its excessive focus on enhancing consumer welfare. This chapter is concerned to critically examine technological advances in market segmentation. Of particular interest is the growth of Geographic Information Systems (GIS) and the attendant productions of consumer subjectivity. The chapter critically engages with a particular reading of Michel Foucault's (1977) *Discipline and Punish*. Analysts of GIS segmentation have often interpreted Foucault's writings here to mean that marketing applications of GIS allow for 'the classification of all individuals in society by spatial inference, achieving a total ordering of social life from which no consumer escapes' (Goss, 1995: 190). Foucault's writings do indeed provide an important analytical tool to conceptualize marketing technologies, but Foucault's analyses of time and regulation are an account of 'discontinuity' in the application of regulatory technologies. Foucault challenged the line of inevitability through which modernist analysis seeks to resolve enquiry. Chapter 6 applies Foucault's concept of 'discontinuity' to the analyses of postmodern time/space and the making of consumer subjectivity in market segmentation.

Chapter 7, Sign of the Times: Postmodern Disruptions in Advertising Times, identifies the diaphanous spaces of multifarious shopping arcades, theme parks and multi-media advertising as radically challenging modernist traditions in advertising practice. Modernist demarcations are predicated on boundaries which delimit the real from the unreal, inside from outside, culture from nature. These delineated market spaces struggle to contend the frenetic assault and irrepressible play of the pure sign. In modernist advertising, time and space can be brought immediately under our control and provide a context for the products of our imagination and desire. The postmodern hyperspaces of shopping arcades and theme parks transcend 'the capacities of the individual human body to locate itself, to organize its immediate surroundings perceptually and cognitively to map its position in a mappable external world' (Jameson, 1992: 44). Our experience of advertising on-line is a vivid example of decentred consumer subjectivity. There is little doubt that electronic advertising communication presently involves a more intense compression of time/space than we have previously experienced. Virtual reality is clearly beyond concrete linearity and our ways of relating to cyberspace technology rarely take a linear temporal sequence as we allow ourselves to be controlled by its random routines, feeling the ever demanding pressures to provide instant responses to messages. Can it be that postmodern advertising is the drug that truly ties us to a machine-like existence?

Part One

Marking Time in the Making of Modern Advertising

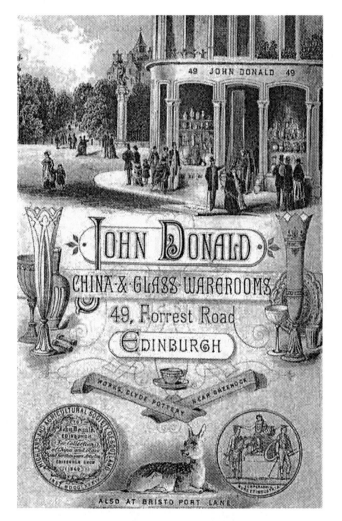

Part I *Commodity culture of Victorian Britain, 1880*

1

Selling-Spaces in Advertising History

It is customary to argue that pre-modern advertising developed to sell goods, in a particular form of economy. The fall of the Roman Empire and the invasions by barbaric Teutonic tribes had arrested the spread of education, rendering word of mouth and pictorial signs the main method of advertising in the Middle Ages. Designated trades were often confined to particular streets and the desideratum then was to differentiate shops through the use of signs, which were vivid and easily understood (Sampson, 1874). Gaily coloured signboards informed people of the whereabouts of particular tradesmen. It was considered customary to include objects typical of the trade: a stocking for the hosier, an anvil for the blacksmith and scissors for the tailor were commonly noted street signs. Others, whose trade could be appropriately linked, adopted historical events; a good example is the golden spheres of the prawn broker. This would appear to have originated from the insignia of three golden coins used by the Lombard merchants who settled in England in the thirteenth century (Preston, 1971). These merchants raised capital against valuable goods and were said therefore to be the forerunners of the pawnbroker. Elsewhere, portraits of noblemen, paintings of towns, articles of dress, all constituted a seemingly endless portfolio of symbols, which were used to attract attention and publicize trade (Sampson, 1874). In an age in which the majority were illiterate, signs were an important means of conveying ideas of space and place in visual communication. The streets of medieval cities were full of brightly coloured imagery radiating from street signs. While the signs took on various forms, their meanings defined systematic resemblances connotating space and place. Signs were therefore a natural medium to publicize trade. These pictorial images, however mimetic, were governed by historical structures of custom and style. They were simple shorthand devices for allegorically rendering a particular way of being in the world.

While it is customary to regard advertising as a comparatively modern phenomenon, there is evidence available tracing advertising to the medieval era, to ancient Greece and even Babylonian scriptures (Nevett, 1982). Nevertheless, this chapter argues that the advent of the Industrial Revolution marked a far-reaching transition in the character of advertising. From being something of a curiosity, advertising progressively began to gain acceptance as a commercial instrument for regulating demand. The increased commercial viability of advertising in the nineteenth century was mainly linked to Britain entering an era when concentrated mass consumption would necessitate mass production. Factory production had precipitated an unprecedented growth in the market for manufactured goods. At the same time buoyancy of demand was being encouraged by a growth in population from about 6 million in 1740 to over 10 million in 1811 (ibid.: 15). Advances in agrarian production had also reduced the labour intensity of farming. Consequently, population growth coincided with a transition in the mode of production and the large-scale redeployment of workers into manufacturing industries. At the end of the seventeenth century, about three-quarters of the population earned most of their livelihood from some type of agricultural work, with the majority living in villages and small towns. By the eighteenth century, a decline in agricultural work had resulted in the large-scale relocation of workers into the new industrial towns. The major growth in trade constituted the town, not only as a pool of available labour but also as a convenient concentration of consumers. This chapter has as its focus these processes. It seeks primarily to examine advertising history and the establishment of an advertising industry in the United Kingdom. It is argued here that our current advertising industry historically emerged through cultural practices and legislative enactments, intent on fostering a rationalized relation to the spaces and places of commerce.

This chapter focuses on key transformations in the regulation of space-selling during the eighteenth and nineteenth centuries. It commences with a descriptive analysis of billboard advertising. Seemingly novel features of billboard advertising are revealed to have foreshadowed the establishment of influential forms of regulated street advertising, described as 'advertising stations'. Then the chapter focuses on space-selling in the newspaper industry. The mid-1800s saw the abolition of taxes which had been levied on newspapers and on their advertisements. Imposed by the Stamp Act of 1712, the taxes had been an immense constraint on newspaper advertising. In 1855, Stamp Duty was scrapped and in its wake sprang forth a flood of new periodicals and heightened competition for advertising revenue. Newspaper proprietors were nevertheless reticent to disrupt traditional column formats and placed strict controls on advertising format. Advertisers countenanced these editorial restrictions by developing intriguing typographical styles designed to maximize the spatial presence of the advertisement.

Newspaper editors often harboured a deep-seated suspicion of advertising, which was not helped by the unscrupulous practices of unlicensed street advertising. Nevertheless pressures on newspapers to adopt the editorial display of illustrated magazines became increasingly difficult to ignore. By the mid-nineteenth century, many leading papers had abandoned their column rules and allowed large print type and illustrations. Display advertising inaugurated a new aesthetics of space, which had a significant bearing on popular culture. The chapter examines a semiotics of space characteristic of imperialist display advertising. It is a widely recognized truism that the production, consumption and commercialization of commodities were essential components of British imperialism. The diverse regions of the British Empire were cornucopias of natural riches, ripe for commercial exploitation. But enormous efforts were needed to persuade nineteenth-century Britons to populate otherwise inhospitable places and accept the need for their economic colonialization. Advertising featured here as a commercial mechanism for promoting, and publicizing, the Empire through spectacularly stylized tropes of exotic paradises inhabited by 'noble savages'. Direct links can be made here to an Enlightenment cultural chauvinism, which treated other societies in its own image. To the extent that historical time expressed the teleologies of Western development, any culture deemed entrapped in tradition was relegated as backward. The chapter identifies 'synopticism' as informing the advertising of British colonial spaces in the nineteenth century. Synopticism refers to the practice of viewing any phenomena from the same standpoint (Fabian, 1983). In imperialist advertising, it refers to a Western visual culture that 'gazes' on other cultures from its own vantage point. The detached observation of imperialist advertising, characteristic of this time, was often isolated from the exploitation and impoverishment of indigenous populations. This chapter describes the advertising of the British Empire, during the nineteenth-scentury, as epitomizing an imperialist ideological bias towards synopticism. The dehumanizing effects of this visual–spatial reduction were undoubtedly germane to sustaining the political hegemony of one society over another. Indeed, the classification and hierarchical ordering of culture give method to a denial of coevalness between the West and its Other. A central theme linking an analysis of imperialist capitalism with an analysis of advertising in nineteenth-century Britain is that both these instances in advertising history were predicated on the rationalization of commercial space.

Industrialization, space-selling and advertising practice

In nineteenth-century Britain, urbanization presented commodity providers with attractive economies of scale. The average population density of industrial towns had nearly doubled between 1721 and 1821 (Nevett, 1982: 15). In London, population density at the beginning of the nineteenth century was approximately 1 million, by 1821, the figure had reached 1.27 million (ibid.: 15). For product providers, the concentration of consumers in industrial areas meant that the costs of distribution and selling were made cheaper. This was a consequence of a declining unit cost for the communication and transportation of commodities. Innovations in transportation infrastructures had accelerated the movement of manufactured goods across greater distances and at reduced unit cost. Some of the most profitable trade emerged from wealthy provincial families, among whom it became fashionable to order merchandise from London stores. Inevitably this meant a loss of trade for local provincial merchandisers. These businesses responded to the competition presented by London-based manufacturing firms by the establishment of trade journals. One such journal was *The Family Goldmine*, which circulated throughout the Home

Counties. *The Family Goldmine* was described as 'a compendium of useful household and general knowledge' (quoted in Hindley and Hindley, 1972). The Introduction contained a lengthy encomium intended to steer local consumers away from merchant companies in the capital. Yet despite these promotional endeavours, the provincial merchants were usually outdone by their London rivals.

Industrialization meant that vast amounts of capital were invested in the machinery used to produce commodities. Selling goods at a value greater than their cost of production is the primary mechanism for accumulating returns on capital invested. Given that labour power produces wealth, returns in the investment of capital were predicated on the manufacture of greater quantities of products than would be produced by hand. This surfeit of goods presented manufacturers with the threat of a declining rate of profit as existing markets became saturated. During the Industrial Revolution, manufacturers responded to a potential crisis in the accumulation output of production by extending their catchment areas into the new concentration of populations in urban towns (Nevett, 1982). As more manufacturing firms extended their product ranges, so fierce competition ensued between manufacturers to try and secure orders from retailers. Given that most goods sold by the retailers in those days were unbranded merchandise, the retailer was often the primary point of product differentiation. Nevertheless, increased production levels had heightened the need for differentiation as existing markets were becoming saturated by a burgeoning mass of unbranded merchandise, largely indistinguishable to the general public.

Advertising provided manufacturers with a vital resource in the struggle for market share. First, advertising was used to entice retailers to buy stock from specific manufacturers. Nevett (1982: 23) describes how in the 1780s William Jones, a London pharmaceutical supplier, was offering free advertisements in local newspapers to any stockist buying a dozen bottles of his product called Tincture of Peruvian Bark. Alternatively, manufacturers used advertising to promote the virtues and distinctions of their own product ranges, in an attempt to establish consumer confidence. It was conventional for information identifying supporting retail outlets to be incorporated into these advertisements. In cases where the manufacturer was the sole provider of a product to a retailer, it merely sufficed for the retailer's insignia to be displayed on packaging. Even at this early stage in industrial capitalism, manufacturers realized the commercial potential of associating their product with a particular retail outlet.

Monopoly capitalism, space-selling and advertising practice

The materialization of advertising, as a fully incorporated system of commercial information and persuasion, appeared in the nineteenth century with the emergence of monopoly capitalism. Certain characteristics of monopoly capitalism can be traced to the economic depression, which dominated the period from 1875 to the middle 1890s. The aftermath of the economic recession witnessed a dramatic fall in prices and furtive measures to reorganize the productive capacities of manufacturing industries into larger units and combines (Williams, 1980: 197). Industrial production had reached a turning point in its approaches to distribution. Advertising became a crucial component of this systemic transformation. Williams describes how full-scale advertising was an integral feature of mechanisms geared towards the control of markets by manufacturing cartels, and the growth of a form of economic imperialism which assured markets overseas (ibid.: 197). These aspects of market control were closely linked to radical changes in the organization of advertising during the nineteenth century. Of particular significance was the systematic regulation of street advertising and newspaper advertising.

Street life in nineteenth-century advertising

The streets of nineteenth-century urban Britain witnessed the vivacity and dexterity of free trade. Casual workers in their thousands, armed with placards, sandwich boards and posters, defaced every available space with their advertising wares. At one time, it was said that billposting in London had reached such extraordinary intensity of coverage that it seemed impossible to locate a building at all. The following extract describes billstickers in the 1850s:

> The billstickers never heeded the notices to beware, and cared nothing for the privacy of 'dead walls', or for the matter of that, of dwelling houses or street doors. Though he himself was rarely seen, his disfiguring work was a prominent feature of the metropolis. Early morning was his busy time, and if he could cover up the work of a rival, so much better. (quoted in Dyer, 1993: 32).

Billboard advertising and streetcar car circulation featured prominently among the bustling spaces and places of the new metropolises. Posters were a popular medium of advertising communication as they were not subject to advertising duty. Posters also avoided the commercial restrictions imposed by newspapers on column inches, which had resulted in the crowding together of advertisements and prevented the use of illustrations. Figure 1.1 is a pictorial representation of a billsticker characteristic of this era.

Little information exists on the effectiveness of posters, apart from various derisory complaints concerning the rapid speed with which posters could be distributed. In 1808, a writer observed that 'within six hours, by means of printed bills, the inhabitants of a great city can be advertised of a thousand things necessary to be publicly known; and in cases of fugitive robbers, traitors, spies etc., the hue and cry, or notice of their apprehension is circulated throughout the kingdom in four or five days' (quoted in

Figure 1.1 *A man pasting up a poster*

Source: William Henry Pyne, London, 1808. Reproduced by permission of the British Library.

Nevett, 1982: 53). Of curious relevance here is the often recounted swagger of a self-proclaimed 'King of Billstickers' who in 1851 asserted that some 150 stickers were operating in London and that they could post around one hundred bills a day (ibid.: 55). It is difficult to ascertain how long a bill would remain in public view before it was plastered over, although it was customary in the trade for a billsticker not to over-stick a wet poster. But the bonhomie which had traditionally managed relations between members of the poster trade was fatally disrupted in 1826 with the abolition of the National Lottery and with this the legal restrictions preventing over-sticking on anyone else's posters. Thereafter it became normal practice for billstickers to over-stick, as freelance operators competed to plaster their signs on the street walls of the new metropolises.

Hardly a dwelling house or street wall escaped the hurriedly plastered signs of the billstickers. Competition between billstickers exacerbated the nuisance factor presented by fly postering. Unscrupulous twilight raids by rival billstickers could mean that by daybreak the public walls of whole districts would be bedaubed with an unintelligible clutter of signs. Sampson, in his account of advertising history, quotes a then popular song which satirized the billstickers' audacious escapade and the art of exaggerated publicity (i.e., puffery):

> I'm Sammy Slap the billsticker, and you must all agree, sirs,
> I sticks to business like a trump while business sticks to me, sirs.
> There's some folks calls me plasterer, but they deserve a banging,
> Cause yer see, genteelly speaking, that my trade is paperhanging.
> With my paste, paste, paste! All the world is puffing,
> So I'll paste, paste, paste! (Sampson, 1874: 26)

The advent of the Metropolitan Paving Act of 1817 considerably circumvented the avocations of the predatory billstickers. The Metropolitan Paving Act certified that 'Hoardings shall not be erected without licence' (quoted in Elliott, 1962: 164). This Act encouraged the establishment of advertising contractors who would purchase the legal rights to adhere posters to hoardings. These contractors established 'advertising stations' on which bills and announcements were ordered, with regulated mathematical precision. But their attempt to impose order on the spatial province of the advertising hoard was a difficult battle. For as soon as a contractor had completed an advertising station with meticulous efficiency, swarms of illegal billstickers armed with posters, pots of glue and brushes would transform the orderly arrangement into chaos (Sampson, 1874: 27). Nevertheless, the advertising contractors' efforts at spatial regulation were not in vain. Over time, and aided by a swathe of magisterial decisions, and the intriguing alacrity of the police, the contractors succeeded in institutionalizing their advertising stations (ibid.: 27). Figure 1.2 is a picture of an advertising hoarding located in a London railway station in 1874. It is on record that with the establishment of advertising stations, hoardings on which posters were pasted adopted an orderly and attractive display.

Much of the credit for the sustained regulation of billposters is attributed to the internal market controls of billposter associations. Examples of leading collectives here include the United Kingdom Bill-Posters Association, founded by Edward Sheldon in 1862, which enforced a strict code of ethics designed to contain the more objectionable aspects of the industry. These attempts at self-regulation were part response to stringent legal controls on street advertising, which gathered pace in scope and severity. The

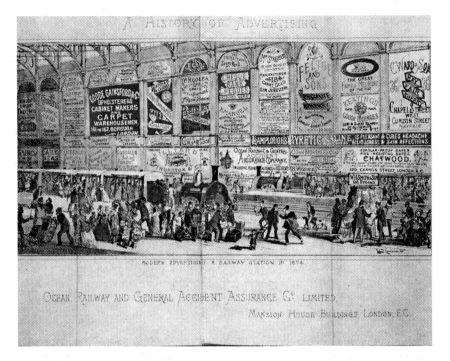

Figure 1.2 *'Modern advertising': a railway station in 1874, Ocean Railway and general Accident Assurance Co. Ltd.*

Source: Reproduced by permission of the British Library.

Metropolitan Paving Act of 1817 had in previous years empowered parishes to appoint individuals called Surveyors of the Pavement (Nevett, 1982). They had the authority to issue licences for the erection of hoardings and to remove distasteful unlicensed hoardings. In later years amendments to this Act, namely, the Metropolitan Paving Act of 1839 witnessed far more stringent policing of bill postering. Under Section 54 of this Act, any individual carrying the tools of the billposter trade would be deemed to have intention. Judging by the successive attempts to fine tune this legislation, it appears to have experienced difficulties in its efficient enforcement.

In 1889, the Indecent Advertisement Act was passed, marking a moral dimension in the concerted attack on the 'horrors of walls' (Elliott, 1962: 165). Such was the bill-postering industry's concern over pending threats of legislation and restrictive practices that in 1890 two leading bodies – the United Kingdom Bill-Posters Association and the London Bill-Posters Association – set up the Joint Censorship Committee. The committee's regulatory efforts included establishing a directory of responsible billposters and insisting on checking the quality standards of posters distributed by affiliated members. This appears to have been deemed insufficient, for in 1898 the National Society for Checking the Abuses of Public Advertising

(SCAPA) was established. SCAPA achieved some notable successes in removing illegal billposters and checking the quality of outdoor signs. The activities of SCAPA were premised on the need for advertisers to find a middle way between the outcries of the defenders of 'good taste' and the needs of commerce. While the crusades of SCAPA were instrumental in setting the boundaries of advertising decency, more heavyweight legal intervention was needed to regulate the extraordinary growth in street advertising. Parliament eventually gave way to pressure for more stringent regulation of street advertising and it passed the Advertising Regulation Act of 1907. The Act empowered local authorities with the jurisdiction to construct bylaws for the regulation of hoardings. Towards the end of 1914, approximately 30 counties and around 34 boroughs had made use of the 1907 Act to create bylaws regulating street advertising (Nevett, 1982). Elsewhere important signs of reforms in space-selling were evident within the printed press.

The abolition of stamp duty makes its mark on newspaper advertising

The rapid growth of advertising during the Industrial Revolution is closely linked to the development of the newspaper industry. Initially the population density of London attracted the majority of newspaper business. Gradually, however, newspaper circulations extended into more towns and cities. At the same time the combined circulation numbers of newspapers printed were rapidly increasing from 1,500 in 1700 to 7,314 fifty years later (Nevett, 1982: 17). Table 1.1 shows statistical data on newspaper circulations during this era. The vast expansion of newspapers offered lucrative opportunities for advertising but these opportunities were significantly limited by the fiscal restrictions which had been imposed by the government's first newspaper tax in 1712.

In the early eighteenth century, heavy duties were imposed on newspapers and advertising, which would prove to be a substantive limitation to the circulation of notices. The Stamp Duty on newspaper announcements was first imposed in 1712 and was one shilling an announcement. By the time of the Napoleonic Wars, Stamp Duty had increased to 4d a sheet and Advertisement Tax was 3s 6d (Williams, 1980: 173). The imposition of the tax had arrested the development of advertising, but it had not stopped it completely. During the period from 1700–1720, newspapers are recorded to have carried on average a total of 15 advertisements an edition, and by 1720–1745, this had increased to 35 (Bruttini, 1982: 21). This number continued to rise despite the fiscal restraints of Stamp Duty and, between 1750 and 1800, London newspapers had an average of 45 advertisements. Further evidence of the surprising growth of advertising during this era is provided by the increasing presence of newspapers entirely dedicated to carrying advertisements. In February 1731, the *Daily Advertiser* was first published in London. The launch of this newspaper was particularly significant as it was entirely dedicated to carrying advertisements. The *Daily*

Table 1.1 *Numbers of newspaper titles published and combined circulation 1700–1800*

Year	Number of titles	Cirulation (000)
1700	25	1500
1710	53	2000
1720	84	3500
1730	76	4600
1740	75	6000
1750	90	7314
1760	103	9464
1770	133	–
1780	159	14217
1790	208	14036
1800	258	16085

Source: Nevett (1982: 17) Reprinted by permission of the Random House Group Ltd.

Advertiser developed some noticeable appeal among the general public affirming the intentions of the publishers. The following quotation provides some indication of the *Daily Advertiser*'s circulation, distribution and organization of advertising space:

> It being intended to render this Paper equally Useful and Acceptable; As well to entertain our Readers, as to serve those who Advertise in it; At the earnest Importunity of Both, we design for the future to publish Daily the best and freshest Accounts of all Occurrences Foreign and Domestick. The Account of Goods Imported and Exported to be inserted in the Papers of Tuesday and Friday, and the Course of Exchange on Wednesdays and Saturdays. The Advertisement to be taken in at Two Shillings each, and to be pasted up at the several Publick Parts of the Town in the Usual Manner. And for the better Dispersing and Publishing the Usefulness of this Undertaking, This Paper will be left Gratis for some Days at most of the Houses of the Nobility and Gentry, and the Coffee-Houses; and such who are pleased to approve thereof, are humbly desired to signify the same to the Person who leave it. (Quoted in ibid.: 12).

The extent of advertising coverage provided in the *Daily Advertiser* amounted to around 70 per cent of the paper's surface space, compared to around 50–55 per cent of other newspapers. This suggests the existence of a burgeoning market for advertising despite the imposition of 'advertisement duty'. Indeed, the 1730s witnessed the continued development of newspapers bearing the title of 'Advertiser'. Many of these advertising newspapers also appeared in the provinces where the Industrial Revolution had precipitated increased commerce and trade. It is recorded that at least 50 newspapers bearing the title 'Advertiser' appeared in London and the provinces during the 1730s (ibid.).

By the mid-eighteenth century, advertising's popularity had excited the interests of academics and market analysts. Newspapers of some intellectual calibre had begun to publish essays concerned to focus attention on the need for intellectual debate about advertising. Newspapers such as the *Universal Chronicle, The Rambler* and *The Adventurer* published articles by

notable academics, many of whom were making links between the desires
of man (*sic*), wealth and the creation of artificial appetites. Advertising was
once again colonizing newspaper space but its promotional activities here
were of a different kind. Social commentators mused over the persuasive
capabilities of advertising, often concluding that advertising success was
largely due to an ability to tap into hidden aspects of human character.

During the 1740s, the prominent social commentator, John Fielding,
published regular articles in *The Champion*, extolling the enormous persuasive power of advertising (ibid.). Fielding drew attention to how advertising's influence had begun to impact on the editorial world, so that, in
order for an author to become famous, it was often necessary that they
adopt the art of 'puffing' (ibid.: 15). It had become conventional for lengthy
extracts from publishers' catalogues to be included in the end matter of
books. This practice met with some disdain, encouraging one critic to state
that book reviews were 'nothing now but vehicles for the puffing of trash
books' (Stuart, 1889: 4, quoted in Bruttini, 1982). By the nineteenth century, social commentators were increasingly vocalizing their indignation at
the commercial connections between advertising, newspapers and the book
trade. Among these concerned critics is the work of Thomas Babington
Macaulay, who in 1830 published 'Mr Montomery's Poems and the Modern
Practice of Puffing'. According to McFall (2002: 541), Macaulay lambasted
what he perceived to be the shameful artifice of book advertising. His
indignation was not merely with the affront of puffery (McFall, 2002).
Macaulay equally disdained the networks of interest linking publishers,
advertisers and authors (ibid.). Macaulay perceived this connection was
leading to 'the construction of an elaborate promotional machine where
the notoriety of authors could be carefully constructed and managed in
what would appear to be an independent editorial' (ibid.: 541). These links
between literary circles, advertising and publishing are extensively examined elsewhere (cf. McFall, 2002). It might suffice here to state that by the
nineteenth century the organization of advertising was increasingly extending economic calculation into the scholarly spaces of literary production.

In other quarters, considerable intellectual weight had been given to the
'Institution of Rhetoric, or the Art of Persuasion'. The social commentator
Fielding, in an article published on 19 December 1741, affirmed advertising
to be a universal practice with its trajectories in Greek and Roman culture
(Bruttini, 1982). Advertising, he argued, 'is the practice of "the whole Species"
almost from the cradle to their graves, the grand science of Life, what com-
prehends, mixes with, or assists all other; that we are taught in our infancy,
what we cultivate every hour we live, and what we never quit till we quit
the Stage' (quoted in ibid.: 15). Such penetrating prose must have given
considerable weight to advertising as a pervasive force in society.

A series of articles which attracted significant notoriety first appeared on
20 January 1760, in the fortieth number of the *Universal Chronicle*, in a
column entitled 'The Idler'. The author, a Mr Johnson, in the first of a
series of similar publications, begins by formulating a narrative of public

transactions which traces the skill of advertising to a humble heritage. He stated that 'the man who first took advantage of the general curiosity excited by a siege or a battle to betray the readers of news into knowledge of the shop where the best puffs and powders were to be sold had a profound skill for the nature of man' (quoted in Bruttini, 1982: 16). By the 1750s, Johnson's academic reflections in many respects anticipated an advertising revolution which was still merely in its infancy. In 'The Idler' (no. 30), published on 11 November 1750, Johnson stated that 'the desires of the man increase with his acquisition ... and no sooner are we supplied with everything that nature can demand, than we sit down to create artificial appetites' (quoted in ibid.: 17).

 During the 1760s, newspapers enjoyed higher rates of circulation than recorded in previous years, mainly due to structural improvements in the postal service. England was becoming a formidable trade power as it extended into markets in the colonies. Workers were migrating in greater numbers into the towns and the spread of elementary education was decreasing the rates of illiteracy. Advertising mirrored many of these transformations. Steady increases in the flow of newspapers had signified an upturn in economic conditions. And the income gained from advertisement tax had no doubt filled the State's coffers. Advertising can also be said to have directly contributed to the economic expansion of the mid-eighteenth century. First, through its attempts to create a need or desire for consumption. Such practices were admittedly crude compared to contemporary selling technologies, nevertheless, the advertisers' intention to persuade had attracted the interests of leading social commentators. The *Adventurer* on 26 June 1753 published an essay by Johnson, cautioning against the practice of promotional advertising, stating that 'the multiplicity of criers that stun him in the street and the variety of merchandise and manufacturer which the shopkeepers expose on every hand' can only temporarily satiate happiness (quoted in Bruttini, 1982: 17). Johnson argued that new needs are easily created: 'that every man in surveying the shops of London sees numberless instruments of which, while he did not know them, he never felt the need' and yet 'when use has made them familiar, wonders how life could be supported without them' (quoted in ibid.: 17). Johnson's incisive academic enquiry was intent on drawing attention to advertising's role in the creation of needs which had fuelled some increased commercial prosperity during this era.

Advertising's contribution to the Industrial Revolution extends even further than the artifice of 'need'. It has been argued that advertising played a prominent role in the circulation of the technical knowledges necessary for a wider public understanding of the Industrial Revolution (ibid.). Newspaper circulation increased significantly in the provinces, particularly from the mid-eighteenth century onwards. Quality newspapers published in the provinces were not restricted to these areas but were often distributed to the remotest parts of the kingdom and the important coffee-houses of London. There is some evidence that the circulation of newspapers from large and small towns was important in the diffusion of technical knowledge and expertise. An illustration of this proposition is provided by the activities of Thomas Yeoman (1704–1781), who was a surveyor, a mechanic for agricultural machinery, a prominent member of the 'Northampton Philosophical Society' and a distinguished Fellow of the Royal Society. In the *Northampton Mercury* of 27 April 1747, Thomas Yeoman included an advertisement, which publicized that he made and sold 'ventilators for Hospitals, Gaols, Graineries or Ship, Back-heavers for expeditiously winnowing of Corn, Hollow stick for Ventilating Corn in Stacks' (quoted in ibid.: 20). Another advertisement in the *Northampton Mercury* earlier in December 1743, and also linked to Yeoman, states that: 'Among the many excellent and useful Machines invented by our own Countryman, the Ventilator by the Ingenious Dr Hale … this is to inform the Publick that Tho. Yeoman, operator for Mr Cave's Cotton Engines … will undertake to make any sort of them' (quoted in ibid.: 20). In the same *Northampton Mercury* of 27 April 1747, Yeoman circulated news of 'Bridge Weighing Engines for all Sorts of Carriages' (ibid.: 20). And in the *Birmingham Airis's Gazette* of 29 December 1746, Yeoman advertised a course of lectures in 'Electricity' (ibid.: 20). It is clear from these examples that advertising operated to publicize the activities of innovators while also communicating technological change to an enquiring general public. In the absence of a state-sponsored national education system, advertising become a principal instrument in the spread of technical knowledge which would form the spring-board for future technological innovations.

However, Stamp Duty had significantly constrained the development of an advertising industry. It placed advertising out of the reach of most commercial speculators and reduced the numbers of notices appearing in newspapers. This was evident when in 1833 Advertisement Tax was reduced to 1s 6d. A comparison of figures recording advertising notices between 1830 and 1838 reveal in the former year a total of 877,972 advertisements in mainland Britain's newspapers and this rising to 1,491,991 in 1838 (Nevett, 1982: 27). In 1855, by an Act 18 & 19 Vict. C,27, the Stamp Duty was abolished and with this occurred a rapid rise in the circulation of newspapers and advertising. Stamp Duty had significantly hampered the growth of newspapers, much to the delight of successive governments which had experienced blistering attacks from the press. Indeed, Stamp Duty had been described by editorial proprietors as a 'tax on knowledge' and a forthright attempt to muzzle the press (Hindley and Hindley, 1972). Nevertheless the allure of commercial profiteering prevailed over a desire for government censorship and the Stamp Duty was lifted. No doubt studies conducted during this era, suggesting that a single small advertisement could attract as many as 200 letters of request, excited the coffers of the Exchequer (Turner, 1952), especially as each of these client contacts would have to bear a postage stamp.

Guaranteed circulations; and other late nineteenth-century transformations in space-selling

The abolition of Stamp Duty in 1855 precipitated a flood of new periodicals onto the market and fierce competition for advertising revenue. Advertisers were unsurprisingly attracted to those newspapers that could demonstrate impressive circulation figures. Publishers, eager to outshine their rivals, often resorted to the disclosure of over-stated circulation figures. Equally mystifying was the tendency of publishers to claim that they were the primary periodical for a given community of adults. Nevett (1982) describes one such claim made by the publishers of *The Primitive Methodist* who would regularly claim that they were the official religious periodical for a community of over 200,000 adults, without stipulating how many members of this community read the periodical. Similarly, some publishers relying on the London business person's lack of knowledge of the provincial press, would produce two or three editions of the same newspaper with little differences in content. Such unscrupulous practices were intent on increasing the number of advertising outlets derived from a single newspaper publication. Indeed, discreditable publishers would charge advertisers multiple insertion fees under the pretence that the newspaper commanded wide circulation, when in reality they were often paying for different editions of the same newspaper. It was clear that advertisers required some guarantee that a newspaper's circulation figures were reliable.

One of the earliest recorded attempts to extract reliable circulation figures from newspaper publishers was instigated in the new *Advertiser's Review* of 8 April 1899 (Nevett, 1982). In an article entitled 'Guaranteed Circulations; Are they Frequently a Myth?', the authors drew attention to widely known practices used by publishers to over-rate their newspaper's popularity. Tricks of the trade included quoting figures that were out of date, and misrepresenting peak circulation figures – for specialist issues – as indicative of the norm. The authors were clearly cognizant of the problems these practices presented to advertisers, stating that 'It is quite possible ... that if a really thorough and searching investigation as to the circulation could be obtained, the advertising value of many publications now in good repute would be heavily reduced' (quoted in ibid.: 59). Publishers responded to pressures for more reliable circulation figures by promoting their use of controlled circulation, which emphasized that the paper was distributed in public establishments such as hotels where each copy could be read by several readers. An example of one such controlled circulation notice is provided by *The Illustrated London News*. In 1900, it stated that, 'In every club in England you will see the ILN. In most big hotels you see it also and the result is that not only one individual who pays sixpence for it, but perhaps 50 or 60 people a day, turn over the pages and their eye is caught by some striking advertisement' (quoted in ibid.: 11). Controlled circulation claims nevertheless proved insufficient protection for a burgeoning advertising industry keen to galvanize the highest circulation of promotional literatures. Towards the latter part of the nineteenth century the newly established advertising agencies were increasingly inclined to litigate against newspaper proprietors who had gained their advertising accounts through fraudulent circulation figures. Examples include T.B. Browne, a leading agent who, in April 1899, took representatives of the Morgan Publishing Company to court for conspiring to defraud by means of false circulation certificates (ibid.: 60). In 1917, the Association of British Advertising Agencies was established, but it was not until 1931 that the Audit Bureau of Circulations was put in place to systematically address this problem. Elsewhere, a number of advertising agencies had begun to incorporate into their newly evolving business profile the publication of newspaper circulation figures. These lists and directories were to become an integral feature of the evolution of advertising agencies.

Editorial controls on display advertising

Having overcome the constraints of Stamp Duty, advertisers faced a new nemesis: newspaper editors keen to stifle the spread of display advertising. There remained a fierce distrust of advertising among newspaper editors. Indeed, much documented evidence exists to suggest that this distrust was justifiably based on the unscrupulous practices of an advertising industry in dire need of regulation. Examples of just some of the scandalous activities of advertising practitioners included the practices of 'farming', 'puffery' and 'fly-by-night' operators. These practices are briefly described as a means of illustrating conditions which precipitated editorial restrictions on the place of display advertising within the printed press.

In the practice of 'farming', an advertising agent would be contracted to a newspaper to buy advertising space in bulk over a given period of time (Hindley and Hindley, 1972). The arrangement suited the newspaper as the bulk purchase of space guaranteed fixed revenue. The arrangement was also of benefit to the advertising agent who would purchase selling space at a cost lower than the standard rate and resell at higher rate of profit. In this capacity, the relationship between the agent and newspaper was rather akin to that of manufacturer and retailer. But abuses of the system were rife. First, having committed to buying spaces in bulk, the advertiser sometimes struggled to fill them. In these instances, the advertiser could, and often did, approach other agents for clients to fill surplus advertising spaces. This would sometimes be to the client's detriment. Clients tended to rely upon the agent's skill in positioning their advertisements in a manner which would maximize customer contacts. When an agent 'farmed' among other agents for clients to fill surplus spaces, much of the attention to the client's account would be readily abandoned. Additionally, farming often involved the promotion of cheap advertising spaces as a mechanism for attracting clients. But these cheap spaces were invariably an illusion, as they tended to be loss leaders. At best, the smaller agent would find that their initial financial outlay would rise considerably, and, at worst, the agent with the

Figure 1.3 *'Taken in and done for', 1865*

Source: Spellman Collection of Victorian Music Covers. Reproduced by Kind permission of Reading University Library.

advertising franchise could approach the smaller agent's clients directly and offer them a cheaper rate of advertising space (Figure 1.3).

Such practices advocated the implementation of controls in which agents were encouraged to disclose whether they practised farming. However, these controls were often facile attempts at reform and invariably unsuccessful (Hindley and Hindley, 1972). Additional examples of unscrupulous practices included the profiteering of the 'fly-by-night' operators and confidence tricksters who would use advertising 'puffery' to sell goods of negligible benefit. Both practices were particularly devious in their efforts to entice unsuspecting members of the public seduced by the mysteries of advertising. Naïve investors, having parted with their money, would invariably find that the confidence trickster had scurried away to ever more gullible prey.

Given advertising's burgeoning reputation for unscrupulous practices, it is unsurprising that newspaper editors treated agents with suspicion. Few editors were eager to admit that it was advertising rather than journalistic endeavour which enabled a paper to publish at a penny a sale. It was widely felt that advertising's presence in newspapers should be disciplined as much as possible. Newspaper advertisements of the time were discrete when compared to the transformations in display advertising, which were soon to take hold of the industry. Typically newspaper advertisements were laid out like classifieds. They were rarely illustrated, and were confined to specific parts of the newspaper.

The 1800s progressed into an era of unparalleled expansion in trade and a substantial increase in manufacturing. Advertising also witnessed steady growth and innovation. More attention was being paid to the design and layout of advertisements, and the art of 'copyrighting' was now considered an expertise exclusive to advertising professionals. Nevertheless editors were still reluctant to encourage the new styles of advertising, especially where designs extended beyond the width of a standard newspaper column (Dyer, 1993). Requests for display advertisements were also treated with immense incredulity, as if the newspaper might be transformed into a public hoarding by the presence of images. Editors were immensely reluctant to break up the column layout of their newspapers. And in an attempt to prevent display advertising, editors imposed stringent column rules, restricting advertisers to the use of big black type. Advertisers responded to these restrictions by filling columns with the endless repetition of their clients' trade name, thus:

WALTER JONES AND SON
WALTER JONES AND SON
WALTER JONES AND SON

WALTER JONES AND SON
WALTER JONES AND SON
WALTER JONES AND SON

Advertising columns might be filled with as many as 1,000 repeated lines announcing a firm's name (Turner, 1952). But the efforts of editors to restrict the appearance of advertising to within the format of the editorial column were being significantly challenged by the 1880s. Dazzling pictorial advertisements in illustrated magazines had transformed readership cultures. The 1860s had already witnessed impressive advances in colour lithography and the ability of posters to dazzle spectators. In 1886, the proprietors of Pears astounded the art world by purchasing Sir John Everett Millais's 'Bubbles' picture for their exclusive use in promoting Pears Soap (Elliott, 1962; Dyer, 1993). Artists had previously been reluctant to enter into the world of commercial enterprise, fearing that such links might be detrimental to their reputation. Consequently, Pears, success in commissioning Millais was a monumental achievement. Nevertheless, Millias was one of the most eminent artists in late Victorian England and horror was expressed that he would lend his work to such commercial endeavours. Further hostility was generated when it was publicized by T.J. Barratt (then chairman of Pears), that the purchase price and reproduction of the 'Bubbles' picture cost £20,000 (Elliott, 1962). T.J. Barratt was later noted to have said that the poster had 'dissipated the delusion that art was lowering itself by an alliance with commerce' (quoted in ibid.: 166). Writers have since identified the 'Bubbles' advertisement as perhaps 'the first example of advertising which associated a product with (high) culture' Dyer (1993: 37). In 1891, Pears also produced an annual designed to bring serialized narratives and advertising to the general public. Slowly a now familiar world of signs and imagery was forming, and newspapers could hardly ignore the changing milieu. By the 1890s, newspapers were abandoning their column rules and allowing display advertisement, often in light-face type across several columns with the increasing occasion of illustration (Turner, 1952). Towards the latter part of the nineteenth century, *The Times* in 1897 announced that it was permitting 'advertisements in type which three years ago would have been considered fit only for street hoardings' (quoted in ibid.: 153). Although editors continued to resist changes to editorial column rules, display advertising had become standard practice by the end of the nineteenth century. Indeed, display advertising was increasingly an integral feature of popular culture and to some extent national culture. Of particular relevance here was the use of advertising display, during the Victorian era, to ensure economic imperialism and the concerted expansion of British companies into markets overseas. The following section highlights these practices as part of a concerted imperialist effort to commodify 'other' non-Western spaces as part of capitalist accumulation in the late nineteenth century.

Rationalizing 'Other' non-Western spaces in advertising history

British imperialism was a pivotal cause of the exploitation and environmental degradation associated with the expansion of Western capitalism. Historians have elsewhere provided detailed descriptive accounts of imperialist production and the attendant features of merchant ships overflowing with luxury goods destined for Western consumption (O'Connor, 1974; Larrain, 1989). Nevertheless, an often neglected aspect of imperialist expansion has been the promotion of the Empire through advertising communication. Late Victorian Britain was, by all reports, a 'prodigiously abundant society' (Richardson, 1991: 119). Substantial increases in manufacturing had improved productivity and endowed Victorian commodity culture with a surplus of commodities available in many varieties. For the upper and middle classes, abundance was a familiar reality, but for the

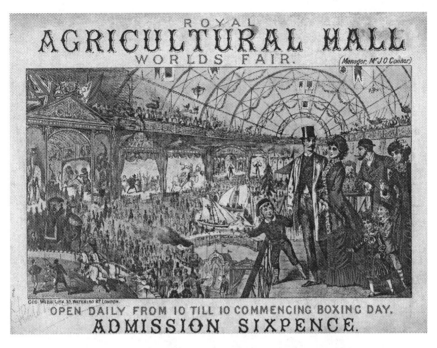

Figure 1.4   *Royal Agricultural Hall World's Fair*

Source: Henry Evanion, 1880. Reproduced by permission of the British Library.

lower classes the possession of material goods increasingly became an aspiration to strive for (ibdi.: 120). Victorian economists and politicians fostered the culture of abundance and channelled it into an ideology of the
Empire. In this ideological configuration, proficiency in the production of
commodities (even to the point of surplus) was equated with the interests
of the Empire and the economic expansion of Britain (ibid.: 120). The
Great British exporting industries needed to ensure home markets as a
source of investment capital. Consequently, it was efficacious for the political establishment to propagate an ideology of citizenship which claimed
that 'Empire buying was a duty no citizen could afford to neglect' (Freeman,
1977: 14). Figure 1.4 shows a poster for the Royal Agricultural Hall World's
Fair in London, 1880. The poster is illustrative of the use of advertising to
foster the incorporation into popular culture of an ideology which equated
economic wealth with the growth of the British Empire.

   In the late nineteenth century, plenitude in the abundance of commodities was conceived to be the driving force of imperialist domination.
Victorian advertising drove home this new imperialism and its attendant
endeavour to transform commodities from a necessary utility to the 'extraordinary profusion of an indigenous industry' (Richardson, 1991: 130).

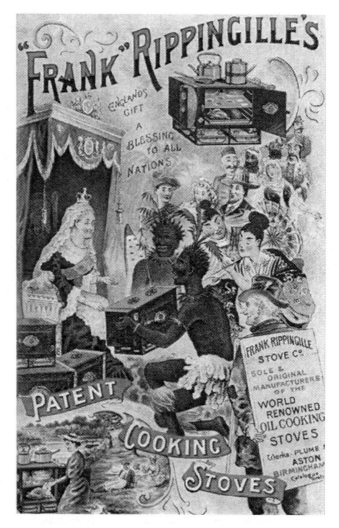

Figure 1.5 *Victorian imperialist advertising aesthetic*

Source: Reproduced by permission of British Empire.
(www.britishempire.co.uk/images)

Figure 1.5 provides an example of Victorian Empire advertising. The advertisement epitomizes a specific Victorian aesthetic evident in the Empire advertising that characterized this era.

The consumption and commercialization of commodities were essential components of British colonialism (Auerbach, 2002). Advertising provided a means of packaging the geographic spaces, peoples and products of the Empire into exotic objects. In the sociology of tourism, Boorstin (1964) identifies these processes as linked to the emergence of packaged tours in the mid-1800s. Prior to the nineteenth century, visits abroad were uncertain adventures. Travellers to new and exotic places directly experienced indigenous cultures. Communication systems in these new territories were often limited and few amenities existed to welcome the traveller. These stark conditions meant that travel was virtually unknown to everyday members of the public. Boorstin's (1964) analyses of tourism often celebrate the naïveté of a time before packaged holidays. Boorstin devised the concept of the 'traveller' to distinguish the adventurers of a bygone era. For him, the 'traveller' was a member of an elite group of privileged individuals who actively sought authentic cultural experiences in their travels abroad. Boorstin observes how in the mid-nineteenth century this form of dedication to travel decreased markedly. He argues that mass-produced packaged tourism has overshadowed the authentic pursuit of travel and replaced this with a facile stereotypical 'pseudo-event'. Direct links exist here with advertising imagery and media. Tourism packaging involves a reductionism of complex cultures into marketable commodities which can be displayed in advertising brochures. In so doing, the tourist gaze is constituted into a closed self-referential system, which tourists draw upon in order to render meaningful their touristic experiences (Urry, 1990). This is partly what Boorstin (1964) describes as the 'pseudo-event'.

The British government publicized the colonies of the Empire through carefully commissioned artistic displays portraying these diverse non-Western colonies as Edenic paradises (Auerbach, 2002). Instrumental in this campaign was the work of professional artists such as William Hodges and Benjamin West who publicized the Empire through ostentatiously heroic paintings. Their idyllic depictions of exotic cornucopias and languid tranquil havens were befitting of a British Empire keen to inculcate its citizens into an ideology of colonial capitalism. In this imperial gaze, the colonies of capitalism were 'Edenic paradises, cornucopias of natural riches, empty lands available for settlement' (ibid.: 30). These visual images operated to sell the spaces of the Empire and legitimize capitalist commerce. In this sense the battle for imperialist control was never exclusively fought on the imperial frontier; it also took place at home on the canvasses of artists (ibid.: 20). Unsurprisingly, therefore, indigenous people fared much worse in the battle for cultural representation. They were either depicted as noble savages or degenerate heathens in desperate need of religious salvation. Figure 1.6 shows an advertisement for a circus performance entitled 'Farini's Earthmen'. The poster is indicative of Western imperialism's trajectories in the Enlightenment's representational chauvinism.

Enlightenment cultural chauvinism treated other societies in its own image. Explanation was defined by a framework of structural relationships, which imposed on things a temporal order attuned to the teleogies of Western development. Knowledge corresponded to the accurate ordering of representation. It was involved with the representation of identities, difference and their calibration (Cousins and Hussain, 1984: 33). In the early modern era, 'signs are knowledge tools of analysis and means of representing order' (ibid.: 33). Signification is the product of a binary sign composed of a signifier and signified. Foucault (1970) describes how, by the end of the

Figure 1.6   *Farini's Earthmen*

Source: Henry Evanion, London, 1885. Reproduced by permission of the British Library.

eighteenth century, knowledge and representation begin to uncouple (Cousins and Hussain, 1984). The elucidation of phenomena can be the object of knowledge yet 'no longer amenable to a single elaboration through the category of representation' (ibid.: 49). The relations of knowledge are now the productions of a knowing subject and unknown object. It is within these confines of such totalizing visions that a certain conception of 'otherness' could be admitted and even flourish.

It is the Enlightenment differentiation between the subject and object, between the self and world, which inspires the representational aesthetic of the advertisement in Figure 1.6. The ambiguity of landscape is critical to the success of this advertisement and the 'Othering' of the indigenous people illustrated. Given that 'the pigmies or dwarf earth-men' would probably have been forcibly transported to Europe, the landscape of the advertisement is an imaginary place. The harsh deleterious consequences of imperialist exploitation would have most probably destroyed the original homestead of these indigenous people. Thus, the landscape depicted in the advertisement merely mourns the passing of a space destroyed by racial domination. Rosaldo (1989: 68–9) provides important theoretical reflections on colonialism and visual imagery. She observes how nostalgic visual imagery idyllically depicting bygone eras, which have since been destroyed by colonial expropriation, are evidence of 'imperialist nostalgia' (ibid.: 68–9). MacCannell (1999) provides an account of touristic display which develops the concept of 'imperialist nostalgia'. Commenting on modern-day touristic cultural display, MacCannell argues that commercial exchanges of this nature ameliorate a collective guilt that moderns hold for the systematic destruction of primitive societies (Dicks, 2003: 60). In this sense, 'imperialist nostalgia' is a response to a mythic ideal intent on sustaining the idea of the primitive in modern times.

A form of nostalgia is certainly at work in the advertisement's cultural aesthetic. In a typically imperialistic display, the space and culture which had been taken away (by the colonial expropriation of natural resources) are returned through the theatrical performances of the indigenous showmen. Our attention is also drawn to the gradient of differentiation separating the status of the white male from the black subjects. Race is clearly being depicted here as a trope of ultimate irreducible difference. The landscape is an exotic geographic space populated by wild animals and dark-skinned 'primitive' people. The driving force of the Enlightenment age is the search for certainty, the effort to use reason to establish absolute and universal truth. Since Descartes, that quest for certainty has been embedded in the rationality of the transcendental knowing subject (Bordo, 1986). Descartes' *ego cogito ergo sum* located the modern episteme's Cartesian rationality within the context of 'man' himself (Hekman, 1990: 62). The aristocrat depicted in the advertisement clearly symbolizes a definition of subjectivity enshrined in the Cartesian *cogito ergo sum*. His stance and relation to the dark-skinned subjects epitomize Enlightenment sensibilities, and the ascription of reason with the role of exercising power over the unknown rather than escaping from it. In this sense, the advertisement's visual representation is ordered so as to celebrate the liberation of 'man' as a free and active individual endowed with consciousness and will. The commodification of an Other's space, place and belonging is but a logical extension of this abstract instrumental reason. In summary, the visual tropes of nineteenth-century British imperialist advertising clearly hearkened back to an Enlightenment view of Western identity and civilization. Similar patterns of advertising aesthetic are evident in the promotional campaigns of the Empire Marketing Board, which was established by the British Government in the 1920s and existed from 1926–1933. The Secretary of the Empire Marketing Board, Sir Stephen Tallents, secured the services of Crawford Limited, which was widely recognized at that time to be an 'enlightened' advertising agency with a 'distinctly international approach' (Freeman, 1977: 12). The Board's activities involved research, publicity and education. Nevertheless, the Empire Marketing Board is best known for its poster campaigns. The narrational style of these posters broke with the avant-garde abstractionism of the late 1920s (ibid.: 12). Indeed, the linear narrational aesthetic reproduced in the Empire Marketing Board's poster campaigns displayed little trace of the Cubist abstractionism which was, at

Figure 1.7   *Empire Marketing Board poster, 'Highways of Empire', 1927*

Source: Artist: MacDonald Gull. Reproduced by permission of the National Archive.

that time, captivating the art world. Figure 1.7 is a reproduction of a marketing poster distributed by the Empire Marketing Board in 1927.

The Empire Marketing Board's main objective was to promote the sales of Empire produce and consolidate the incorporation of Empire trade into the popular culture of the British people. One of its much acclaimed promotional endeavours was a poster campaign that sought to foster commercial links between Britain and its colonies by urging consumers to 'Buy Empire Goods from Home and Overseas' and to 'Buy Empire Every Day' (quoted in Auerbach, 2002: 16). Other similar initiatives include the 'Buying Brings Prosperity' campaign (quoted in Freeman, 1977: 13). While product promotion featured in the Empire Marketing Board's poster campaigns, it also had a sustained commitment to educate the public about the Empire. Indeed, the Board frequently stated that its primary intention was to create 'Empire-conscious people' (ibid.: 13). Accordingly, poster illustrations focused on depicting the commercial activities of the Empire. Figures 1.8 and 1.9 are reproductions of posters distributed during the reign of the Empire Marketing Board.

The imagery contained in Figures 1.8 and 1.9 is evocative of transformations which had taken place in the commercial representation of colonial markets. Whereas earlier advertising had suggested colonial regions to be pristine Edenic paradises suffuse with natural riches, by the turn of the twentieth century these spaces were being sold through more industrial

Figure 1.8 *Empire Marketing Board poster, 'Tobacco plantation in S. Rhodesia'*
Source: Artist: Frank E. Page. Reproduced by permission of the National Archive.

Figure 1.9 *Empire Marketing Board poster, 'Our trade with the East'*
Source: Artist: Kenneth D. Shoesmith. Reproduced by permission of the National Archive.

allegory (Freeman, 1977; Auerbach, 2002). Britain's industrial dominance had begun to dwindle and attention was turning to colonial suppliers and markets as sources of labour and raw materials necessary to refuel Britain's industrial challenge. In promotional literatures the trend was now to emphasize colonial spaces as extractable resources rather than pristine untouched lands (Auerbach, 2002: 17). These changes in advertising imagery nevertheless continued to invoke a sanitized history of the British Empire, one which concealed the deleterious consequences of imperialist expansion into markets overseas (ibid.: 4).

Conclusion

This chapter has focused on key transformations linking the evolution of modern advertising to economic relations, geared towards the control of markets by manufacturing cartels and the growth of a form of imperialism which ensured markets overseas. One consequence of the Industrial Revolution was that manufacturers were presented with economies of scale unforeseen in previous productive epochs. Manufacturers generally attempted to absorb the surpluses of heightened productivity through geographic expansion. This equates with 'spatial displacement', which 'entails the production of new spaces within which capitalist production can proceed' (Harvey, 1990: 183). Geographic displacement often coincides with 'temporal displacement' which is defined by 'a switch of resources from meeting current needs to exploring futures uses' or a speeding up and 'acceleration in turnover time' (ibid.: 182). Nineteenth-century imperialism was a formidable example of geographic expansion fuelled by a crisis of accumulation in British commodity capitalism.

The rationalization of space-selling, which accompanied the evolution of the advertising agency, also appears to have been an integral feature of capitalist development. Manufacturers eager to extend into wider areas of the country needed to have knowledge of market competition, distribution outlets, newspapers published and their respective circulations. In essence, they required advertising agents with knowledge and familiarity of newspaper publishers, who were also capable of writing advertising copy, simplifying accounts and managing cash flow. In its institutional form, the early advertising agency started with the buying of space by individual agents as part of the emergence of 'classified advertising order offices' (Hindley and Hindley, 1972). Initially, agencies were virtually agents of the press. The advertising agent would place an announcement for a client, check its appearance in designated publications, pay the proprietors of the publication and present the client with a bill. Alongside this basic space-selling service, advertisers were enabling city clients to expand beyond their immediate markets and into the provinces. Before the advent of nationally circulated newspapers, a nationwide campaign required the manufacturer to make links between city-based publications and the provincial press, but this required the business operative to possess a vast amount of knowledge about hundreds of local newspapers. Advertising agencies increasingly began to specialize in supplying provincial editors with notices of city trade. In the City of London, advertising agents operated as vehicles for channelling London advertising to the provincial newspapers.

Gradually and with an increasing emphasis on untied consultation services, advertising agencies were to become more independent from the press. Newspapers developed their own advertising managers. Towards the end of the nineteenth century, advertising had evolved from publishers' space salesmen (*sic*) into a more developed system of space-brokerage and consultation (Williams, 1980). Further advances in the rationalization of advertising were evident in 1904 with the establishment of the Incorporated Society of Advertising Agencies (Dunbar, 1979). This was formed largely as a response to the scathing critiques of the Society for Checking Abuses of Public Advertising (SCAPA), founded in 1898 (Hindley and Hindley, 1972). ISAA put pressure on the advertising industry to regulate the proliferating numbers of agencies and stem the inexorably competitive rate-cutting. The establishment of an organized system of commercial information and persuasion ultimately emerged in 1917 with the setting up of the Association of British Advertising Agencies (ABAA).

2

Selling Time in Advertising History

Figure 2.1 *Prudential Insurance advertisement, 1960s*
Source: Reproduced by permission of Prudential PLC.

Chapter 1 provides a historical account of dialectical links between industrial capitalism, the regulation of commercial spaces in the nineteenth century and the emergence of large-scale advertising. This chapter also has a historical theme, as it focuses on advertising with respect to the emergence of insurance as a socially acceptable commercial enterprise. Insurance is the art of transforming our lived experience of time into an abstract economic form of commodified relation. Indeed, it is striking how insurance makes possible a general economic ordering of the future. The 'openness of things to come', a colloquial representation of modernity, 'expresses the malleability of the social world and the ability of human beings to shape the physical setting of our existence' (Giddens, 1993: 111). As a socially dependable quantity, the 'open' future terrain of modernity lends itself to colonial invasion through counterfactual thought and risk calculation (1993: 111). Insurance plays an active part in this attempt to secure identity well into the unknown future. It is one of the principles of insurance that human life and health can be subject to financial evaluation (Defert, 1991; Ewald, 1991). Considered as suffering, the death of an individual or loss of a sentimentally valued object is all beyond price. And yet it is one of the principles of insurance to offer financial compensation for such a loss. In this sense, insurance operates through a dualization of the lived and the indemnified (Ewald, 1991: 205). Death and injury are at once unique events and indemnifiable risks. Axiomatic to this form of alchemy is the commodification of time. What is insured is not the injury or loss suffered by an individual but the 'value of a possible damage in a determined unit of [commodified] time' (Ewald, 1991: 205). For example, the practice of life, health and accident insurance often involves financially compensating an individual for 'work time' lost through injury. In this respect, insurance refers to a particular type of closure. It invokes a form of closure inextricably bound up with commercial instrumentality and directed towards rendering the future amenable to predictable controls. As Ewald puts it, 'to calculate risk is to master time, to discipline the future' (ibid.: 207).

The mid-nineteenth century is generally recognized as constituting the Gilded Age of insurance (Pope, 1983). At that time the selling of insurance was transformed from a practice of ill repute with unsavoury links with gambling, into a reputable moral enterprise. The first section of this chapter provides some illustration of advertising's role in promoting the now obscure speculative roots of insurance. Up until the late eighteenth century, advertising allied the legal association of insurance with the speculative possibilities of gambling. Insurance was mere speculative folly and advertising bolstered this image. From the late eighteenth century, cultural and legal expectations of insurance changed dramatically. The vision of insurance as a form of gambling troubled moral sentimentalities because it represented a presumptuous assault on prudence and financial self-discipline. More fundamentally, the Gambling Act of 1774 was intent on polarizing the practices of insurance and speculative gambling. This changing legal climate provided a strong incentive for a decisive transformation in the insurance industry's image. The second section of this chapter identifies advertising ingenuity as playing a crucial role in the fortuitous re-branding of the insurance industry in the nineteenth century. Insuring oneself from future hazard was transformed from mere speculative folly into a morally responsible task. Advertising promotion is largely accredited with having engineered a turnaround in the image of the insurance industry. In so doing, advertising represented a vital component of disciplinary technologies keen to make links between the buying of insurance and the adoption, by individual subjects, of a responsible relationship to the future (Knights, 1988). Insurance was transformed into a moral imperative and advertising was a key instrument in the creation of subjects, self-disciplined in the moral efficacy of financially managing their future.

Advertising chance in the history of insurance

Early writers on insurance, annuities and other risk ventures equated time with uncertainty, 'for time brought unforeseen changes in crucial conditions' (Daston, 1995: 115). Directed to this purpose, the early forms of risk sharing such as guild-administered aid and maritime insurance operated in terms of cumulative short-term risks. Prudent judgement based on experience, and the particularities of each case and, above all, personal knowledge, dictated the practices of early dealers in risk. These practitioners of risk acted as if the world were a mosaic of individual contingent events, each subject to the ordered restrictions imposed by moralists and theologians for hundreds of years. Thus, although the sixteenth-century manuals on maritime insurance were replete with detailed guidelines on particular cases, they contained limited material on standardized premiums (Gigerenzer et al., 1989). The early practice of risk sharing was not merely a-statistical, it was emphatically anti-statistical in its focus on short-term individual risk and neglect of long-term statistically informed predictions (ibid.: 26). Indeed, insurance amounted to little more than a wager on the price of a future contingency, on the basis of intuition and a thorough versing in the minutiae of an individual case. The association between insurance and gambling was common as is evidenced by the peculiar tradition of betting on lives. Up until the Gambling Act of 1774, it was common for insurance offices to serve as the primary site, from which to establish life insurance wagers on the life of a third person. Celebrities, cardinals or even sovereigns provided the subjects of these curiously contrived wagers on life. Insurance covers were available on the infamous lives of notorieties ranging from Sir Robert Walpole to the succession of Louis XV's mistresses. Premium rates rose or fell in accordance with their subject's circumstances. It is little wonder that these aleatory contacts were routinely accused of 'impiously anticipating providential outcomes', especially given that the third party insured was not required to be acquainted with the buyer (Clark, 1999: 44). The dilatory pace of news travel compounded the speculatory nature of these aleatory contracts and provided immense opportunities for the exploitation of insider knowledge. Evidence of such insider dealing was revealed in an exposé by the *London Chronicle* which stated, 'It is a well known fact that a certain ambassador insured £30,000 on Minorca in the war of 1755 with advices at the same time in his pocket that it was taken' (Flower and Wynn Jones, 1987: 53). In 1768, the *London Chronicle* published a leading article criticizing the illicit gambling at Lloyd's Coffee House. Nevertheless Lloyd's, and indeed the industry as a whole, thrived on the business of supplying aleatory contracts based on unknown future contingencies. It is fair to say that the marketing of life was as little interested in calculable probability as the purchaser of a lottery ticket. Indeed, merchants were offering insurance covers against losing at the lottery and were perhaps prosperous as a direct consequence of advertising ingenuity.

Lottery insurance and advertising puffery

The origin of lotteries is obscured by myth and legend, but it is generally believed that lotteries of various sorts had been known for centuries. Early recorded evidence of lotteries recount the activities of fifteenth-century Venetian merchants who held lotteries to avail themselves of costly but unsaleble commodities (Daston, 1995: 141). In due time, lotteries found favour in England and were adopted by the State as a lucrative source of government revenue (Sampson, 1874: 423). The State lottery was framed on the simple principle that the State offered a given sum, which would be repaid by a larger sum derived from losses incurred by players. Players inscribed a piece of paper with their names or some lucky invocation, this was then ascribed a number and registered at a designated lottery office (Daston, 1995: 142). On the occasion of the grand draw, a container held prize tickets and an equal number of blanks. An individual was deemed to have been successful if their registered number corresponded with a prize ticket. The inclusion of blanks into the selection process multiplied the possibility of no prize numbers being selected. As might be expected, the average player paid little attention to the improbability of success, preferring instead to believe advertising puffery exhorting the provident fortunes of lucky players. The promoters of lotteries were – even at these early stages – thoroughly cognizant of the persuasive value of advertising.

Scintillating advertisements were sedulous in their desire to convince each and everyone that they had the same pretensions to good luck. Indeed, it has been suggested that few things appear, at that time, to have had as intimate a connection with advertising than lotteries (Sampson, 1874). The advertisement shown in Figure 2.2 provides some indication of how advertisements allied with a profound belief in providence to obscure the improbability of success from the majority of players:

The advertisement in Figure 2.2 provides some indication of advertising's role in the spread of lottery participation across demographic groupings. It

> *"Dama Fortune presents her Respects to the Public, and assures them that she has fixed her Residence for the Present at CORBETT's State Lottery Office, opposite St. Dunstan's Church, Fleet Street; and, to enable many Families to partake of her favours, she has ordered not only the Tickets to be sold at the lowest Prices, but also that they be divided into Shares at the following low rates, -*
>
> | | | £ | s. | d. |
> |---|---|---|---|---|
> | *A Sixth-fourth* | .... | *0* | *4* | *0* |
> | *Thirty-second* | .... | *0* | *7* | *6* |
> | *Sixteenth* | .... | *0* | *15* | *0* |
> | *An Eighth* | .... | *1* | *10* | *0* |
> | *A Fourth* | .... | *3* | *0* | *0* |
> | *A Half* | .... | *6* | *0* | *0* |
>
> *By which may be gained upward of one hundreds and fifty to upwards of five thousand Guineas, at her said Office No., 30*

Figure 2.2 *Lottery dividends*

Source: Sampson (1874: 455).

was customary for lottery contractors to divide the shares of a registered number among individuals. Each ticket could be divided into halves, quarters, eighths and even sixteenths. A person with only 'thirty shillings to spare' was able to purchase a sixteenth of a ticket, thus providing the lottery contractor with huge profit margins among the lower classes (ibid.: 424). Contractors also profited from charging relatively more for these aliquot parts (ibid.: 424). In order to avoid a declining rate of profit resulting from saturated markets, contractors depended upon a wide geographic spread of these poorer customers. Changes to the older patterns of trade and demography had already begun to break down medieval parochialism. Regional self-sufficiency struggled to withstand the advent of early industrialization and the emergence of specialized commodity production. Advertising of all types flourished as the public taste for news exceeded the capacities of word-of-mouth communication. Promoters of the lottery were not oblivious to the potential of advertising to expand existing customer bases and increase the circulation of shares in lottery tickets. But few large fortunes were ever derived from the aliquotian parts of a lottery ticket. Nevertheless caprice was found to act in the place of reason and with the aid of advertising, lottery organizers enticed huge numbers of people into the groundless imaginary belief that their number would be selected. At the heart of the speculative lottery fever of sixteenth- and seventeenth-century England, hardly a day would pass without fresh projects for players to subscribe to. Sampson (ibid.: 443) describes how some of the projects 'were so barefaced and palpably gross as not to have the shadow of anything like feasibility'. Such instances include subscriptions to an insurance against divorce; another for making butter from beech trees and a scheme guaranteed to teach men to cast aside nativities (ibid.: 443).

Advertising provided the keepers of these obscure books with the levels of circulation required to attract subscriptions. Having generated speculative fever from an advertisement posted the previous day an unscrupulous agent could open a subscription book, net a quick profit and disappear.

Elsewhere advertising allied with the practice of insurance to provide an adjunct to playing lotteries. Although this 'sporting' part of insurance could be exceptionally complex in practice, it was in principle quite straightforward. Having secured the payment of an agreed premium, an insurer would be contracted to compensate a lottery loser for the cost of the ticket. If sufficient attention was paid to the rate of premium and enough policies issued, the insurer could be guaranteed to turn a tidy profit. The complexities of practice arose because lotteries were frequently drawn over several days and were often not sold out (Clark, 1999: 49). This meant that the ratio of blank tickets to prizes would change as the lottery progressed. Thus the value of undrawn tickets fluctuated and in so doing adding another layer of speculation to the aleatory contract. Nevertheless, the business of lottery insurance was immensely popular. Sampson (1874: 456) describes how between 1770 and 1775 the practices of insurance and lottery office-keeping had become largely indistinguishable. The social commentator, Thomas Mortimar, observed: 'There is hardly a 'prentice boy, or a waiter to a tavern, or coffee-house, in the neighbourhood of the [Exchange] Alley, that is not a sporter [in this kind of insurance]' (quoted in Clark, 1999: 49).

The insurance offices in London numbered over four hundred and many practised with dexterity the highly profitable exercise of insuring lottery tickets (Sampson, 1874). Circulation was in part based on the door-to-door trading of insurance agents. Advertising provided an additional medium through which to publicize the lucrative marriage of insurance and lottery in the occasioned speculation of chance and fortune. But this alliance was beset with problems. Lottery critics of the day catalogued a number of deceptive practices intent on defrauding the public. A noticeable feature involved the practice of bribing lottery personnel to conceal a registered number, with a view to insuring the same ticket in as many available offices (ibid.: 456). Public indignation directed at these duplicit practices precipitated intense debates among legal professionals, concerning the legality of insuring lottery tickets. In 1778, Parliament (having vehemently debated the problematics of insuring) passed an Act for the regulation of lottery offices. The legislation designated it illegal for office-keepers to operate without a licence and prohibited the sharing of any ticket by less than a sixteenth (Sampson, 1874: 460). Many other regulations featured in this Act and the legality of insuring was raised again the following year. Notwithstanding these initial attempts at regulation, the practice of advertising lottery insurance continued unabated. Advertising ingenuity was now of prime importance as office-keepers were forced to side-step the letter of the law in order to continue their pernicious trade. Advertising creativity rose to this challenge as lottery proprietors employed persons with the literary ability to attract public attention by verse, decoy paragraphs in

---

November 7th 1781

MODE OF INSURANCE

*Which continues the whole time of drawing the Lottery, at CARRICK'S STATE
LOTTERY OFFICE. Kings Arms, 72 Threadneedle Street. At one Guinea each
NUMBERS are taken to return three Twenty Pound Prizes, value Sixty Pounds, for
every given Number that shall be drawn any prize whatever above Twenty Pounds
during the whole drawing*
*Numbers at half a Guinea to receive half the above

&

*J. COOK respectfully solicits the Public will favour the following incomparably
advantageous plan with attention, by which upwards of thirty-two thousand Chances
for obtaining a Prize (out of the forty-eight thousand tickets) are given in one Policy.
POLICIES OF FIVE GUINEAS with three Numbers, with the first Number will gain:*

20000	*if a Prize of*	*£20000*
10000	*"*	*£10000*
5000	*"*	*£5000*

with the second number will gain

6000	*guineas is*	*20000*
3000	*"*	*10000*
1500	*"*	*5000*

with the third Number will gain

3000	*guineas is*	*20000*
1500	*"*	*10000*
1200	*"*	*5000*

Figure 2.3   *Lottery insurance advertisers, post-1778 Regulatory Act*

Source: Sampson (1874: 460–1).

newspapers and smart allusions to topical events (ibid.: 463). Evidence of
the use of advertising to evade the trading restrictions of the 1778 Act is
shown in Figure 2.3.

The later part of the eighteenth century witnessed a flurry of Acts seeking to prevent the practice of insuring lottery tickets. Parliamentary reports
in 1807 declared lotteries to be indistinguishable from illegal insurances
(Sampson, 1874: 462). It seemed an anomalous proceeding by the State to
reject the lucrative revenues obtained from lotteries and to declare gambling scandalous. But a dramatic change was occurring, an indication of
which is provided in the following excerpt from the 1807 Parliamentary
report:

> [T]he Lottery is so radically vicious, that under no system of regulation which
> can be devised will it be possible for Parliament to adopt it as an efficient
> source of revenue, and at the same time divest it of all the evils and calamities
> of which it has hitherto been so baneful a source ... idleness, dissipation, and
> poverty were increased – the most sacred and confidential trust were

betrayed,–domestic comfort was destroyed, madness was often created, suicide itself was produced, and crimes subjecting the perpetrators of them to death were committed.

(ibid.: 462)

Even during the heady heights of its popularity, the lottery had attracted vehement criticism. Speculating on chance provoked concern among the English intelligentsia, who set in print a chorus of denouncements declaring the lottery to erode the links between hard work and temporal reward. The winner 'many tymes is driven to wonder how hee wane' in the absence of 'industrie or overreaching wit', declared the sixteenth-century religious philosopher Daneau Lambert (quoted in Daston, 1995: 148). Elsewhere, the irrationality of occasioned speculating invoked vehement criticism from Daniel Defoe who called for mathematicians to contribute to 'a Weekly paper … highly necessary and useful to instruct the People how to lay their money, and very instrumental to the abolishing of Gaming' (ibid.: 147). Lottery critics of the day appeared tremendously troubled by the implicit message of social subversion represented by the lottery. In 1816, Sir Nathaniel Conant (a chief magistrate of Bow Street, London) stated, to a Committee of the House of Commons, that the lottery was one of the primary causes why 'the people of the metropolis were vitiated' (Sampson, 1874: 462). Occasioned speculation on chance was said to have encouraged theft, losses, disappointment and the continued proliferation of illegal insuring practices. The intensification of gambling regulation merely heightened the ingenuity of advertising as lottery proprietors generated ever more captivating devices, to exorcise the notoriety of lottery schemes and tempt public participation. The following specimen of advertising puffing is of particular quality and provides an indication of the advertising creativity, which characterized this regulatory era (Figure 2.4).

Advertising ingenuity is evidenced in Figure 2.4 by the complex processes of meaning transfer, whereby the rational linearity of Newtonian theory comes to be imbued with cultural meanings only arbitrarily linked to the referent that they originally signified. The clever allusions to rational science and metaphysics illustrate the ability of advertisers to attach

---

Before the time of Sir Isaac Newton, various notions were entertained concerning colours. Plato said colour was a flame issuing from bodies, the Indians of America believed the same, and when any person read a letter they believed it spoke, and blessed the paper in proporation as they were moved by it. What emotions would the following billet excite? "The bearer may receive one hundred thousand pounds" This would make a deep impression on the natives of every country, and may now be realised; for by the present Grand Lottery a single ticket may bestow on the Bearer One Hundred Thousand Pounds.

Figure 2.4 *Lottery insurance advertising puffery*

Source: Sampson (1874: 463)

signifiers to disparate objects and infer association in the most arbitrary of occasions. At a further level of analysis, the advertisement appears to represent a defensive response to a new sensibility of time discipline, order and causation.

With the rise of industrial capitalism, a new time consciousness emerges. Time becomes 'a commodity of the industrial process' (Hassard, 2001: 33). It is translated into an economic construct and ascribed symbolic reverence as an indicator of economic capital. Central to this transition is the commodification of productive labour and the economic imperative equating 'acceleration and accumulation' (ibid.: 133). In industrial capitalist production, labour time is the common measure of value and the expropriation of surplus labour time is the basis of profit. Technological innovations in manufacturing consolidated the hegemony of linear time to the productive economy and the notion of scarcity 'enhances its worth' (ibid.: 133). Human agents were now 'obliged to display good stewardship; time was scarce' and a powerful sign of capitalist progress, therefore, it must be used rationally (ibid.: 135). Thus, Mumford (1955: 5) writes, 'time-keeping passes into time-serving and time-accounting and time-rationing. As this took place, Eternity ceased gradually to serve as the measure and focus of human actions.' Similarly, Thompson, in his seminal essay, wrote:

> Puritanism in its marriage of convenience with industrial capitalism was the agent which converted men to new valuations of time; which taught children even in their infancy to improve each shining hour; and which saturated men's [sic] minds with the equation, time is money. (1967: 95)

Thompson's writings suggest that the asceticism associated with the emergence of time discipline is one of rationally calculable, future-orientated action. Puritan theologians had, in previous centuries, admonished the godly to interpret their daily conduct as a succession of deliverances superintended by God (Clark, 1999: 36). But by the end of seventeenth century God's providential plan appeared more inscrutable (ibid.: 36). Providence was increasingly perceived as operating through intermediate natural causes, necessitating a focused mental gaze on the workings of chance and accident. Consequently it became ever more difficult to attribute misfortune to God's punishment of sin. Thus providential thinking became attenuated with human agency, and the moral obligation to adopt higher standards of private and public morality so as to avoid the calamities of vice. It is no wonder that the polemical literatures of eighteenth-century philosophers berated the lottery for its implicit message of avarice and idleness. Daniel Defoe is said to have lamented the association of wagering with insurance, stating that gambling

> [had] become a Branch of Assurance ... and the [Nine Years] War providing proper subjects, as the contingencies of Sieges, Battles, Treaties and Campaigns, ... offices were erected on purpose which manag'd it to a strange degree and with great Advantage, especially to the Office-keepers. (quoted in Clark, 1999: 35)

A new providentialism had emerged. The idea of a world based on contingent processes seemed abhorrent to the enlightened free-thinking exponents of a mechanically driven, deistic universe (ibid.: 34).

It is this differentiation between self and world that constitutes the great 'Cartesian anxiety' (Bernstein, 1980), concerning the possibility of 'intellectual and moral chaos' (Bordo, 1986: 440). The medieval sense of ontological security, derived through relatedness with the world, had not relied upon objectivity, but on 'continuity between the human and physical realms, on interpretations, through meanings and associations of self and the world' (ibid.: 449). Conversely, the rationalist knowledge of the Enlightenment espoused a discontinuity between the 'self' and the 'world', which created a distinct sense of time as an 'indeterminate' future. It is within this context of anxiety that a new role is envisaged for reason, the role of exercising power over the natural world rather than escaping from it or rising above it through death or prudent actions. In this sense, time and space had to be organized not to reflect the infinite wisdom and all-consuming glory of God but to celebrate and facilitate the liberation of man (*sic*) as a free and active individual endowed with consciousness and will. As Descartes put it: 'We could be freed from the innumerable maladies, both of the body and of mind, and even perhaps from the infirmities of age, if we had sufficient knowledge of their causes and of the remedies provided by nature' (1952: 152).

The mechanical philosophy dominated scientific thinking in the seventeenth century and provided a convenient convergence between physicists and philosophers. Whether they regard matter as atomic and infinitely divisible or the accomplishment of metaphysical forces, scientists agreed with mechanistic philosophy that all phenomena in the physical world are the outcome of objective, causal relations between matter and motion (Adam, 1990). Moreover, such statements dictate the existence of universal temporality, for they specify that causal relationships define the logical form of a category of events, and this deterministic relationship can be applied to the past, present and future. As Peirce argues, this assumes that 'the state of things existing at any time, together with certain immutable laws, completely determines the state of things at every other time' (1892: 323) Sullivan, 2006). Everything that happens to spatial substance is inexorably determined. Hence all spatio-temporal phenomena are (re)constituted, as a consequence of the universal laws of determinism. A new world is constructed, one in which generativity and foresight are the preserve of objectively identifiable causal relations rather than the passionate attachments and malevolent virago of a supernatural cosmos. 'Chance', by the 1800s, 'was a mere word, signifying nothing – or else it was a notion of the vulgar, denoting fortune or even lawlessness, and thus to be excluded from the thought of enlightened people' (Hacking, (1990: xiii). Few eighteenth-century thinkers were prepared to embrace the idea of providential contingency. David Hume ([1739]1967) produced a sustained critique of chance, defining it pejoratively as the absence of established cause and directed by the imperfection of human reason (Clark, 1999: 37). Hume was committed to the belief in causation even when the determinant indices of effect were obscured by irrational logic. Alexander Pope (1734) also derided chance as mere illusion, stating that 'All nature is but Art unknown to Thee; All Chance, Direction, which thou canst not see' (quoted in Clark, 1999: 37). Numerous other polemical Enlightenment writers put in print their critique of the idea that God's will was meaningfully manifested in the outcome of aleatory practices. Meanwhile, scepticism concerning the moral efficacy of gambling was spreading among the middle classes (Clark, 1999). Successive gambling legislation had already encouraged the professional middle classes to withdraw from the public gambling scene. By the latter part of the eighteenth century, this group had become vehement critics of gambling. In anti-gambling literature, an emerging emphasis on moral matters provided a logical extension to the theological and philosophical discourses on the existence of fortune. The middle-class anti-gambling critique made connections between the national welfare and the time-disciplined actions of individual citizens. Gambling represented a direct threat to familial responsibility. It was perceived as eroding social trust and undermining links between hard work, talent and gain (Daston, 1995: 161). Gambling not only offended the tender conscience of middle-class morality, it also unleashed wild impetuous desires that upset the abstemious demeanour 'expected of the godly' (Clark, 1999: 40). Public indignation against gambling was especially inflamed by the widely held belief that certain humans harboured speculative impulses, which increased the possibility that they would be 'both incapable of calculation and incalculable' (Daston, 1995: 162). The enlightened self-controlled mind was apt to rely upon future prospects, involving the calculation of long-run probabilities and consequences. Conversely, speculation on chance presupposed a future proportionable to what we may be and not what we are, with the hope of instant fortune seldom realized or desired. Aleatory contracts like gambling agreed upon the price of a future contingency based on intuition, experience and the minutiae of the individual case. Such speculative practices ran directly counter to the calculable probabilities of middle-class morality. To the middle classes, gamblers were derided as undisciplined beings driven by an insidious passion for moral uncertainty, which, if left untempered, could erode familial trust and responsibility.

Eighteenth-century moralists tried to tame the acquisitive passion driving gamblers by inculcating the undisciplined soul into affirming a prudent relation to time. The gambler's narcissistic desire to disregard familial responsibilities epitomized a foreshortened attitude to the past, present and future. Speculation made uncertainty a necessity by choice, and was irreconcilable with the calculation of stable conditions or constant probabilities (Datson, 1995). To voluntarily succumb to chance symbolized a direct assault on the stable orderly world of the probabilists and arrested the calculating reason they sought to inculcate. In 1826, these middle-class sentiments supported the abolition of the state lottery in Britain.

By the early nineteenth century, speculative aleatory contracts had largely become associated with precarious financial circumstances and irreconcilable with the indissoluble bonds between cause and effect, past and future. Against this background of moral indignation it is hardly surprising that gambling and insurance had come to be seen as antithetical approaches to risk. Modernity had ushered in a new relationship to the future, one based on the desire to control the possibilities of life. Conversely, the proprietors of aleatory practices equated the future with uncertainty and unforeseen change. Their attitude to risk seemed to be less prudential than reckless, fuelled by the evanescent passions of gambling. Daston (1995) describes how the acceptance of probability calculus by these insurance practitioners required a profound shift away from a reliance on situationally contingent, finite time frames towards a conception of time as abstract, quantifiable and infinite.

Advertising prudence

In the marketing of insurance as a moral prerequisite, advertising played an important role both in controlling distribution channels and in marketing a new kind of product. Insurance was one among many types of commercial contracts that had accelerated the commercial growth of Western economies in the nineteenth century. But the flurry of prosperity, which defined the Gilded Age of insurance business, came at the cost of differentiation. Advertising provided key players with the means to centralize control over operations. In the United States the insurance firms which emerged out of the Depression in 1870 had accumulated billions of dollars of revenue (Pope, 1983). Corporations at the top of the industry had amassed vast pools of capital and built organizational structures of a size and scope virtually unparalleled in the American economy. Among these companies, the Equitable Life Insurance Company and the New York Insurance Company each had over a billion dollars of insurance in force by 1900 (ibid.). Both companies sold through a nation-wide network of general agents and salesmen. But neither of these immense corporations had been completely successful in controlling their individual salesmen and general agents. Given the importance of reputability to the promotion of insurance as a commercial guarantee to sustaining family welfare and financial solvency, controlling the practices of agents was imperative. Advertising became the principal mechanism of centralizing power and controlling the sales domain of corporate activity. First, companies often used advertising to recruit sales personnel. The recruitment advertisements would attempt to screen out undesirable applicants by emphasizing respectable character traits and warning against bad practice. Second, the insurance corporations attempted to standardize product information by requesting that agents use promotional material prepared by central office. Indeed, insurance providers, as early as 1848, emphasized the idea of presenting a consistent

Figure 2.5 *Image used for the Prudential Mutual Assurance Company seal in 1848*

Source: Reproduced by permission of Prudential PLC.

company point of view in all advertising. Stalson in *Marketing Life Insurance: Its History in America* (1942), provides extracts derived from the minutes of key insurance companies in the mid-nineteenth century. These minutes variously describe the efforts expended by companies to gain corporate acceptance of some degree of branding through advertising. Thus, for example, the Connecticut Mutual Board on 5 June 1848 is recorded to have stated the following:

> That the secretary notify Mr Morgan in reply to the application from New York for liberty to publish a pamphlet there; that the Board adhere to their former discussion directing that all pamphlets and circulars are to be published here, but if the Agent in New York desires anything printed adapted for that locality, he is requested to forward the manuscript here for publication. (ibid.: 269)

Pope in *The Making of Modern Advertising,* describes how the advertising literature distributed by agents served the dual purpose of communicating product offerings and disciplining work practices (1983: 58). One such sales brochure, circulated in 1889, contained the message 'no discrimination [in premium rates] is permitted or practiced', and included a notification to readers that 'any agent caught rebating would be summarily fired' (ibid.: 58). Companies also used advertising as a regulatory index in order to counteract the misleading and inflated claims for their policies made by agents. Advertisements would outline – as best possible – the scope and limitations of the insurantial agreement. Insurance advertising therefore performed an important educational function. The insurance policies themselves where mostly front-end loaded (i.e., rewarding long-term continuous investment and penalizing payment lapses and early surrenders). For these reasons, advertising for long-term contractual agreements emphasized financial calculation and promised favourable rewards (ibid.: 58). Advertising, quite obviously, was an efficacious device in the campaign to convince consumers of the prudential benefits of insurance. Similar conclusions are raised in Viviana Rotman Zelizer's (1983) *Morals and Markets: The Development of Life Insurance in the United States.*

Zelizer contends that the reversal of fortunes for the American life insurance industry in the nineteenth century rested on a new public acceptance of 'monetary equivalences for sacred things' (ibid.: xiii). Up until this time families, guilds and voluntary mutual aid groups were deemed responsible for attending to the economic hardship of the bereaved. Charity was perhaps the Church's most beneficent accomplishment as a source of voluntary aid for the destitute. Guilds were occupational brotherhoods of craftsmen and merchants, dedicated to securing economic well-being and social welfare for their members. By the Industrial Revolution, the power and influence of the guild collectives were being challenged by new individualistic forms of capitalist commercialism. And the Church struggled to sustain its commitment to the poor in the new urban economy. It was amidst this transition period from old to modern modes of production that security entered into the cash nexus. Economic security in a capitalist society is predicated upon protecting 'the greatest asset that most men possess … their economic value as earning machines' (Stalson, 1942: 11). Salaried employment therefore constituted both a source of security and risk, in the sense that unemployment would be financially detrimental to the individual and their dependants. It would appear that life insurance in the USA emerged as a direct response to these specifically modern conditions of material insecurity and the need for a device to safeguard against the loss of economic well-being.

Zelizer states that, by 1851, 'the financial protection of American families became a purchasable commodity' (1983: 91). This shift from a gift economy of reciprocity to a market of purchasable securities required a transformation in public attitudes towards the monetary evaluation of death. Zelizer argues that business enterprise instantiated this turn-around in public sentiments, but this required overcoming substantial cultural oppositions to commercial life insurance. Mutual aid and 'brotherhood reciprocity' had for generations provided financial assistance to the bereaved and those experiencing economic hardship. The ideology of altruism, which informed mutual aid, had deep-rooted religious and cultural values. In the pre-capitalist system of economic security, individuals were obliged to abide by the codes of conduct imposed by the system of support to which they were affiliated. Nevertheless, membership was an important source of comfort and security for its adherents. Mutual aid given by a community or religious group amounted to a reciprocal type of exchange regulated by obligation, trust and solidarity rather than by a business contract. The establishment of monetary equivalents to these gift relationships required a systemic shift, from a gift economy to a commercial system of economic provision. Life insurance blurred cultural boundaries between the sacred and the profane (Lubove, 1981). It confronted the traditional rituals of death and 'threatened the sanctity of life by pricing it' (Zelizer, 1983: 151). Consequently, the monetary evaluation of human life introduced by the industry was 'initially rejected by many as a profanation which transformed the sacred event of death into a vulgar commodity' (ibid.: 151).

The development of the life insurance industry in the United States was marked by the struggle between an ideology of altruism that endorses systems of voluntary mutual aid, and a market ideology representing efficiency equity and market relations. The instant wealth reaped by insurance claimants unsettled many people's strong belief in the doctrine of providence, which argued that God determined man's (sic) fate. The savings aspects of insurance were seen as a honourable mechanism for managing economic affairs because 'money was accumulated gradually and soberly' (ibid.: 151). However, the more general aspects of life insurance unsettled deep-seated cultural belief systems and this presented formidable obstacles to the diffusion of life insurance. Nevertheless, Zelizer argues that, by the mid-nineteenth century, the marketing of life had become popularly accepted. Life insurance had successfully aggregated the scared realm of death with the profane and in so doing constituted the value of man as a measurable commodity (ibid.: 150). A dramatic reversal of fortunes had occurred and life insurance 'began its fantastic history of financial success' (ibid.: 149). Historians of life insurance have long since puzzled over the sudden prosperity of the American life industry in the mid-nineteenth century. Insurance companies were offering the same products, terms and conditions as previously, and yet diffusion rates had significantly improved. Zelizer attributes the rapid growth of life insurance after the 1840s to a major change in the marketing and advertising practices adopted by life companies. In an attempt to cope with the conflicting goals of business and altruism, life insurance companies adopted an elaborate rationale to legitimize their 'secularised role in the management of death' (Lubove, 1981: 939). Zelizer (1983) identifies two major trajectories of changing marketing practices, the first extending from the early nineteenth century to the 1870s. During this time the marketing of life was keen to minimize the purely economic function of life insurance companies, emphasizing instead their ethical superiority. Life insurance advertising warned against 'dependence on the capricious and stinted aid of friends and neighbours' (ibid.: 95). Companies promoted life insurance as functioning 'to place its beneficiaries above the need of public charity' (ibid.: 96). Secular terminology was avoided in advertising communications, favouring instead a euphemistic alignment with religious, moral and social ideals (ibid.: 939). Indeed, insurance advertising often suggested that irreligiosity was the likely situation of the uninsured. The tendency for advertisers to communicate simultaneously in aleatory and providential terms reflected a desire by life insurance companies to connect their enterprises with dominant cultural values (Clark, 2002). Evidence of this curious mix of morals and statistical calculation is provided in the following advertising extract derived from a newspaper advertisement posted by the Mutual Life Insurance Company of New York in 1844:

> The science of Life Insurance, then rests upon the simple fact, that every individual of the human family has at birth, or at any given age, a certain term of existence which it may be predicted they will live through; this prediction is verified by all observations of the bills of morality, through three fourths of a century.
> The wider the sphere of observation in space and time, the better is the data upon which the system is founded. (quoted in Stalson, 1942: 136)

At a time when poverty was dismissed as dishonourable, life insurance assumed a responsibility to God and to family. Companies promoted the concept of the 'good death' which referred to 'a concern for one's family that extended beyond the grave and increased the probability of an untroubled mortality' (Lubove, 1981: 939). Stalson provides extracts from a newspaper advertisement posted in 1843 by the Mutual Life Insurance Company of New York. The advertisement contains the following admonition for the general public to be cognizant of their moral obligation to ensure the financial security of family members:

> Merchants and traders, officers, civil, military and naval; clergymen and professional men generally, clerks and persons in every station of society, may secure to their families in the event of death a comfortable support and independence by making, with this institution, a small annual investment for an insurance on their lives. (quoted in Stalson, 1942: 132–3)

Zelizer (1983) contends that in this first trajectory of marketing life, companies used moral and theological tropes to undermine the secular connotations of their role in the management of human life and death. This re-branding of the life insurance industry was startlingly successful and by 1851 over $100 million of security had been transacted. Between 1840 and 1860, the US life insurance industry had established itself as 'a morally beneficent institution' (ibid.: 101). But this unprecedented rate of economic success raised questions concerning the conflicting ideologies of economic success and altruism. The vast financial profits accumulated by the industry had transformed life insurance companies into powerful corporations. It became increasingly evident that 'the elimination of commercial self-interest by the mutuals ... had been more illusory than real' (ibid.: 103). Zelizer describes how the 1870s witnessed a second stage in the marketing phenomena of American life insurance. The industry's fortuitous growth enticed advertising communications away from an emphasis on 'disguising its commercialism' in altruistic pretensions, towards an appeal to the 'economic interests of premium payers' (ibid.: 117). Moralistic sentimentality was increasingly perceived to be an ineffectual marketing communication for corporations, which now had to convince a sceptical public of the legitimacy of their financial gains. From the 1870s, life insurance advertising discarded its emphasis on moral persuasion and adopted more 'sober business methods' (ibid.: 94). Life insurance continued to occupy a 'higher stage' in the civilization of mankind but this was now less a function of altruism and more a consequence of policyholders seeking 'personal economic advantage from their purchase' (ibid.: 111). In the ideology of utilitarian advertising, individuals are seen as pursuing their own separate ends and as motivated by the pursuit of private gains. The form of rationality in operation here is the instrumental rationality of efficiency, of seeking efficient means of achieving given ends; and underlying this form of rationality is the assumption of pervasive self-interest (Poole, 1985). It is axiomatic to this form of insurantial knowledge that time and the future should be ascribed the characteristics of abstract, singular units that can be measured and predicted. Time is perceived as a homogeneous unity that is nonetheless divisible into discrete units – a flow which, is however, unaffected by the transformation it charts (Adam, 1993: 166). And the future is a knowable limited entity, the eventualities of which can be mathematically calculated.

Zelizer's (1983) account of the fortuitous growth of the American life insurance industry in the nineteenth century accredits marketing and advertising as having placed 'death on the market'. In both the trajectories which constituted the Gilded Age of American life insurance, advertising operated to rationalize and commercialize cultural values. Advertising is constituted here as corroborating the commercial intentions of the insurance industry, by disguising 'its material mission in spiritual garb' and yielding theology to the capitalist ethos (ibid.: 153). Significant parallels exist between advertising's role in establishing the insurance industry in the USA and the relevance of advertising to the evolution of the UK insurance industry.

Although unremarkable in its ascendancy, the evolution of the UK life insurance industry also mapped onto a shifting moral climate. During the sixteenth and seventeenth centuries, life insurance was typically issued for short periods of time, often ranging from a few months to several years (Clark, 2002: 82). These restricted insurantial time-frames corresponded with the use of life insurance to cover discrete periods of time (e.g., the duration of a voyage). Maritime insurance underwriting epitomized short-term risk analysis as it was based on a view of the world as a 'mosaic of individual cases' (Gigerenzer et al., 1989: 24). Short-term risk analysis was also a consequence of the *ad hoc*, serendipitous associations of the insurers who underwrote risks. Then, as now, the market was constituted by brokers and underwriters. Insurance cover was obtained by brokers drawing up the details of the policy and then marketing the risk until convincing a body or individual to underwrite it. Underwriting tended to be carried out in a haphazard fashion by bankers, merchants and any individual prepared to subscribe to a policy. Such practices are easily likened to the touting of bets in racing establishments, as underwriting was open to any punter who fancied a flutter. The emergence of permanent life insurance collectives at the end of the seventeenth century partly arrested the short-termism inherent in the marketing of life. Permanent life collectives extended the temporal horizon of insurance because they enabled cover to extend the entire extent of an individual's life-time (Clark, 2002: 82). This form of long-term risk management required a profound shift in beliefs. Daston argues that long-term life insurance was directed at 'a growing middle class of salaried professionals – clergymen, doctors, lawyers, skilled artisans who were respectable but not of independent means' (1995: 175). This might partly explain why the marketing of life insurance appeared so receptive to the changing moral order. Permanent life collectives required mutual obligation in the management of risk profiles and a commitment to regular premium payments. This form of life insurance created a level of social cooperation distinct from the *ad hoc* affiliations, which linked the constituents of a risk pool in the wild-cat operations of individual underwriters (Clark, 2002: 82). Mutual obligation assumed a moral connotation quite at odds with the insurantial culture of aleatory speculation. It was presumed that the working classes lacked the social and moral resources necessary to sustain, unassisted, the long-term financial commitment necessitated by insurance policies (O'Malley, 2002). Marketing to the middle classes was thus a necessary mode of doing business and a disciplinary strategy for cultivating prudent moral values. In its pre-actuarial phase, the industry was keen to represent insurance as establishing a necessary civic virtue aligned with the middle-class values of thrift, parsimony and self-discipline (Clark, 2002: 88).

By the early eighteenth century the deleterious effects of insurance gambling, crime and fraud encountered vehement hostility. In a world in which 'even clergymen could not count upon communal charity', financial catastrophe was the proper fate of the imprudent gambler (Daston, 1995: 175). Bourgeois moral sensibility vociferously deplored the impropriety of gambling and this would have direct consequences for the marketing of life. Clark (2002) describes how, in order to demonstrate legitimacy, life insurers were increasingly intent on abandoning links with gambling. Lloyd's coffee house for some time had been linked to gambling racketeering. But, in 1769, a group of Lloyd's brokers decided to break adrift from the Lloyd's group and establish a rival to Lloyd's which they promoted as 'a more tightly controlled body that refused to issue gambling policies of insurance' (ibid.: 85). An increasing feature of advertising promotion was the enticement for buyers to recognize their moral obligation to provide a source of permanent protection for their beneficiaries. The Amicable, founded in 1706, set forth the following moral reasons for buying insurance:

> To Clergymen, Physicians, Surgeons, Lawyers, Tradesmen, and persons possessed of employments for life; and others whose income is usually subject to be determined or lessened at their respective deaths; who by insuring their lives may be morally certain of leaving to their families a claim not less than £100 on each member insured. (quoted in Stalson, 1942: 39)

Notable life insurers were also inclined to make explicit appeal to the values of the Enlightenment. For example, the prospectuses of the Paternal Society for the Provision of Children (1710), and the Amicable Society (1706) variously appealed to 'wise and judicious persons' (quoted in Clark, 2002: 85). Nevertheless if risk were to be domesticated and insurance respected as a 'pious and charitable undertaking' (ibid.: 85), measures were needed to sever its links from gambling.

The milestone legislation of 1774 (the Gambling Act) was intended to distinguish legitimate life insurance from gambling. It prohibited the insuring of persons or events where the policyholder could not show a legitimate interest in the life assured. In so doing, it foreshadowed new horizons in the marketing of life insurance. The image of life insurance was increasingly less allied to speculative values. In the aftermath of the 1774 Act, life insurance represented the triumph of technical and financial foresight over gambling (Daston, 1995). Insurance was transformed into legally authorized rational practices directed towards the mastery of time and disciplining the future. To conduct one's life in accordance with moral self-discipline was already a defining feature of middle-class culture. By the mid-eighteenth century pious middle-class culture was also refusing to ally 'the use of prudential institutions for speculative ends' (Clark, 2002: 85).

During this pre-actuarial stage of the UK insurance industry's evolution, advertising promotion was largely concerned with rationalizing and commercializing existing informal economic assistances and gift economies. Insurance as a commercial pursuit rationalizes spontaneous assistance through bureaucratized systematic risk-bearing techniques. In order to establish the legitimacy of the insurance enterprise, companies had to justify the shift from mutual aid and reciprocity to a commercial market for securities. Promotional appeals to the middle-class ideals of moral obligation and self-reliance were used to market insurance companies as beneficent institutions concerned more with the welfare of clients than the pursuit of profit. This beneficent image of the insurance industry appealed to an increasingly industrialized economy dominated by the cash nexus.

With the rise of probability calculus, guarding against ill fortune now also necessitated 'mathematizing one's commitments' (Ewald, 1991: 207). The founders of early life insurance societies in the UK focused on the particularity of each case, and thus were concerned with security in the short term and thought in terms of cumulative risks; a growing sum over cases and time (Daston, 1995: 115). Conversely, the probabilists asserted the opposite. Probabilistic concerns with symmetric deviations from an average encouraged long-term projections (ibid.: 115). Time was thought to reveal the formative regularities which underlaid change. With the rise of probability calculus, the future becomes an object of rational instrumental action. The surest way to advancement is shown, for a secure social order is now conceived in terms of rational actions guided by financially disciplined future-orientated goals. If buyers were to be convinced of the efficacy of an aleatory contract, it had to be seen to uphold the cardinal virtues of prudence, foresight and self-discipline.

It was no longer deemed acceptable to resign one's fate to providential forces. For even in misfortune one retains the possibility of calculating risk and repairing future eventualities. The combination of rational calculability and liberal prudence made insurance a formidable technology for human enterprise. An example of this shift in insurance discourse is evident in the promotional activities of the Equitable Society for the Assurance on Lives Survivorship. Established in 1762, the Equitable Life Assurance Society was one of the earliest mutual life assurance companies in the UK. It was also one of the first companies to use mathematical regularities in the calculation of risk. In 1750, the mathematician James Dodson (Fellow of the Royal Society) fundamentally transformed the practice of risk analysis by developing a statistical basis for calculating premiums (Equitable, 2006). Dodson was to become the moving spirit behind the Equitable's ground-breaking application of mathematical probability. Most annuity and life insurance providers were charging flat rates, regardless of age and largely oblivious to the available mortality statistics (Daston, 1995). Armed with mortality tables and probability studies, Dodson set out to introduce a refined analytical technique geared towards the production of standardized annual premiums. Probability calculus supplied insurers with the mathematical regulations upon which fixed premiums could be calculated, and guaranteed payments made. Thus, 'the policyholder's premium was fixed throughout the term of the policy and the amount paid on death was guaranteed' (Equitable, 2006). Dodson's mathematical ingenuity was eventually to form the basis of modern life assurance, despite initially experiencing significant reservations.

Although Dodson died in 1757, his backers were intent on carrying his project forward and presented a petition for a Royal Charter to the Privy Council on 1 May 1760 (Daston, 1995: 176). The verdict of the Privy

Council was emblematic of the seasoned judgements which characterized risk calculation at this time. For it was stated that the Equitable's mathematical basis 'whereby the chance of mortality is attempted to be reduced to a certain standard: ... is a mere speculation, never yet tried in practice and consequently subject, like all other experiments, to various chances in the execution' (ibid.: 177). Unrelenting in their endeavours, in 1761, the directors of Equitable produced a prospectus outlining the benefits of the new statistical procedures for calculating premiums. Daston provides an account of the published prospectus, which, as a form of advertising, is of relevance to our enquiry. The promotional literature is said to have invoked the language of moral virtue, appealing to the Equitable's mutual status as a pious charitable undertaking. The prospectus announced that the Equitable was to be a mutual established for its members 'the assured being mutually assurers one to the others' (ibid.: 177). Probability calculus and the mathematical calculation of risk would, in turn, facilitate the equitable distribution of dividends and the accurate application of annual premiums.

During the eighteenth century life insurance had fostered a uniquely modern means by which individuals could form affiliations in order to 'exert control over nature and the ineluctable hazards of human life' (Clark, 2002: 201). In pre-modern times, mutual guarantees of economic security were based on economic liaisons between individuals joined together by a committed sense of community and reciprocity. In the modern era, the spread of technologies that capitalize on the mathematical calculation of chance reduce future security to a monetary payment between members largely unknown to each other (Stalson, 1942: 15). This new imaginary served the individualistic and competitive aspects of capitalist society. The capitalist regime of individualism requires a subjective conviction and contractual guarantee that each member will pursue self-reliance both now and into the distant future (1942: 17). Indeed, in order to forestall a decline in long-term profitability, capitalism is compelled to convince its members to make provisions for their future retirement and for periods of non-productivity (Knights, 1988). Thus, in the modern era, the marketing of life is designed to inculcate a belief in the statistical calculation of life's contingencies and to promote the adoption of a financial self-disciplined relation to the future.

Nineteenth-century expansion

By the nineteenth century the enterprising opportunities proposed by insurance offered a means of ameliorating the rapacious effects of capitalism. Industrial capitalism had brought poverty, squalor, deprivation and abundance in equal measure. If left unabated, the poverty beneath the surface of Victorian prosperity threatened to undermine the foundations of the capitalist system. Life insurance presented a means of ameliorating capitalism's tendency toward corrosive aridity. It does by providing a commodified means of averting the risk of impoverishment and thus avoiding the social

NORTH BRITISH

AND

MERCANTILE

INSURANCE COMPANY LTD.

CHIEF OFFICES

EDINBURGH .   64 Princes Street

LONDON . . . 61 Threadneedle Street, E.C.2

Figure 2.6   *Re-branding insurance in the Gilded Age: North British and Mercantile Insurance Company Ltd, 1809–1959*

Source: Reproduced with acknowledgement to Peter Stubbs, www.edinphoto.org.uk

embarrassment of financial dependency on others (Knights, 1988). The nineteenth century had witnessed significant transformations in public attitudes to the provision of financial assistance to the poor. Liberal capitalism harnessed the enlightened pursuit of self-interest as a justification for inequalities in the dynamics of wealth creation. Enlightenment philosophers defined human beings as inherently predisposed to acquisitive behaviour. In this

71

sense, the uneven way in which wealth is distributed is justified as an outcome of natural human instincts and the natural laws of the market. The social analyses of Adam Smith epitomized the assertion that economic efficiency followed from the actions of self-interested subjects. Axiomatic to enlightened self-interest was an indifference to the poor and the tendency to blame the poor for their own impoverishment. The dissonant attitude of the British to poverty partly explains the erratic system of charity relief available in the nineteenth century. Charitable offerings were available from churches, missions and settlements but this was haphazard, often requiring claimants to demonstrate that they were deserving of assistance (Sheppard, 1983). Such degrading processes of interrogation 'cumulatively helped to make the poor believe their was nothing they could do to affect their destiny' (ibid.: 177). Indeed, liberal social philosophy defined each person as responsible for his or her own fate. This is largely the basis on which insurance came to be perceived as a means of buying freedom from the demeaning philanthropic paternalism of charities and misery of the labouring pool (Knights, 1988). The purchase of insurance is thus productive of life, as it protects the living against misadventure (ibid.: 53).

Evidently insurance is only one of many institutional relations producing instrumentally rational subjects, but what is especially illuminating is the relationship between this possessive mode of subjectivity and the commodification of social relations that characterize capitalist production. Offe and Ronge (1984) claim that the main strategy for state institutions to sustain their interest in accumulation is by advancing the widespread public participation in commodified relations. The greater the proportional share of the population engaged in the exchange of personal labour for abstract property, 'the more they become constituted as subjects whose sense of what it is to be socially significant involves them in pursuing material and symbolic possessions' (Knights, 1988: 60). Advertising makes possible the production of a certain form of acquisitive possessive individualism that leads to the 'adjustment of the accumulation of men to that of capital, the joining of the growth of human groups to the expansion of productive forces and the differential allocation of profit' (Foucault, 1979: 141). It is in effect a means of inserting subjects into the machinery of production and its economic ordering of the future (Knights, 1988: 60). Insurance advertising encourages the spread of commodified forms of exchange, to the extent that each new measure of protection creates a new form of insurable insecurity. This involves the continuous extension of insurantial technology through the exploitation of anxieties.

Conclusion

In the eighteenth century, buyers and sellers of insurance were no more interested in probability than were the purchasers of a lottery ticket. Insurance relied upon the speculation of chance and misfortune. By the early nineteenth century, these aleatory practices were perceived as clearly subverting the virtues of prudence and the need for foresight, 'from provision of self to provision for family' (Daston, 1995: 173). The calculation of risk through probability calculus was seen as analogous to the calculation of self-interest and the virtues of reliability (ibid.: 173). Quantifying perplexity by the adoption of probability may have attenuated the margins of profitability, but it also provided insurers with direct connections to changing moral values. The calculation of self-interest was an increasingly influential moral prerequisite and a crucial aspect of promotional imagery. Insurance advertising in the nineteenth century invoked the language of moral virtue in its appeal to self-imposed regularities on social and economic arrangements. In so doing, advertising attested to an alliance between capitalism and linear representations of the future.

In the modern era, insurance becomes the art of transforming our lived experience of time into an abstract economic form of commodified relation. Scales of compensation are fixed in advance so as to anticipate the indemnity entitlement for every form of crisis (Ewald, 1991). Hence it is a major feature of insurance that an event considered as suffering can be transformed into a cash price. Moreover, calculating something as a statistically desirable event enables risk to be continuously elaborated, differentiated and expanded by the practice of insurance (Knights and Vurdubakis, 1993). It would appear that every eventuality can be transformed into a risk, so long as the event can be classified in accordance with the principles of insurance technology (Ewald, 1991). Indeed, it is hard to imagine all the things which insurers have managed to invent as classes of risk. As Ewald puts it:

> for certain thinkers insurance is called upon to extend indefinitely the field of guarantees it affords against risk and to attain the form of an 'integral' insurance. Here, in fact, it tends to the character of an infinite, unlimited guarantee. (ibid.: 200)

Advertising is efficacious in this respect, especially in its ability to transform the present into a moment of lack and disenchantment. Indeed, the marketing of life insurance invites consumers to objectify their future as something that can be managed through rational instrumental action. The future is transformed into a series of risks that can be managed in the present. Nevertheless, advertising discourse diverts our attention from the fact that what is insured is not a subjectively meaningful loss as experienced by the individual, but rather 'a capital against whose loss the insurer offers guarantee' (ibid.: 204). The event, defined through insurantial technology as a statistically probable occurrence, becomes an indemnifiable risk, amiable to financial reparation. It is clear that the overall impact of offering financial compensation for life's eventualities is to advance the spread of commodified relations. And insurance advertising is a primary vehicle for these purposes. Indeed, the marketing of life gives rise to forms of commodity relations, which reflect and reinforce acquisitive materialism as a moral imperative.

Part Two

Dialectics of Advertising in Modern Times

Figure Part II *Utility, style and the commodity-sign*

Source: Reproduced by courtesy of Whirlpool, photographer Tessa Traeger.

3

Time and the Commodity-Form

Marxist analysis of time and commodity culture reveals advertising as directly implicated in capitalist accumulation. *Capital* (Volume 1) begins by telling us that the foundational form of capitalist society derives from 'an immense accumulation of commodities'. But the commodity presents itself to us as 'an object outside us'. 'A commodity is ... a mysterious thing, simply because ... the relation of the producers to the sum total of their own labour is presented to them as a social relation, existing not between themselves, but between the products of their labour.' (Marx, 2003: 77). Marx believed that people should be fulfilled as creative beings in their work. Under capitalism, however, we neither control the things we produce nor do we recognize them as products of our labour. What particularly interested Marx was that in capitalist modes of production, social relations between people become transformed into a relation between things. This Marx refers to as commodity fetishism. Commodities are the outcome of labour power, but this disappears into them as they transform into an alien force which rules our lives. Marx established the value of a commodity to be defined in its magnitude by the amount of socially necessary labour time invested in its production. It is labour time which produces value. Embodied in the commodity these exists an abstract unit of socially necessary labour required to produce it. This also represents a source of profit in addition to any that may be made from the 'exploitation' of labour. But labour misrecognizes its basis as a source of value. The products of modern capitalism are sold as commodities which are fetishized in appearance so as to obscure their basis in the exploitation of labour. This chapter examines critical theorists who have located advertising within the network of economic processes dedicated to reproducing capitalism's expropriation of surplus labour time.

Time and the commodity-form

Modern consumption can be observed as an extension of what Marx called 'commodity production'. Part 1 of *Capital* begins with an examination of what Marx calls the 'two-fold aspect' of commodities: 'those of use-value and exchange-value'. For Marx, a commodity is 'a thing that by its properties satisfies human wants of some sort or another' (Marx, 2003: 43). Marx defines a use-value thus:

> The utility of a thing makes it a use-value. But this utility is not a thing of air. Being limited by the physical properties of a commodity, it has no existence apart

from that commodity. A commodity, such as iron, corn or a diamond, is therefore, so far as it is a material thing, a use-value, something useful … Use-values become a reality only by use or consumption: they also constitute the substance of all wealth, whatever may be the social form of that wealth. In the form of society we are about to consider [i.e., commodity producing society], they are, in addition, the material depositories of exchange-value. (Sayer, 1989: 50)

Marx also defines exchange-value thus:

at first sight, [it] presents itself as a quantitative relation as the proportion in which values in use of sort are exchanged for those of another sort, a relation constantly changing with time and place. Hence exchange-value appears to be something accidental and purely relative, and consequently an intrinsic value i.e., an exchange-value that is inseparably connected with, inherent in commodities, seems a contradiction in terms, (ibid.: 50)

Marx proceeds to unravel this contradiction between use-value and exchange-value (see *Capital* Vol. 1, 2003: 44–8). To commerce with, Marx contends that although exchange-value necessarily manifests in a purely relative form (i.e., subject to market forces), the value-relationship which commodities bear to one another has expression in an absolute form. This requires that some common quality either inherent in or attached to commodities must be identified as constituting the substance of value. This common quality must also take upon the 'substance that manifests itself in the exchange-value of commodities' (ibid.: 46). These forms, Marx argues, are 'abstracted from' in the exchange. In effect, commodities, regardless of their specific use-values, have the capacity to pass as equivalents in market-based relations (Meek, 1979). We need only consider the popular two-for-one offers at supermarkets to gain a sense of products passing as equivalents. Marx argued that the substance which constitutes a common element across commodities was quite apart from a natural property such as weight, volume, etc., 'such properties claim our attention only in so far as they affect the utility of these commodities' (Sayer, 1989: 51). Once the option of constituting 'that common something' as a natural property is excluded, commodities have only one quantifiable common property left that fulfils the requirements that Marx identifies with value. That inherent quality can only be the quality of being products of labour. But the exchange of commodities is an act totally abstracted from use-value. Consequently, labour in capitalist production is a distinctive form of labour. The commodity is no longer regarded as the product of the carpenter, the joiner, the mason 'or any other definitive kind of productive labour' (ibid.: 51). Irrespective of the various forms of labour embodied in them, all commodities are reduced to one form of labour, 'human labour in the abstract' (ibid.: 52).

Labour theory of value

Marx contends that it is labour that produces value, and surplus labour is converted into monetary profit by the capitalist during the circulation of products on the market. Pivotal to Marx's concept of value is an important distinction between 'useful' and 'abstract' labour (Meek, 1979). Use-value can be defined objectively as the utility of the product or subjectively as the usefulness of the labour required to produce it. When use-value is considered subjectively, the concept of 'useful' labour emerges (ibid.: 165). Marx defined 'useful' labour as 'productive activity of a definite kind and exercised with a definite aim' (2003: 49). Labour in this form creates use-value, but the labour which finds expression in profit, according to Marx, 'does not possess the same characteristics that belong to it as a creator of use-values' (ibid.: 49). Commodity production's primary aim is not the creation of use-value as such, but the manufacture of goods for sale. In this sense, use-values are of relevance to the commodity producer in so far as consumer expectations need to be taken into account.

Marx distinguishes 'useful' labour from 'abstract' labour. The latter's distinguishing characteristics are axiomatic to production within modern capitalist societies. As Marx puts it, the concept of 'abstract labour' is 'truly realised only as a category of the modern society' where 'individuals pass with ease from one kind of work to another, which makes it immaterial to them what particular kind of work may fall to their share' (quoted in Meek, 1979: 165). This abstraction expresses a relation which in fact dates back to a much earlier time when products first started to be turned into commodities. Indeed, the exchange of goods for money designated the essential precondition for capitalism and marked a historical disjuncture with the mode of production which had occurred in the feudal era. The economic and social structure of pre-industrial Britain was organized around a system of feudal agriculture in which land was given as a reward for service. Goods produced in pre-capitalist social formations were typically for immediate consumption and not to be exchanged in the market place. Thus, in feudalism, it is precisely because 'personal dependence forms the ground-work of Society, there is no necessity for labour and its products to assume a fantastic form different from their reality, (Marx, 2003: 81). They take the shape, in the transactions of society, of services in kind and payment in kind. After the Industrial Revolution and with the inception of factory-based production, the goods produced were legally defined as the property of the owners of the means of production. With growing commodity production, where tasks began to be performed for future needs or for trade, there occurred a more ridged demarcation between the workers and owners or controllers of capital. This was a time when labour first started to 'acquire its social character from the fact that the labour of the individual [took] on the abstract form of universal labour' (Marx, 1971: 29, quoted in Meek, 1979: 165). The point of significance here is that whereas labour begins to assume a social character from the moment men [*sic*] begin to work for each other, the special form in which this social character manifests itself differs from epoch to epoch (Meek, 1979: 165). Following this, Marx identifies how in a commodity-producing society, the social character of each producer's labour manifests itself in the fact that this labour is reduced to abstract labour, and the social character that his [sic] particular labour, has of being the equal of all other particular kinds of labour, takes the form that all the physically different articles that are the products of labour, have one common quality, viz that of value. (2003: 78)

The distinction between useful and abstract labour is axiomatic to Marx's account of the expropriation of profit through surplus value. If a use-value derives value 'only because human labour in the abstract has been embodied or materialised in it', the magnitude of this value is therefore measured by 'the quantity of the value-creating substance, the labour, contained in the article' (Sayer, 1989: 52). The quantitative measure of labour is derived by the expenditure of time and 'labour-time in its turn finds its standard in weeks, days and hours' (Sayer, 1989: 52). Thus:

> Labour has been equalized by the subordination of man to the machine or by the extreme division of labour … the pendulum of the clock has become as accurate a measure of the relative activity of two workers as it is of the speed of two locomotives … Time is everything, man is nothing; he is at most time's carcass. Quantity alone decides everything; hour for hour, day for day. (Marx 1967: 151)

If human labour creates value, the clock is its measurement. The mechanistic metaphors of time used by Marx are commensurate with the objectification of labour in capitalist production. For the logic of the capitalist mode of production 'is and remains – the mass of direct labour time, the quality of labour employed, as the determinant factor in the production of wealth' (Marx, 1973: 704). Labour power is defined by Marx as 'the aggregate of those mental and physical capabilities existing in a human being, which he [sic] exercises whenever he produces a use-value of any description' (2003: 164). In capitalist production, what Marx calls 'the dull compulsion of economics' coerces individuals to sell their labour power as there is little other means of survival other than to enter into a subordinate relationship with capital. Conversely, the owners of the means of production retain control over capital and in so doing possess – for the working day – the bodies tied to labour power. The worker for a proportion of the working day is paid back, in the form of wages, the value which is generated from their labour. The capitalist, however, only pays the worker the value of the reproduction of labour power (the sum cost of maintaining the worker at a socially determined level of subsistence). But labour has the curious ability to generate more value than it needs to survive and reproduce itself. The difference between the value of the commodity, created by labour power and the salary supplied to the labourer is surplus value. Thus, in capitalist production, the exchange of equivalences has been turned around to produce a generalized system of commodity production, based on wage-labour and the conversion of surplus value into profit. The worker is doubly bound to work both necessary labour time (in which value is created sufficient for the reproduction of labour power) and surplus labour time (in which value is created for the appropriation of profit). In summary, Marx argues that it is labour time which produces surplus value and provides the basis for wealth. But because the objectification of human labour in production is disguised by the market system, labour is drawn to investing the wages it has earned into the purchase of non-productive property (consumer goods) which have been produced by other workers. The ability of the market system of generalized production to obscure the centrality of surplus labour-time to capitalist exploitation is a key aspect of Marx's concept of commodity fetishism.

Commodity fetishism

What particularly interested Marx was that in capitalist modes of production, social relations between people become transformed into a relation between things. This Marx refers to as commodity fetishism. Commodities are the outcome of labour power, but this disappears into them as they transform into an alien force, which rules our lives. Marx saw the reality of capitalist society as one dominated by commodities, which take the place of the free flow of relations between people. As Marx put it:

> The mystical character of commodities does not originate, therefore, in their use-value. Just as little does it proceed from the nature of the determining factors of value. For, in the first place, however varied the useful kinds of labour, or productive activities, may be, it is a physiological fact, that they are functions of the human organism … Secondly, with regard to that which forms the ground-work for the quantitative determination of value, namely, the duration of that expenditure, or the quantity of labour, it is quite clear that there is a palpable difference between its quantity and quality. In all states of society, the labour-time that it costs to produce the means of subsistence, must necessarily be an object of interest to mankind … And lastly, from the moment that men in any way work for one another, their labour assumes a social form. (2003: 76)

It is clear from this quotation that the fetishism of commodities refers precisely to the relations between labour time, use-value and exchange-value. In *Capital*, Marx is conclusive about the materiality of use-value as he expresses it 'so far as it [the commodity] is a use-value, there is nothing mysterious about it'. Marx defines labour time as producing use-values which, in turn, have a clear, quantifiable materiality. Conversely the mysteries of fetishism flow from the commodity's exchange-value. To 'make a fetish' involves investing something with properties it does not have in itself. In this sense, fetishism does not equate with illusion, but rather the misrecognition of properties as belonging to a commodity directly. For example, if we think that the value of a house is an inherent quality, we misrecognize that its value is only a result of a market system created by humans. In essence, fetishism involves failing to recognize that the properties of things are not an inherent part of their physical existence, but in fact 'created by their integration into a system of meaning' (Jhally, 1987: 29). The mystery arises because the social character of production is manifested only in exchange. For example, the many individual labour hours invested in the building of a house are carried out by private individuals or groups of individuals labouring independently of each other. The social character of production is revealed in the process of sale, within which the individual labour hours are aggregated and appropriated as profit. In this sense, the market operates as a distributing force transforming the total labour invested into a socially unifying element, which can be expropriated as profit. Commodity fetishism consists in disguising the fact that in essence humans produce value. In so far as labour produces capital, the sale of a commodity in a market place is just the fetishized offspring of 'congealed labour time' (Marx, 2003: 47).

It would seem then that commodity fetishism is as much a product of market relations as it is a product of labour producing itself as object and subject of capital (Wayne, 2003: 191). The fact that social relations between producers take the form of value relations between commodities is testament to how consumption is part of alienation. Nevertheless one consequence of capitalist economic production is that workers have to enter into market relations in order to survive. The sense of estrangement which workers experience in the production process is, for Marx, in itself a negation of freedom. Yet this sense of estrangement is compounded by the fact that exploitation in capitalist society is mediated through the active participation of workers in the purchase and sale of commodities. For this denotes a 'labour in which man alienates himself' (Cohen, 1978: 120). Individuals partake in paid work because they assume that the products of their labour have value, to which they relate, and which regulates their lives as producers. The social reality of oppression becomes invisible as workers, in quite a specific sense, become alienated from their own power, which has passed into things (ibid.: 120).

The three volumes of *Capital* develop the theme of exploitation and the generality of commodity relations. The resulting picture is that of a proliferating array of technologies, which are exploitative of the subjective anxieties of the alienated subject. The fragmentation of society into 'material relations between persons and social relations between things' is a vivid recurrent theme in *Capital*. According to Marx, capitalism is an 'enchanted, perverted, topsy-turvy world' (quoted in Holloway, 1992: 152). It is a fragmented world, sustained by the activities of alienated subjects endeavouring to seek security through the accumulation of material wealth, yet oblivious to these actions as reproducing 'the political and economic substructures of capitalist society' (Offe and Ronge, 1984: 121).

Advertising history, time and the commodity-form

In Marxist analysis, it is at the level of commodity fetishism and the corresponding cultural collaborations of subjects that we find the powerful ideological effects of advertising. Marxist analysts identify the capitalization of commodity production as unleashing powerful incentives for the development of techniques, which create new territories for producing exchange-value. Modern advertising is said to have emerged as a response to particular historical crises in the reproduction of exchange-value. Of significance was the transition to monopoly capitalism in 1900 which entailed a shift from 'absolute surplus value' to 'relative surplus value' (Goldman, 1995). Early forms of capitalist expropriation of the means of production entailed a strategy of absolute surplus value extraction, which demanded extended working hours at reduced rates of pay. In this situation, socially necessary labour time contained within the working day remains constant, while surplus labour time is significantly increased. Absolute surplus value also has a direct bearing on the technologies of production, as it attempts to yield an increased magnitude of output, while retaining the rate of variable capital inputs at a level which does not threaten the rate of surplus value. Broadly speaking, absolute surplus value is defined technically 'as any increase in the sum of surplus labour-time worked, regardless of the form that this takes, and without any alteration of the rate of variable capital that is required to generate that surplus labour time' (Lee, 1993: 121).

The quantity of labour time necessitated in the appropriation of profit through absolute surplus value quite clearly runs up against certain concrete barriers of time and space. At its bare minimum, labour requires some portion of the working day to be set aside for its recuperation. Consequently, a strategy of absolute surplus value extraction will inevitably encounter formidable problems. An indication of these limitations is provided in E.P. Thompson's (1967) seminal essay 'Time Work Discipline and Industrial Capitalism'. He identifies the transition from agricultural production to industrial production, in the eighteenth century, as having created a radical disruption to the qualitative rhythms of agriculture and artisan craft-based work. Thompson argues that the rise of industrial capitalism precipitated a marked transformation in the dominant 'task-orientated' temporal consciousness, towards a greater synchronization of labour and more exact time routines. These changes entailed the internalization of a more rational, quantitative 'time orientation' to labour and life. Thrift and abstemiousness were enjoined on all workers as the new time ethic combined with the Protestant work ethic to produce a utilitarian economic approach to time. As early industrial production progressed, tensions emerged between the abstemiousness values of the Protestant work ethic and capitalism's desire to draw all members of society into distributing commodities through the market (Ewen, 1977). The long hours of work demanded by absolute surplus value extraction, coupled with an interest in savings and investments among the workforce, arrested the spread of the commodity-form. Consequently, many reproductive activities (e.g., preparing food) and social activities (e.g., leisure pursuits) continued to exist outside of the cash nexus. Capitalist development under these conditions was not successful in absorbing the population into fully commodified relations. And patterns of consumption adequate to permit subsistence persisted in the form of non-commodity relations (Goldman, 1995).

The transition to monopoly capitalism in 1900 witnessed a systemic transformation in capitalist accumulation from a strategy of absolute surplus value to 'relative surplus value'. Relative surplus value extraction entails reducing working hours through an increased productivity of labour and the development of technology in the mechanization and rationalization of the labour process (Goldman, 1995: 16). Broadly speaking, relative surplus value involves increasing surplus labour time without extending the duration of the working day. It is predicated on the introduction of strategies designed to achieve the curtailment of socially necessary labour time, through the reorganization of the mode of production (Lee, 1993). Inevitably this will involve the rationalization of the labour process and a redeployment of the activities of labour (ibid.: 121). A regime of relative surplus value also necessitates the stimulation of growth through the technological development of productive forces. Collectively, these changes will dramatically modify the appearance of commodities. Marx argued that embedded in goods are located the social relations of production which in turn constitute the commodity-form. The historical transition from absolute to relative surplus value extraction greatly reduced production time and enabled the increased circulation of mass-produced standardized articles. These developments, combined with higher rates of pay, significantly extended commodified relations. In the *Critique of Political Economy* (1971), Marx anticipated the need for modern capitalist accumulation to maintain specific and corresponding social formations, in order to sustain their pursuit of profit and existing relations of production.

The rise of advertising as a vehicle for inculcating time discipline

Marxist analysts of advertising history identify the transition to monopoly capitalism as witnessing an unprecedented level of capitalist expansion into new markets. Monopoly capitalism required the creation of more avenues to absorb an abundance of new commodities and provide outlets for capital investment. Axiomatic to these processes was the development of an ideology of industrialism, which was intent on stabilizing working cultures and inculcating them into a system of synchronized labour. The clock time of industrial work was an assault on the senses of industrial workers. The rhythms of the seasons, movements of the sun, and other qualitative categories of predominance in pre-modern societies, largely governed agricultural production. Conversely, industrial production required workers to become acclimatized to the precise divisions of clock time but this was no easy task and cultural historians have variously documented how the transition to a greater synchronization of labour, and a greater exactitude in time routine, was fraught with resistance and agitation.

Ewen (1977) provides a particularly engaging account of the USA and the widespread working-class resistances to industrial capitalism in the early twentieth century. His book, *Captains of Consciousness: Advertising and the Social Roots of the Consumer Culture*, is an oft cited account of the

American advertising industry and its conditions of emergence. Ewen contends that the early history of industrialization was marked by tensions between the working lifestyles of a pre-industrial order and the mechanized rhythms of factory production. Workers largely resisted the invasion of capitalist ideals into work and lifestyles. These tensions 'precipitated crises of widespread social unrest and violent clashes between workers and those employed to protect the interests of capital' (Ewen, 1977: 8). Within this context, the factory struggled to become an arena of reliable production. Legislative responses to these conflicts were unabated in attacking organized labour, and restricting the rights of working-class people to challenge a lack of self-determination in the industrialized labour process.

In these early stages of industrial capitalism, dissension manifested in the form of disgruntled resistance. As industrial capitalism progressed in its imposition of time discipline, resistance among the working classes shifted from a 'fight against time' to oppositions 'about time' (Thompson, 1967). Similarly, Ewen observes that by the early twentieth century the real issue that confronted workers 'was the development of an industrial system which would be geared toward meeting people's needs; a system in which work and misery would no longer be synonymous' (1977: 9). What is of particular interest here is the response of the business community to this historical crisis of social control. Ewen states that the 'move in industrial thought was in the direction of "human management" – a more affirmative approach to discipline' (ibid.: 12). "Human management" required that businessmen confront the issue of industrial management through strategies, which coordinated a manipulation of markets with the systematic control of the labour process. In the United States, industrial leaders contended that traditional approaches to managing labour had been unsuccessful in conjoining consumption and industrial discipline. It was deemed necessary to imagine ways of linking the need to establish a well-assimilated organization with strategies geared towards achieving commercial success. Under these conditions, business leaders began to explore the possibilities of a 'science of human engineering', which would respond to the exigencies of the productive system and the necessity to control human conduct. Evidence of this move in industrial thought is provided by the implementation of the time and motion studies of Frederick W. Taylor. Ewen describes how these studies 'attested to the new interaction of business and the social sciences in confronting the problem of making an often antagonistic work force behave stably and predictably' (ibid.: 13).

Similar conclusions are evident in E.P. Thompson's analysis of time-discipline and the English Industrial Revolution. Thompson argues that the Industrial Revolution caused disquiet among workers, because they had no model of synchronized work against which to measure the benefits of the dislocations they were suffering. Pre-modern patterns of work had emphasized an 'essential conditioning in different notations of time provided by different work-situations and their relation to "natural" rhythms' (1967: 59). Conversely time measurement in industrial capitalism is defined not by the task but the value of time when reduced to money. It is only through an exactitude in time that labour can be conditioned into the mechanical rhythms of synchronized technology and their surplus labour time be extricated with maximum efficiency. As E.P. Thompson puts it, 'time is now currency; it is not passed but spent' (1967: 61). Thompson observes how the imperative of synchronized labour translated into a determined assault on the irregular labour rhythms of the pre-industrial order. Within the intellectual culture of Western Europe, there had occurred important changes in the apprehension of time. In the Renaissance, intellectuals depicted time and change in terms of a predetermined system of providential forces. For example, in Chaucer's Knight's Tale, Egeus reminds the sorrowing society that the world is but a highway 'And we been pigrymes, passynge to and fro'. With the growth of industrial capitalism, science and a technological intervention into the 'natural' flow of events, Western intellectual orthodoxy begins to adopt a sense of time's all-consuming power; *Tempus edax rerum* was no idle imagining but rather 'present and real' (Quinones, 1972). Elsewhere, the propagandists of discipline within the manufacturing classes imposed time-sheets, time keepers, informers and fines in their attempt to tame the irregular labour rhythms of the working classes. Thompson (1967: 38) details a disciplinary measure administered by Josiah Wedgwood in 1810 to his workforce. It stated that 'Any of the workmen forceing their way through the Lodge after the time allow'd by the Master forfeits 2/-d'. Sloth was construed here as a shameful devourer of money. Schools featured among the many non-industrial institutions involved in the inculcation of 'time-thrift'. Officials recommended that schools aspire to become spectacles of habituated regularity. Elementary schools were a particular site for the systematic indoctrination of the young into time-disciplined subjects. E.P. Thompson observed that exhortations to punctuality were written into the day-to-day rules governing elementary education.

The avalanche of criticism, from so many different sources, directed at traditional work rhythms was not uncontested. Cultural historians forestall have documented how the cementation of synchronized labour was besieged by resistances (Pollard, 1965). Confrontations over discipline threatened to disrupt not only the productive system, but also capitalism's need for steady distributive channels and a definite indication of demand. Ewen (1977) argues that the issue of neutralizing social unrest became a strategic concern of early industrialist. Social science appeared to provide an intellectual means of rectifying this situation. Its analyses of human conduct presented business leaders with an attractive means of linking the need to produce pacific social relations and the need to expand consumer markets. Business corporations envisioned an order in which commodity production and industrial discipline might operate in conjunction with each other rather than in continued opposition (ibid.: 18). Such responses required a redefinition of the worker. No longer were workers primarily conceived as producers. They increasingly came to be regarded as potential 'citizens of a new industrial civilization' (ibid.: 14). The shift to a market economy had already redefined work relations, removing customary elements of reciprocity and social obligation. The conversion of workers into 'citizens of a new industrial civilization' (ibid.: 14) was but a mere extension of these capitalist processes intent on establishing exchange as the dominant form of social interaction. As citizens, workers were increasingly subject to the laws of the market which separated labour from other activities and annihilated organic forms of existence (Hemingway, 1996). Exchange heralded a distinctly atomistic form of existence and a shifting sense of control over the labour process. Business communities had begun to explore the activities of working people beyond their factory roles. And the studies of human behaviour, conducted by social scientists, proved to be a valuable resource for business communities now keen to examine the social and psychological make-up of workers (Ewen, 1977).

'Progressive' social analysts of factory production emphasized the exigent value of extending social control beyond the factory into the communities in which workers lived. Ewen provides extracts from business documents written in the early twentieth century which announce a 'new profession for handling men' and advocates a rationalization aimed at the communities inhabited by workers (1977: 18). It was thought necessary to provide an affirmative image of industrial production, one compatible with the dictates of the workplace. Ewen observes how the business community substituted its early aspirations to be 'captains of industry' for 'a position in which they could control the entire realm' (ibid.: 19). They now craved 'to become captains of consciousness' (ibid.: 19). By the early twentieth century the ideological vanguard of the business community were assured in the belief that 'pacified social relations could be the products of the industrial process' and that this could be achieved with a scientific knowledge of consumer markets (ibid.: 14).

As the Industrial Revolution progressed, wage incentives became a palpable reward for the productive consumption of time and a device for organizing and ensuring markets. Capitalism's response to the dilemmas of working-class indiscipline and the need for a system of market control was 'consumerism'. Historians of advertising trace the formation of modern advertising back to the emergence of monopoly capitalism and its time-disciplined systems of market control. The following sections provide a detailed introduction to the work of key cultural historians who have examined the rise of mass advertising and linked this to capitalism's 'need' for time-disciplined subjects.

Advertising and the mass production of time-disciplined consumers

Marxist advertising historians in the UK and the USA identify modern advertising as having emerged during a pivotal economic transition from 'competitive' capitalism to 'corporate' capitalism (Ewen, 1977; Goldman, 1995, 1994, 1987; Williams, 1980). These writers variously identify the

1900s through to the mid-1920s as an era in which key Western economies were transformed from 'market economies' to a 'corporate economies'. These transformations heralded the emergence of capitalist society and the reconfiguration of community relations to map the logic and dynamics of the market.

The social structure of accumulation had historically fostered a rising technical composition of capital which generated an increased rate of production (Goldman, 1994: 191). This was matched by corresponding rates of consumption, thus stabilizing the circuits of capital investment. By 1910, burgeoning productivity had effectively saturated the demand for the primary commodities of daily reproduction (e.g., food, clothing) and capital was facing a crisis in the reproduction of the commodity-form. Table 3.1 contains statistical accounts of GDP growth during the 1870–1973 in both the UK and the USA. In the UK, GDP growth had increased by over 50 per cent between the period 1870–1913 and 1950–73 (Maddison, 1987). Similar increases are evident in Table 3.2, which contains statistical accounts of GDP per hour worked during the period 1870–1973. In the UK, the annual compound growth rates of GDP per hour worked increased from 1.2 in the period 1870–1913 to 3.2 in the period 1950–73 (1987). Rifkin (1996: 18) states that between 1920 and 1927 productivity in the US industrial economy rose by 40 per cent. The growing capabilities of US manufacturing enabled significant increases in the output per man-hour which rose by an incredible 5.6 per cent between the period 1919 and 1929 (1996: 18).

Heightened rates of productivity ordinarily would have presented capitalist firms with more opportunities to sell things to people. But a series of crises tendencies had triggered a transition towards a 'disaccumulation' stage of capitalist formation (Goldman, 1994). Before the advent of mass production, commodities were produced for a largely middle- and upper-class market. Mechanized production had exceeded demand among wealthier consumers and 'outstripped the middle class capacity to consume' (ibid.: 191). Market saturation was now of particular concern to the leaders of corporate industrial thought, as one exponent presented it:

> that was in the days when it was socially necessary to divert wealth from consumption to the uses of capital. That is no longer necessary. With our present rate of productivity, in fact, it has become foolish and is no longer good business. Continuing in that could would destroy capitalism; for there can be no adequate saving unless there is adequate spending, and spending on a scale which only the masses, with mass leisure can achieve. (Ernest Elmo Calkins, quoted in Goldman, 1983: 84)

Capitalism faced a formidable structural crisis in its endeavour to reproduce the commodity form. The disjuncture between the productive capacities of capital and a declining rate of consumption threatened the key variable of circulation time (Goldman, 1994: 191). Capital investment was perilously concentrated in the sphere of production (Pope, 1983). This

Table 3.1 *Phases of GDP growth, 1870–1973 (average annual compound growth rates)*

	1870–1913	1913–1950	1950–1973
UK	1.9	1.3	3.0
USA	4.2	2.8	3.7

Source: Maddison (1987: 650)
Reproduced with permission of *Journal of Economic Literature* and Professor Angus Maddison.

Table 3.2 *Phases of growth in labour productivity (GDP per hour worked), 1870–1973 (average annual compound growth rates)*

	1870–1913	1913–1950	1950–1973
UK	1.2	1.6	3.2
USA	2.0	2.4	2.5

Source: Maddison, (1987: 650)
Reproduced with permission of *Journal of Economic Literature* and Professor Angus Maddison.

meant that industrialists were investing much of their resources in machinery and in finished products in anticipation of consumer demand. Any machinery left idle due to seasonal or unexpected fluctuations in demand would extend circulation time and threaten the rate of profit (Goldman, 1994). Capital intensivity and high fixed costs equated to a risky combination of contingencies, which were only exacerbated by the absence of a consumer market of corresponding scale. Some capitalist firms tried to offset these contradictions by producing and selling more goods. But this merely exacerbated the problem because saturated markets require even more down-time in the productive process thus rising circulation time still further. Elsewhere, capitalist agencies embarked on the more ambitious task of overcoming the barriers to capital circulation by systematically transforming 'cultural meaning in the interest of extending the domain of exchange-values' (Goldman, 1987: 691). This required extending the underlying structure and ideological hegemony of the commodity-form into the realm of culture (ibid.: 691).

The new 'corporate economy', with its loads of cheap mass-produced goods needed to produce what Ewen calls 'a continually responsive consumer market' (1977: 32). Ewen observes how by the 1920s it was largely recognized that mass production needed more dynamic market growth both horizontally (from provincial to national demand), vertically (away from an upper-class customer base) and ideologically (ibid.: 25). The modern mass producer needed to adopt a nationwide plan which extended beyond the traditional dependence on local markets. Manufacturers had little option other than to create national marketing strategies, especially if they were to compete successfully with other manufacturers of the same goods (Ewen 1977). The construction of 'national markets' became a definable response, by business communities, to the exigencies of the productive system.

As avarice replaced thrift in the ideology of industrialism, so 'it became imperative to invest labour with a financial power and a psychic desire to consume' (ibid.: 25). But this required overcoming a culture of parsimony which had tended to define consumption in the literal sense in which it meant 'to pillage', 'to subdue' and 'to exhaust' (Rifkin, 1996: 19). Consumption was a word steeped in negative meaning, and it needs also to be recognized, that as late as the 1920s it was a word used to denote the deadly disease tuberculosis. This ominous linguistic history highlights the immense metamorphosis of consumption. Businesses were no longer merely concerned with providing for existing markets; rather, foresighted companies began to adopt the creation of new markets as a function of massification. It is within this context that the advertising industry emerged as a tool of social order with the purpose of 'solidifying the productive process while at the same time parrying anticorporate feeling' (Ewen, 1977: 19). Advertising in its corporate era materialized as a specialized vehicle for reproducing and expanding the commodity-form. The first generation of advertising was engaged in the process of appropriating and reworking the sphere of culture into utility constructs for the purpose of expropriating exchange-value. Figure 3.1 is an example of this generation of reason-why advertising. Reason-why advertisements were designed to appeal to the rational utility of discerning consumers. They emphasized objective calculable properties embodied by the product and encouraged reasoned judgment. Quaint as many of these advertisements may now seem, their form defined the industry's burning ambition to formulate a science of persuasion based on rational utility.

As the momentum of capital investment came to be skewed towards intensive capital production, it was imperative that social life be harnessed to fuel the engines of capitalist expansion (Goldman, 1994: 190). During these early stages of corporate advertising, cultural meanings were appropriated and reworked 'to establish the legitimacy of commodity consumption while they also labored to put the stamp of legitimacy on personal desire' (ibid.: 193). Where once consumers sought out reliable commodities, now goods manufacturers mobilized advertising expertise in the pursuit of reliable consumers. As Ewen puts it:

> The functional goal of national advertising was the creation of desires and habits. In tune with the need for mass distribution that accompanied the development of mass production capabilities, advertising was trying to produce in readers personal needs which would dependently fluctuate with the expanding market place. (1977: 37)

Advertising promoted itself as an effective instrument for the creation of a society composed of people self-motivated to consume an endless supply of

Figure 3.1 *Reason-why advertising and the utility of time, AGA cooker advert, 1932*

Source: Reproduced by permission of AGA. Image courtesy of the Advertising Archives.

commodities. It was seen as the key to creating cultural homogeneity, a feature which at the time appeared vital to sustaining national markets. Advances in this direction had already been made by advertising academics in their endeavours to identify a general conception of human instincts. In a series of seminal publications extending from 1901 to 1908, Walter Dill Scott introduced direct links between advertising and psychology. Advertising, according to Dill Scott (1908), functions to 'influence human minds', consequently, its scientific basis could only be psychology. Indeed, the establishment of advertising psychology as a field of expertise is accredited to Scott's highly acclaimed book, published in 1908, and entitled *The Psychology of Advertising*. This book made claims to the existence of human instincts which motivated individuals to consume in identifiably predictable ways. Advertisers merely had to create promotional devices which would appeal to the right instincts and excite the urge to buy. It is here that we see the establishment of further links between advertising, capitalism and the creation of time-disciplined consumers.

The question of time in advertising psychology

In the early twentieth century, advertising knowledges were largely informed by a technical-rational view of consumers as knowable, limited entities, whose characteristics could be captured in the same way as could the characteristics of natural phenomena. The linear rationality of this model of consumption is illustrated as thus. 'Felt need'/problem recognition' – the start of the 'decision-making process' – is described as a felt disparity between a present and an anticipated state. An everyday example here might be realizing the 'need' for a new domestic appliance. This disparity, or 'need', is reconciled through 'search' (i.e., product information gathering and its deliberation). Once the 'need' for a new domestic appliance has been realized, the 'rationally motivated' discerning consumer then sets about deliberating and choosing between a plethora of options. This search is facilitated by approaching a particular space (e.g., the supermarket) and drawing upon a specific past experience – stored information, or memory. Buyer behaviour is thus a product of past experience, present simulation (e.g., advertising) and future anticipations. It is understood as a chronological event-based process brought about by deliberate, cognitive activity. Knowledge of the consumer resides in the elicitation of those objective variables, which govern decision-making. While decision-making models continue to be informed by a technical-rational view of consumers, early challenges to this orthodoxy appeared in 1908 with the publication of Dill Scott's *The Psychology of Advertising*. This publication famously challenged the rational decision-making models of its era. Consumers were defined in Dill Scott's advertising discourse as non-rational beings who could be persuaded to purchase through the tactical use of a 'strong impression', which appealed less to their reasoned judgement and more to their 'desires'. Consumers in this discourse were not infinitely malleable, but rather impulsive beings with an insatiable appetite for irrational buying appeals. By the 1920s the new gospel of behaviourism was being widely adopted by advertising professionals. The challenge to reason-why advertising was appealing, not because it represented an advance in consumer psychology, but because it advanced efforts to differentiate fundamentally equivalent products in an increasingly oligopolistic market place (Pope, 1983: 14).

For advertisers, the creation of 'desires' among consumers involved motivating them not only to buy products but also to experience a self-conscious reflection, both socially and psychically. Elements of this approach can also be traced to the psychologist Henry Floyd Allport (1924) who argued 'our consciousness of ourselves is largely a reflection of the consciousness which others have of us ... My idea of myself is rather my own idea of my neighbour's view of me' (1924: 325, quoted in Ewen, 1977: 34). Allport's 'social self' departed from the self-contained individual of classical bourgeois ideology. In contrast to the classical conception of self–reliance, he theorized a concept of the 'self' as dependent upon the perceptions of others. Ewen (1977: 34) observes how 'this notion of the individual as the object of continual and harsh social scrutiny underscored the argument of much of the ad texts of the decade [the 1920s]'. It was assumed that that people could be conditioned to seek respite from the objectifications of public scrutiny through consumption. A surfeit of such advertisements is widely available in archives, but one example is as follows:

> Madame A.T. Rowley's TOILET MASK (OR FACE GLOVES). Is a natural beautifier for bleaching and preserving the skin and removing complexional imperfections. It is soft and flexible in form and can be worn without discomfort or inconvenience. It is recommended by eminent physicians and scientists as a substitute for injurious cosmetics. Complexion blemishes may be hidden imperfectly by cosmetics and powders, but can only be removed permanently by the Toilet Mask. By its use every kind of spots impurities, roughness etc., vanish from the skin, leaving it soft, clear, brilliant and beautiful. It is harmless, costs little and saves pounds uselessly expended for cosmetics, powders, lotions etc., It prevents and removes wrinkles and is both a complexion preserver and a beautifier. (quoted in Nevett, 1982: 68).

In this advertisement one can see how it is entirely in the interests of manufacturers to espouse a construct of the self as always being scrutinized. The statement that 'Complexion blemishes may be hidden imperfectly by cosmetics and powders' constructs a notion of 'being' in which every moment is defined in response to the unceasing 'gaze' of others. And the intention to eliminate 'Imperfection' clearly appeals to a desire for self-perfection in a scrutinizing world. The manufacturer presents the Toilet Mask as a solution to problems which arise only through the consumer's identification with a particular construct of the social world. Yet the consumption of the product is also an objectified action defined through the tentative gaze of other consumers, who are also keen to affirm their self-identity amidst public scrutiny. These tensions are heightened in the swift, swirling *Gesellschaft* of capitalist societies, in which the first impression of strangers may be all that one has as an indicator of character (Corrigan, 1997: 68).

Roland Marchand's *Advertising the American Dream* (1985) examines advertising in the 1920s and the 1930s and its role in assimilating immigrant populations into commodity culture. His analysis develops the concept of the *'tableau vivant'* (or living tableau) prominent in literary analyses of nineteenth-century theatre. Marchand reminisces about an era before the mass circulation of signs, when theatre operated to provide its audiences with visual images of things known only through verbal description. Theatre performances would often enact historic events, re-create spectacular occurrences and the lives of important ancestors in living tableaus. Marchand reminds us how the living tableau would attempt to capture the time of the event, through frozen poses which would be held for extended durations. The advertising aesthetics of the 1920s and the 1930s are identified by Marchand as having direct trajectories in the frozen forms of the living tableau. Audiences, less accustomed to a surfeit of signs, are thought to have fastidiously observed advertising imagery in the search for guidelines to the latest cultural standards (O'Barr, 1994). Advertising psychology begins to play a pivotal role in the creation of the eternally fearful social actor, with an insatiable desire to consume products that deceptively appear to ameliorate the negative conditions of social objectification.

Consumer motivations: the psychology of the world of objects

During the 1950s there continued to be an intimate connection, both institutionally and intellectually, between advertising and psychology. Psychologists at that time were raising intellectual questions which mirrored advertising's concern to gain scientific knowledge of decision-making in order to predict buyer behaviour. The psychological disposition of the consumer became an integral feature of commercial discourse. And advertising was keen to adopt psychology's accrescent constructions of human behaviour. With the advent of Freudian analysis, the intellectual field of psychology increasingly began to articulate challenges to the rational psychic operator (a *homo economicus*). The assumption that there are unconscious mental processes which motivate people to act towards certain goals achieved a significant level of orthodoxy in advertising circles. Indeed, by the 1960s, advertising professionals generally acknowledged the belief that it was insufficient to merely know the market facts or technical information about a product. Advertising experts also had to 'learn to understand the deeper meaning of the products and services' (Dichter, 1964: v). Freudian analysis directly informed the theoretical contributions of the Institute of Motivational Research, established in 1946. Its director, Ernest Dichter, declared the purpose of the institute to be that of 'finding answers to the "why" of human actions in order to develop appropriate strategy to bring about desired results and goals' (ibid.: vii).

An appreciation of this era of advertising discourse and the specific forms, in which motivations are related to drives, requires an understanding of Freud's psychoanalytic theory. Freud's theories concerning the ego (basis of consciousness) and the id (basis of the subconscious), emphasized the significance of symbolic and unconscious motivations to the formation of subjectivity. Freud's theories of the ego, the id and the superego (the moral and judicial aspects of personality) introduced a new dimension of analysis into the analysis of human psyche. Nevertheless, the concept of unconscious aspects of the human psyche was not unique to Freud. Philosophers had debated for centuries the reverential status of consciousness relative to non-consciousness. In classical Greek philosophy, time represents an infinite form of consciousness available to the gods, whereas non-infinite consciousness (subconscious) was reserved for humans (Krishnan and Trappey, 1999: 452). What distinguished Freud's account of the unconscious was its substantive status as a phenomenon of infinite form and not merely 'the name of what is latent at the moment' (Jacobs, 1998: 31). In Freud's analysis, the subconscious is an important aspect of the human mind with its own peculiar characteristics not in evidence elsewhere. Freud believed that it was imperative to human civilization for there to be a psychical realm where that which is deemed unacceptable to the conscious mind can be held. The human psyche involves a constant struggle to balance the desire for immediate gratification with the need to follow social convention and adhere to the normative order.

This Freudian model was further developed by behavioural scientists, so as to formulate links between the human psyche and observed behaviour. Human behaviour was seen as a result of unconscious efforts to control inner drives and instincts motivated by petty emotions, sexual desire and anxiety. Advertising readily embraced this development in psychodynamic discourse and eagerly placed irrationality at the heart of consumer behaviour. Individuals were conceived as differentiating from one another on the basis of the unconscious nature of personality and motivation. And consumers were increasingly assumed to be 'motivated by symbolic as well as economic-functional product concerns' (Michman, 1991: 22). Thus, alongside the recognizable rational psychic operator of classical consumer theory was thought to exist a polymorphously hedonistic subjective component of the self, unperturbed by a sense of obligation and driven by pleasure (Bowlby, 1993: 115). This belief in the existence of intimate connections between the psychic characteristics of consumers and their product responses spawned a proliferation of psychographic methods. Psychographics refers to the empirical application of the behavioural and social sciences to marketing research (Gunter and Furnham, 1992: 34). Psychographic methods take the form of interpretative techniques, such as in-depth interviewing, specifically designed with the aim of gaining access to subconscious motivations. Armed with an array of psychodynamic methods, advertising practitioners attempted to penetrate the consumer's inner world of fantasy and dynamic processes.

The prospect of delving into the consumer's psyche and finally knowing the paradoxical mix of motivations for buying astounded clients and enticed advertising practitioners. Dill Scott (1908) had paved the way for advertising psychologists to recognize the role of suggestion as a motivation in purchasing. He had already pronounced that 'Man has been called the reasoning animal but he could with greater truthfulness be called the creature of suggestion' (quoted in Pope, 1983: 240–1). Dill Scott called into question the linear temporality of reason-why advertising by stating that 'it is very difficult ... to get the public to think along a new line, because they cannot connect the new fact with their previous experience, i.e., they cannot apperceive it' (quoted in Pope, 1983: 242). During the 1950s, psychodynamic conceptions of consumer subjectivity gained increasing support, achieving its zenith in the 1960s, in the form of motivation research.

The incorporation of motivation research into advertising practice was largely pioneered by the clinical psychologist Ernest Dichter. Motivation research, in contrast to reason-why advertising, emphasizes the psychological and symbolic aspects of consumption. In essence, motivation research is premised on the idea that the consumer's psyche is governed by irrational insecurities and erotic desires which take the form of suppressed and repressed motives. Suppression and repression are attendant features of the conscious and subconscious mind. It was presumed by these early proponents of motivational theory that a causal link existed between intrinsic human drives and consumer behaviour. As Dichter puts it:

> The number of human motivations is limitless. Most of them play a role in the activities of communication, such as selling, advertising and persuasions. Everything that is human is the subject and object of human action and thus of motivations. (1964: 385)

Advertisers have to navigate the deepest recesses of the self in order to entice the consumer. The presence of the id, in the human psyche, was believed to encourage in consumers an infantile predisposition to discerning *how* something was communicated rather than *why* (Leiss et al., 1990: 144). Indeed, Dichter proclaimed that our basic motivations 'have their explanation in a protest against the very smoothness, cleanliness and freedom from friction that we daydream of as the ideal world' (1964: 2). Rational orderliness 'are deep-down threats to our desire for independence' (ibid.: 2). Consequently, consumers do not calculate the cost and benefits of products; rather, they are easily persuaded by suggestion and image. Motivational advertising messages were designed to be 'hidden persuaders', which have the propensity to stimulate a chain of responses. They should stimulate attention, bombard consciousness, arouse central association and affect action (Pope, 1983).

The advertisement in Figure 3.2 is emblematic of the impact of psychodynamic discourse on the advertising aesthetic, which epitomized the 1950s and 1960s. In psychodynamic discourse, time is presumed to represent a kind of synoptic view of events residing in the peculiar nature of the human consciousness, the mind or psyche, which therefore precedes all human

UNITED STATES RUBBER COMPANY

Serving Through Science

Welcome to a new world of driving!

Nowhere in the world will you find the kind of driving you enjoy on the U. S. Royal Air Ride.

This great tire is the first completely new development in tire design since the war. It gives you an entirely new kind of tire performance—brings new smoothness to your riding, new ease to your driving, far greater comfort to your car.

The dramatic new Air Ride principle puts up to 14% more air volume at new, lower air pressure under your wheels. Your ride is actually cradled on bigger, softer cushions of air that smother every bump, smooth every mile.

And with its unique design and magnificent balance, the Air Ride achieves a new high in swift, effortless car control. Its narrow tread is more nimble and fleet on the turns, quick to respond to your lightest steering touch.

So take the wheel on the new U. S. Royal Air Ride. Discover a new and thrilling kind of driving on this better, finer kind of tire.

The New

U.S.ROYAL

Air Ride

Ride on more air—Ride in more comfort!

Figure 3.2 *'Welcome to a new world of driving!' US magazine advertisement, 1950s*

Source: Image Courtesy of the Advertising Archives.

experience as its condition (Holbrook, 1986). We live time and are only partially conscious of its passing. Philosophically, this view presumes that 'time is the infinite form of consciousness' (Krishnan and Trappey, 1999: 452). Motivation research in the 1960s acknowledged the importance of time to the subconscious mind and its propensity to significantly determine consumer behaviour. This is effectively exemplified by Ernest Dichter's (1964) account of 'memory'. According to Dichter, memory is a vital component of the self. Memory arises from 'traces' of previous experience, which are stimulated or activated by present consciousness. In advertising communication the individual message might be forgotten on reception, 'but it leaves a trace that will form, together with all other traces, a composite trace system, which is really then the remembered fact' (ibid.: 435).

Advertising psychology had long since been concerned that 'our memories gradually fade with time' (Howard, 1932: 128). In 1932, D.T. Howard published a revised edition of Dill Scott's (1908) classic text. His revised text detailed practical solutions to the fact that memory retrieval is more difficult than storage. Howard identifies three advertising techniques for 'fixing things' in the memories of consumers. These techniques are 'the mechanical', 'the ingenious', and 'the judicious'. Thus, 'the mechanical method' involves the repetition of a message across, days, weeks and months. Howard provides the following guidance on how best to administer this method:

> the name of the product should be clearly repeated over and over, so that it becomes strongly impressed on the memory of the reader, and if possible the chief uses of the article should be emphasized again and again. It is also good practice to include in every advertisement, information as to where the article can be purchased. (1932: 132)

Howard questioned the efficacy of sheer repetition as a method of fixing an impression among consumers. Nevertheless, he went on to argue that 'if as we repeat the item, we give it attention, think of it in its relation to other things, the repetition will aid in memorizing' (ibid.: 131). A second method of fixing an impression in involved the adoption of what Howard called 'the ingenious method'. This approach required the use of novelty rhyme, rhythm and 'motor reinforcement'. Ingenuity was linked to the ability to 'intrigue the reader in the same way that an appropriate nick-name or slogan "catches on" with people' (ibid.: 133). Axiomatic to this approach is the association of time with mnemonics. Thus Howard argued that the 'ingenious method' is capable of making a mnemonic impression 'when the rhyme or alliteration is brief, pungent and undeniably appropriate' (ibid.: 134). The third of Howard's advertising strategies for fixing an impression is 'the judicial method'. Described as the 'natural method of association', 'the judicial method' relied upon the consumer's capacity to classify information by making links to previous experiences (ibid.: 134). The advertiser adopting this method would have to 'show the reader the significance of a proposition or article in his own life and affairs' (ibid.: 136). Howard provides the following guidance on how best to administer 'the judicial method':

> He [the advertiser] must know where he [the consumer] lives, what he does, what he hopes for and what he values. He must have the customer's 'point of view'. Again he must know his product, and its many uses and applications. Finally he must use the utmost inventiveness in discovering how to find a link between the article and the customer's affairs and in exhibiting this relation in a way that will be impressive. (ibid.: 136)

Underlying Howard's account of memory is a notion of time, in which events are ordered in a linear chronology, with prior memory having a causal influence upon succeeding occurrences. In Dichter's (1964) motivation theory, memory traces are also the product of suppressed and repressed motives locked in the deep recesses of the human psyche. Abreaction refers to the release of a buried emotion, which may have been repressed because it is unresolved or in conflict with accepted aspects of the individual's psyche. Psychoanalytic theory describes the process of abreaction as producing a sense of euphoria and experience of lightheartedness as the repressed conflict is resolved. Dichter discerns direct links between abreaction and the manner in which some individuals relate to products. Commodities might run up against the individual's biographical experiences and precipitate 'hidden guilt feelings' (ibid.: 387). Nevertheless, abreaction can be a positive reinforcement, whereby an individual might use a product to gain emotional release. To this purpose, Dichter detailed measures that advertisers should follow in order to facilitate positive abreaction. Such measures include the incorporation of a symbol of the past designed to signify to the next generation that an act is socially acceptable.

The advertisement in Figure 3.3 is resonant with several aspects of Dichter's motivational account of abreaction especially with regards to the statement 'Welcome to a new world of driving!'. Dichter advised that advertisers incorporate parental figures as well as the 'old-fashioned product itself' to overcome the transference of negative abreactions and resistance to the representation of changing times. In this sense the presence of the tyre in Figure 3.1 signifies both an object of utility (as recognized by past generations) and also part of a new uninhibited world of driving. At a further level of analysis, the advertisement connotes a sense of cathexis in which the observer is encouraged to form an emotional attachment with an object, which then forms an outlet for psychic energy. The advertisement's landscape is a field of dreams in which psyche energy may be cathected into narcissism or sexual love for another person. In psychoanalytic theory, cathexis is inextricably linked to self-development. Psyche energy accumulated in the process of individual development can be effectively neutralized through its subjection to reason and the ego (ibid.: 399). But psyche energy, which is ineffectively neutralized through these means, might be directed into obsessive forms of relationships. Dichter defined the tendency for consumers to develop compelling attachments to objects as a manifestation of unneutralized psyche energy. Advertising communication needed to be cognizant of this intimate relationship between self and object. Failing to reciprocate cathexis can literally make the consumer 'feel like a rejected lover, and like a spurned lover, his cathected psyche energy will be transformed from positive to negative' (ibid.: 399). Dichter's belief in the possibilities of drives to propel consumers into action is also evident in his account of 'closure'. He defines closure as 'the inner tension toward completion' (ibid.: 400). Psychoanalytic theory portrays the ego as that part of the self which is driven by a desire to 'organize their world into a simple and complete meaningful entity' (ibid.: 400). Indeed, it has been suggested that 'an effort towards consistency plays much the same role in our cognitive life that homeostasis plays in our biological drives' (Miller, 1962: 296). The apparent existence of such human desires presents advertisers with immense opportunities. Dichter argued that any disruption to the narrative sequence of an advertisement creates a 'tension to closure' in the viewer. In such circumstances the consumer is transformed into an active participant keen to reconcile the 'tension to closure' (1964: 400). Dichter' believed that this dynamic interplay of suppressed and repressed lived experiences has the effect of producing in individuals unconscious motivations that are manifest in observed behaviour.

In motivation theory, consumption is the direct consequence of unconscious motives and drives aroused by outside influences. Advertising functions to unlock the mind's inner experience. Indeed, the task of the advertiser is defined, in this psychodynamic discourse, as revealing the 'connections, conscious bridging experiences or personal references per minute that the subject makes between the content of the persuasive stimulus and the content of his own life' (Krugman, 1966–1967: 584). Motivation theory postulates that our daily decisions are governed by drives, over which we have little conscious control. In this sense, advertising is beneficent, in that it provides a means by which consumers can achieve self-knowledge. Dichter adopts this form of altruistic pros in a chapter entitled the 'Tyranny of Things' (1964). Here he argues that 'modern advertising has to learn to combine personal attitudes toward life with the material thing embodying them' (ibid.: 1). The human mind is a projector of meaning and also 'a receiver of things which surround it' (ibid.: 5). Personal growth is a process of interaction with material objects. Human beings have the propensity to endow material objects with symbolic meaning. Subjectivity is, therefore, inextricably linked with the objects that surround us, for they 'serve as a kind of mirror which reflects our own image' (ibid.: 6). Advertising professionals are urged to delve into the intrinsic meaning that objects have for individuals. In so doing, advertisers will come to recognize that 'the knowledge of the soul of things is possibly a very direct and new and revolutionary way of discovering the soul of man' (ibid.: vi). Advertising's ability to bring to the fore 'the description of the power and meaning of various types of objects' was believed to enable the revelation of 'new aspects of the personality of modern man' (ibid.: 6). And this was quite clearly defined by

Dichter as the beneficent duty of advertising, for 'the more intimate the knowledge that a man has of many different types of products, the richer his life will be' (ibid.: 6). Advertisers were to become 'captains of consciousness' (Ewen, 1977).

Indeed, such was the popularity of the belief that advertisers could sub-liminally control consumer behaviour, that the criticism of manipulation and the ability of advertisers to deprive people of freedom became com-mon currency (Foxall et al., 1998). The sedimentation of this view in popular culture was evident in Hollywood movies and especially the pseudo-documentary *The Manchurian Candidate*. This suspense thriller is set in the early 1950s during the height of McCarthyist political paranoia, which had fuelled the obscurantist fear that the Communists were plotting to control the USA via brainwashing techniques (Dirks, 2006). The film's provocative storyline reflected wider concerns about the emerging role of television broadcasting in determining public affairs and shaping vulnerable minds. The possibility that advertisers could deploy subliminal messages to brainwash consumers, even sparked measures by the government to regu-late advertising (Leiss et al., 1990). In retrospect, such governmental reac-tion seems naïve and unwarranted. Nevertheless the pervasiveness of psychodynamic constructions of consumer subjectivity heralded perturbing new times. Psychodynamic theory had propelled the subconscious mind into advertising discourse and in so doing linked the realm of subjectivity ever more closely to commercial objectives. But this new regime of capital-ist accumulation was distinct in its endeavour to define commodities as 'organic extensions of personality' (Diggins, 1978: 101).

Conclusion

Marx observed the value of a commodity to be determined by the labour time necessary to produce it. 'As values, all commodities are only definite masses of congealed labour-time' (2003: 47). Marx further observed that 'the value of a commodity, therefore, varies directly as the quantity, and inversely as the productiveness, of the labour incorporated in it' (ibid.: 48). In this sense, 'nothing can have value, without being an object of utility. If the thing is useless, so is the labour contained in it; the labour does not count as labour, and therefore creates no value' (ibid.: 48). Advertising's preoccupation with time discipline in the early nineteenth century and then use-value in the early twentieth century provided clear links between the clock-time of the produc-tive economy and consumption. If a commodity can be shown to yield util-ity, then the labour time invested in its production and time required for its consumption can be clearly communicated to the consumer. Time is trans-formed into an object which exists external to the individual, in fixed immutable units (hours/minutes/seconds). These units in turn yield an implicit utility to the consumer (e.g., time-saving products). This implicit utility facilitates the transformation of time and space into monetary values.

The clockwork precision of this mechanistic form of time encouraged its application to reason-why advertising and a wide variety of utilitarian buying instances. In reason-why advertising, time is a controllable scarce resource; a pressure in decision-making; an exchangeable commodity; and a principal component of risk. Consumers were encouraged to perceive objects as embodying substantive utility value. As 'the value of the commodity represents human labour in the abstract' (Marx, 2003: 51), consumption involves workers in the fetishized product of their labour time. Consequently, this first generation of advertising operated to obscure the extent to which the utility value of a commodity derives from the expropriation of labour time.

Corporate leaders of the Fordist era anticipated that advertising communication would create a more homogeneous national market for standardized manufactured goods. Advertising would teach workers the benefits of consumption and ameliorate discontent while also 'breeding consumer consciousness' (Pope, 1983: 258). Once consumers could recognize the technical performance of a commodity-mass production could then achieve its objective to stimulate the mass consumption of manufactured merchandise. Even Henry Ford had recognized that the standardization and rigidity of assembly-line production imposed on consumers the incongruous choice that 'you can have any color you like, so long as it's black'. The hope was that mass advertising would provide an efficacious fit between the mechanistic rhythms of assembly production and the timing of consumer demand. Conversely, the dramatic technological advancements in productivity, during the post-war era, linked prosperity with profusion and not standardization (ibid.: 259). Many of the conditions which forced manufacturers into capital-intensive, large batch production began to disappear. Technological advances meant that it cost less to make small batches. Automation enabled manufacturers to reduce the carrying costs of the huge inventories of machinery parts that mass-production systems require. This, combined with flexible production methods, meant that it no longer cost vast amounts to change the mix of products a factory turned out (ibid.: 260). The cost advantages of short production runs significantly reduced the capital costs of diverse outputs. Lean production also meant that it no longer took as long to change product specifications. Production technology was now less inclined towards standardized homogeneous markets and the nascent appeal to mass consumers (ibid.: 260). Elsewhere developments in marketing knowledge were directly challenging the 'advertiser's dreams that their products would be universally and permanently welcomed into consumers' lives' (ibid.: 262). In the USA, marketing experts had observed that products over time were subject to the laws of diminishing profits, whereby 'products start as novelties, develop into distinctive and protected specialties and then degenerate into undifferentiated commodities' (ibid.: 262). The product life-cycle concept was widely received as a warning to the business community of the need to segment markets, for 'even regular customers are unlikely to stay loyal to the same brand forever' (ibid.: 262). The scale and speed of manufacturing growth required a more diversified

approach to consumer markets and advertising officials responded to this changing climate.

The creation of 'fancied needs' was one means by which the advertising of this early mass industrial period enticed consumers into transcending the desire to satisfy utilitarian needs. The department stores and illustrated magazines of the early twentieth century promised consumers dreams which only manufacturers could realize. This was evidence of advertising's growing expertise in achieving what Thorstein Veblen (1994) called the illusion of existing in the realm of 'being'. Marx's *homo economicus* is designed to apprehend products as part of the continuous pursuit of maximum utility. Use-values are the 'material depositories of exchange-value' and both properties are intrinsic characteristics of the productive process (Sayer, 1989: 50). When human beings are regarded primarily as producers, it becomes difficult to comprehend the location of advertising psychology in capitalist accumulation. Nevertheless, psychodynamic theory was intent on effecting a 'self-conscious change in the psychic economy' (Ewen, 1977: 35).

In Dichter's motivation theory, consumers 'do not buy simply the utilitarian, timber-and-nails value of a chair, a table or a bureau; rather we buy its symbolic meaning' (1964: vii). Advertising incorporates into consumption a semiological dimension, which is conditioned by social status. The driving force of emulation is especially apparent in those societies where the accumulation of wealth 'confers honour' and 'invidious distinction' (Veblen, 1994: 17). But this pressure to consume goods for the purposes of signifying status is an incessant activity. If the incentive to accumulate was driven by the desire for functional utility, then consumption might satiate desire. Given that the motivation to consume 'is substantially a race for reputability on the basis of an invidious comparison', no definite satiate is possible (ibid.: 21). Individuals have to upgrade their consumption to match 'what is expected of them and feel secure in the possession of the goods that authenticate their position in the status structure' (McIntyre, 1992: 45). Veblen observes the growth of conspicuous consumption to have its primary basis in the social and economic transition to industrial capitalism. Even in its most rudimentary form, this 'economic process bears the character of a struggle between men for the possession of goods' (Veblen, 1994: 16). Advertising psychology typically defines this struggle as driven by the human psyche's unconscious drives, instincts and defences. The consumer is both the subject and object of deep-seated motivations. And it is the self-designated role of advertising to 'bridge the world of objects and the world of the mind' (Dichter, 1964: 385). In so doing, advertising functions to transform subjective sensibilities and visual literacies into the currency of exchange-value.

The growth of advertising psychology in the post-war era clearly coincided with economic and social trends which transformed the marketing needs of manufacturing corporations. The business community desperately needed to convert the psychology of parsimony to one of avarice and

advertising psychology was suitably versed in the 'new economic gospel of consumption' (Rifkin, 1996: 19). The notion of intrinsic motives naturalized the pursuit of immediate gratification and provided cultural legitimacy to competitive spending and displays of 'wasted time'. Such circumstances highlighted the paradox of conspicuous consumption in terms of an ability to signify status through waste. A highly priced object of art might have aesthetic utility and lack practical utility. Similarly an advertisement for a vintage antique will appeal to the cathartic delights of impetuosity when prompting a beautiful object with limited serviceability. In each of these examples, the value of the commodity appears less determined by the quantities of labour time required to produce it. Nevertheless, each of these examples is evidence of advertising's trajectories in the struggles of capital to achieve hegemony over labour. Advertising psychology operates to transform subjectivity into an object, which is dislocated from its original context and re-presented to individuals in the form of commodities. The role of symbolism as a feature of the mediating tendencies of the human psyche suggests a distinct form of alienation. Veblen observes how, in order to achieve recognition through consumption, it is necessary that an individual achieve a conventional standard of display. As Veblen puts it, 'a certain standard of wealth in the one case and of prowess in the other, is a necessary condition of reputability and anything in excess of this normal amount is meritorious' ([1899] 1994: 20). But because of the competitive nature of conspicuous consumption, the present object of status ascription decreases in its ability to bestow distinction, as soon as it is widely emulated. Consequently, the tendency becomes one of making 'the present pecuniary standard the point of departure for a fresh increase of wealth' (ibid.: 20). Pecuniary emulation is, therefore, marked by a transient attachment to the present and insatiable desire for a future state of (dis)satisfaction. Indeed, incessant pecuniary emulation is the most disturbing feature of conspicuous consumption. Invidious comparison can never be favourably satisfied so long as the cardinal principle of emulation is directed to exceeding the present standard. Because of its transient attachment to whatever happens to be the 'latest', advertising directly contributes to a logic of invidious comparison predicated on a 'canonisation of novelty' (Eby, 1998: 692). In this sense, advertising is inextricably linked to a form of subjectivity which never 'is' but can only be experienced as incessant 'becoming'.

4

Time and the Commodity-Sign

Advertising in the early twentieth century was firmly embedded within a hermeneutic tradition of rational and utilitarian communication. In seeking to promote the utility of commodities, advertising entered into a mode of communication which subordinated aesthetic value to use-value. Indeed, the golden rules of advertising orthodoxy 'stipulated the necessity to promote products by highlighting their functional utilitarian strength' (Lee, 1993: 151). It was considered essential that advertising practice emphasize the material benefits of commodities demonstrating their unique selling points and distinguishing their attributes from those of rivals (ibid.: 151). In so doing, advertising constituted 'an apparatus for reframing meanings to add value to commodities' (Goldman, 1994: 188). During this period advertising reproduced a wider perception of a 'natural connection between commodified objects and consumer needs' (ibid.: 193). While this involved the circulation of signs, the economy of sign value remained tied to a conception of utility. And the symbolic form of advertising communication was designed to be unambiguous and accessible to the widest audience available (Lee, 1993). Illustrations were designed mimetically to faithfully represent what the consumer could get for their money. For example, if you required a complexion treatment, then the product provider would show the container of what you would get and possibly include some advice on application. Emphasis was placed on displaying the integrity of the product rather than creating a seductive aura to entice the consumer. This first generation of advertising was challenged in later decades by a focus on psychology, signification and symbolism. Williams observes how advertising 'as it neared the centre of the economy ... began staking its claims to be not only a profession, but an art and science' (1980: 179). This second generation of advertising was intent on imbuing commodities with an aura that extended far beyond a notion of function. Indeed, contemporary advertisements dedicate very little space to providing information about the product's utility. Even where factual information is provided, it is mediated through the logic of exchange-value (Goldman, 1995: 18). Figure 4.1 is an advertisement for the detergent Surf. In this advertisement, the utility value of Surf as a detergent capable of brightening both whites and coloured fabrics is a mere adjunct to the image of ideal motherhood. The commodity appears 'as personified expressions of human characteristics' (Kline and Leiss, 1978: 17). The commodity acts on the consumer, not merely as use-value but also as a symbolic entity capable of endowing consumers with perceived

Figure 4.1 *The sign-value of a spotless wash to ideal motherhood, Surf advert, 1950s*

Source: Reproduced by permission of Unilever. Courtesy of the Advertising Archive.

qualities. We have become 'the channels along which the product flows' (Williams, 1980: 187). The creation of consumer subjectivity through the interpretation of signs is now an integral feature of the circulation of capital. Advertising is a primary vehicle for transforming the sphere of culture into new territories for reproducing the commodity-sign. Indeed, advertising's

Can I share a special moment with you?

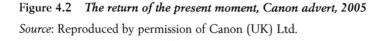

Figure 4.2   *The return of the present moment, Canon advert, 2005*

Source: Reproduced by permission of Canon (UK) Ltd.

reification of the commodity-sign operates to 'gloss over the capitalist moment of exchange' (Winship, 1980: 217). In this second generation of advertising, time does not stand outside of the self as an object of utility and determinant of rational consciousness. Rather, the commodity-sign is trans-forming time–space 'events' in the interest of extending the domain of exchange-values.

Figure 4.2 is an illustration of how advertising symbolically represents time–space 'events'. The 'special moment', to which the advertisement makes an appeal, is an event embedded and embodied in cultural practice. The duration of this moment is defined in terms of 'social time'. The con-cept of 'social time' recognizes time and space as both the medium and the outcome of social meaning which shape identities and the senses we have of ourselves. The commodity-sign operates to colonize the tempo-spatial meaning attributed to an event. In Figure 4.2 we are encouraged to perceive the traces of an event and ascribe to this a sense of duration. Thus, the female subject changes position in space and both bodies appear as if in motion. But are we observing the present, past, or future of the event? Indeed, our apprehension of time, space and the event is defined by our subjective interpretation. For subjectivity is embedded in, and constituted through, time–space events that are themselves in continuous flux and re-formation as the self-reflexive monitoring of action and interaction unfolds. This implies a form of engagement with the socio-symbolic world of images and commodity-signs, which is at once dynamic and constraining

107

of subjectivity. In their determining capacity, time–space events represent structural phenomena – a medium through which we co-ordinate complex meaning structures and reproduce everyday affairs. Consumption, while embedded in a social context, occurs in accordance with responses to specific dimensions of social stratification (age, ethnicity, sex) which then combine in particular places and at specific times (Jackson and Thrift, 1995: 229). Individuals are also active subjects, reflexively monitoring their action through the time–space events, which constitute them. Instantiated through social interaction, the structural outcome of social practices is premised upon their time and space characteristics, since these practices serve simultaneously as patterns of interaction and, through their impacts on human experience as foundations for the motivation to future practices. Agency and structure are, therefore, bound by their temporal and spatial specificity (Gregson, 1997: 61). The encoding and decoding of symbolic meaning are accomplished by individuals and societies embedded in particular, historical configurations of time and space (ibid.). As cultural practices, the encoding and decoding of symbolic meaning are also part of the creation of history, society and social action. It is in this sense that the image in Figure 4.2 operates to define subjective relations to cultural practices, which have little to do with chronometric time. Rather, the commodity-sign operates through the colonization of inter-subjective qualitative times and their transformation into exchange-values. This chapter provides a brief history of time and the commodity-sign.

A brief history of time and the commodity-sign

The concept of the commodity-sign defines consumption as involving the communication of cultural meaning (Douglas and Isherwood, 1978). At the core of this concept lies the idea that material objects embody a system of meanings, through which we express ourselves and communicate with each other. Douglas and Isherwood identify the symbolic meaning of objects as manifesting two main functions. First, material objects involve social processes which 'are needed for making visible and stable the categories of culture' (ibid.: 59). According to Douglas and Isherwood, the central 'problem of social life is to pin down meanings so that they stay still for a little time' (ibid.: 18). Material possessions carry social meanings which enable consumers to construct an intelligible universe of cultural practices and social relationships. Figure 4.3 shows two Patek Philippe advertisements. The narration and semiotic style of these advertisements make a direct appeal to the importance of material possessions to human relationships and their maintenance over time.

Goods not only communicate social categories and hierarchies (e.g., superior/subordinate, avant-garde/conservative), they also transfer a highly varied, specific and symbolically charged range of meanings to do with self-symbolism (Douglas and Isherwood, 1978). Consumers actively manipulate

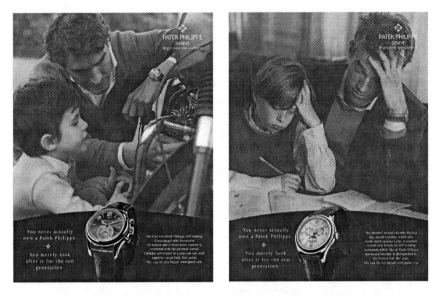

Figure 4.3   *'You never actually own a Patek Philippe. You merely look after it for the next generation', Patek Philippe, 2006*

Source: Reproduced by permission of Patek Philippe.

these meanings with the deliberate intention of sending signs to others about themselves (Campbell, 1995). Consumption is a means of self-construction and 'shopping is not merely the acquisition of things; it is the buying of identity' (Clammer, 1992: 195). The availability of symbolic goods in the modern era presents consumers with a bewildering array of lifestyle choices but at the same time it offers little guidance as to which options should be selected (Giddens, 1993). Thus, the freedom to desire is also a source of anxiety, least we make the wrong choices. The market provides expertise to guide us in our interpretation of commodity-signs. 'Cultural intermediaries' have the capacity to forage the plentitude of traditions and cultures creating a surfeit of new signs and developing lifestyles for their use (Featherstone, 1991). In the modern era, advertisers and marketers have assumed the role of linking products and symbolism. Meaning is constantly flowing to and from material possessions, aided by the collective and individual efforts of designers, producers, advertisers and consumers (McCracken, 1990). Consequently, 'the same market which offers freedom offers also certainty' (Bauman, 1988: 61).

Consumption as the communication of cultural meaning represents a radical departure from the a-social models of reason-why advertising. Axiomatic to reason-why advertising is an economic model of a rational subject exercising sovereignty and dispassionate control. This model of consumer subjectivity is fundamentally a-social as it neglects the social dimensions of self, subject and identity. Conversely, in the writings of Douglas and Isherwood (1978), we come to understand consumption as situated within a social cultural context which shapes consumer trends, the products we consume, and the needs and identities that are constructed, sustained or changed through processes of consumption. While the linkage between consumption and identity is not a new thing, it is argued that a transition has occurred from an ideology of consumption to consumer subjectivity (Featherstone, 1991). Whereas, in the former situation, individuals had to be manipulated to consume to avoid the economic consequences of over-production, in the latter, individuals are continually seeking out commodities with which both to identify almost in conformist fashion (e.g., designer label clothes) and to differentiate themselves from others (e.g., the particular design). Figure 4.4 is particularly interesting in this respect as it epitomizes the centrality of consumer culture to the creation of modern identity, how else might we justify the claim that 'It's your watch that says most about who you are'?

Consumption in Western societies is characterized by a diversified or pluralistic range of consumption patterns, where the search for a degree of distinctiveness through the consumption of highly differentiated products and services is both the condition and consequence of a multiplicity of social identities. Individuals in their capacity as consumers engage with a proliferating multitude of goods for the purposes of 'fashion[ing]' (Bauman, 1988: 808) a distinct and differentiated subjectivity. Identity, in this formulation, does not relate to fixed attributes of personality or self, still less to certain fixed forms of behaviour. Instead, as Giddens states, identity resides 'in the capacity to keep a particular narrative going' (1993: 54). It has acquired the status of an ongoing 'project' (ibid.: 54). Identity construction in the late modern era has become a story: 'which a person writes and rewrites about him/herself, never reaching the end until he/she dies and always rewriting the earlier parts, so that the activity of writing becomes itself part of the story' (Gabriel and Lang, 1995: 86). This conception of identity, self and subjectivity as an almost arbitrary intervention in the flow and flux of social experience through time and space, has significant implications for reason-why advertising's conception of objective time and absolute space. For the self is not conceptualized here as stable, continuous and consistent between distinct linear tempo-spatial frames as is presumed in rational decision-making models. Rather, the self is embedded in and through time–space 'events'. The literature of contemporary geography is particularly helpful here in conceptualizing identity as a fluid reflexive process instantiated through the time–space events, which it also serves to constitute (Giddens, 1979, 1993; Mort, 1988; Lefebvre, 1991). In the urban geography of Mort, for example, we come to recognize time and space as mediums of social meaning which shape identities (1988: 218).

IT'S YOUR WATCH THAT

SAYS MOST ABOUT WHO YOU ARE.

ARCTURA   POWERED BY THE MOVEMENT OF YOUR BODY.
KINETIC   QUARTZ ACCURACY, NO BATTERY CHANGE.
CHRONOGRAPH   SAPPHIRE CRYSTAL. 10 BAR WATER RESISTANT.

www.seiko.co.uk

Figure 4.4   *'It's your watch that says most about who you are'*, SEIKO, 2005
Source: Reproduced by permission of SEIKO UK Ltd

As may have already been discerned, the concept of the commodity-sign draws largely on an interactionist perspective where the meaning of any-thing, including time, is recognized as profoundly to do with language con-sidered as a medium and outcome of social interaction. Material objects embody a system of meanings, through which we express ourselves and communicate with each other. In their capacity as consumers, individuals engage with a proliferating multitude of goods for the purposes of con-structing a distinct and differentiated subjectivity either at the level of the individual or the group and subculture (e.g., youth). Consumption should be regarded as an activity undertaken by conscious subjects, who deliber-ately intend to 'make use' of symbolic meanings embodied by commodities. Consumers employ these meanings to 'make statements' and 'send mes-sages' about their identities and lifestyle.

In the twenty-first century, consumption has become a way of life and one of the most important sources of identity, perhaps displacing the pre-eminence of work and occupation. Identity in our contemporary era does not relate to fixed attributes of personality or self, still less to certain fixed forms of behaviour. Instead, identity assumes narrational qualities. What this signifies is that every person is only as 'good' as their last 'claim' to a particular identity. Conversely, in pre-modern societies where identities were primarily ascribed at birth through kinship and blood lineage or acquired through affinal ties of marriage, this precarious and unending process of achieving and sustaining one's identity through social activity was unknown. Human beings considered themselves as subjects given meaning from stable social relations, skilled crafts and trade. Using a fairly traditional notion of artisanal production Baudrillard notes how during this stage objects are inscribed with the contingent character of need (2003: 18). The objects of human labour were infused with the logic of tradition and cultural heritage. This was an era 'of timeless objects, instruments or monuments which outlived the generations of humans beings' (ibid.: 25). The transition from pre-capitalist societies to a capitalist system initiated a shift in the forms of exchange from utility to 'sign-value'. The exchange of utilities transfers a concrete meaning onto objects. Conversely, capitalist systems of production function to detach objects from a concrete basis of meaning and transform them into signs. The sign object operates as coded difference, a signal of distinction and is neither given nor exchanged: 'the object-become-sign no longer gathers its meaning in the concrete relation-ship between two people. It assumes its meaning in its differential relation to other signs' (Baudrillard, 1981: 66). The objects of consumption gain meaning through their positioning within a sign system and to a lesser extent, their connection with embodied relationships. It is in this sense that Baudrillard makes the claim: 'We live by object time: by this I mean that we live at the pace of objects, live to the rhythm of their ceaseless succes-sion' (2003: 25). Direct parallels exist between the function of sign-value and the Saussurean sign, as both systems of symbolism are constituted differentially and arbitrarily (Baudrillard, 1981: 64). The transition to corporate capitalism witnesses an extension to the circulation of sign-value. The objects of consumption continue to gain meaning through their positioning within sign systems, but systemic structural transformations at the level of capitalist production markedly accelerates the circulation of signs. An inauguration of commodity-sign values opens up new terrains for the expropriation of exchange-value. And culture becomes a potentially limitless sphere of commodity relations. These transformations constituted an important structural adjustment to the commodity-form, made necessary by a period of dis-accumulation (Goldman, 1994). Indeed, the extension of the commodity-form into the sphere of culture provided a crucial structural mechanism for offsetting a declining margin of surplus-value (ibid.: 185). Commodity-sign values became relevant to the parcelling out of needs, as needs were ever more arbitrarily integrated into the matrix of objects. And the commodity-sign became indexed to the commodity-form in such a manner so as to render both indissoluble (Baudrillard, 1981). Historically, advertising has operated to colonize the social world and materialize desire. Advertising captures the effervescence of the commodity-sign, extending its influence to more spheres of social life while also securing its index to the commodity-form. Indeed, the history of the commodity-sign clearly bears the trace in its substance and its form, of the conscious and unconscious dynamics of advertising's evolution.

After the Second World War, developments in manufacturing and distribution were to have a profound effect upon advertising. Nevett (1982) observes how in the aftermath of the war, rationing had preoccupied agency clients with concerns over the management of supply rather than the stimulation of demand. Advertisements were designed merely to fill spaces with lighthearted distraction. By the mid–1950s, market competition had escalated due to the dismantling of wartime controls on commerce and enterprise. Advertising was operating in a new era of corporate capitalist expansion. Manifestations of these changes at the level of advertising strategy were evident in the retail market. In the UK, small independent retailers were competing unsuccessfully with large-scale operations such as supermarkets and discount stores. Declining numbers of independent retailers also impacted on the fortunes of wholesalers as supermarkets dealt directly with suppliers. These shifts in the retail trade placed more emphasis on promoting individual brands, something that the wholesalers in the pre-war years particularly opposed (Nevett, 1982). Alongside these changes was an increasing fashion for self-service in retail outlets. Shortages of retail employees, coupled with higher wages, had made it impractical for retailers to continue the tradition of serving individual customers. Consumers were now provided with an array of products, in pre-packaged form and arranged on shelves awaiting customers to serve themselves from the display. Under these conditions the manufacturer could no longer rely upon advertising to merely motivate the consumer to buy a generic product. Instead, manufacturers commissioned advertisers to design promotions communicating levels of product distinction, which had in previous times been the role of the retailer (ibid.: 178). Elsewhere, dramatic transformations were occurring at the level of advertising aesthetic.

The 1950s witnessed technological advances in the field of media, arts and design. In the arts, photography had become the subject of critical regard. Though the invention of photography can be traced back to the 1830s, it was not until the mid-twentieth century that the medium assumed the accolade of an art form deemed worthy of exhibition in art galleries and museums (Nickel, 1998). In their desire to collect, preserve and display photography, art museums attested to a growing conviction that photography was a 'manifestation of modernism in the arts' (ibid.: 13). From the moment of its introduction in the 1830s, photography defined an era of automation destined to eclipse the syntactical procedures of traditional art forms. Photography constituted a decisive break from 'Typographic Man' to the age of 'Graphic Man' (McLuhan, 1997: 190). Its arrival broadened the scope of uniformity and repeatability in the production of representation. The camera was unparalleled in its capacity to produce rapid, mirror images of the external world. Thus, when photography became the new *ad* icon for the magazine enterprises in the 1950s, few had anticipated the startling transformations that were to come. Until this time, overseas markets had limited influence on fashion trends. But editors were increasingly acquiring diverse representations of contemporary living in an attempt to produce a stylized world of reality. Photography, coupled with increased air travel, had meant that the 'total mosaic of the contemporary world' could be captured in all its resplendent vivacity (ibid.: 195). Some indication of this, altogether new relation of the fashion magazine to its users is indicated by a proclamation in *Vogue* (15 March 1963) which stated, 'A woman now, and without having to leave the country, can have the best of five (or more) nations hanging in her closet – beautiful and compatible as a stateman's dream' (quoted in McLuhan, 1997: 189).

It is one of the quintessential manifestations of photography that it 'isolates single moments in time' (ibid.). It is possible to freeze-frame fast action with an ordinary camera, using an exposure of approximately 1/1000 second (the maximum speed of mechanical shutters). Professional photographers are able to maintain the finest details of a fast-moving subject by controlling the duration of a light flash that exposes the film. The split-second flash of light from stroboscopic units might be more familiar to the reader and thus provide for a more accessible way to grasp the importance of photography in 'creating a world of accelerated transience' (ibid.: 196). The use of stroboscopic units has the capacity to produce exposures thousands of times more rapidly than mechanical shutters. And these techniques illustrate how the camera can be used in ways to manipulate time (Figure 4.5).

The ability of photography to capture accelerated motion has the effect of transcending the limits of time, just as the telegraph and cable had abolished space (ibid.: 196). Observed in this way, the camera has proved an indispensable tool in the erosion of national frontiers and cultural barriers.

Figure 4.5 *'Capture every moment', Olympus, 2005*
Source: Reproduced by permission of Olympus.

McLuhan observes photography to have added a new and surprising dimension to our collective appreciation of the world. We have become integrated into the aesthetic 'family of man' irrespective of our individual points of view (ibid.: 196). Photography, as part of the graphic revolution in art and representation, 'has shifted our culture away from private ideals to corporate images' (ibid.: 230). This graphic revolution extends the circulation of signs to make transparent the realms of taste in both the public and private sphere. Set against the stark realities of post-war Europe, photography provided distraction from the private 'point of view' as it ingratiated individuals into 'the complex and inclusive world of the group icon' (ibid.: 230). Advertising operates similarly. Advertising promotions purposely sacrifice the private vista for a discourse on style that 'is for everybody or nobody' (ibid.: 231). Style becomes a symbolic expression of taste as individuals hastily engage in the practice of fashioning the self.

Advertising and domestic labour time

The 1950s witnessed the start of a boom period in women's periodicals and an unparalleled escalation in domestic consumption. Technological advances in the design and production of home appliances accelerated existing rates of consumer demand. Home appliances such as vacuum cleaners and washing machines were promoted as labour-saving devices. In this sense, they intended to substitute capital for household labour time (Lee, 1993). Advances in domestic equipment were indeed labour-saving as they reduced the amount of time required when completing a domestic task. But feminist cultural historians have questioned the extent to which labour-saving domestic equipment actually reduced the amount of time women dedicated to domestic tasks. Instead of enabling women to trade 'domestic-work-time' for 'non-domestic-time', the revolution in household gadgets appears to have escalated the privatization of domestic labour as part of capitalism's expropriation of women's domestic labour time (Dalla Costa and James, 1975). This observation suggests that domestic labour time has an important place in the capitalist division of labour (ibid.: 33). To this endeavour, feminists working within the tradition of historical materialism have been assiduous in their intentions to incorporate Marxist analysis into the study of household consumption. But they have been equally keen to challenge the assumption that Marx's labour theory of value can only be determined by the capitalist–proletarian relationship. For many, the central challenge has been Marx's distinction between 'productive' and 'unproductive' labour.

In *The Power of Women and the Subversion of the Community*, Dalla Costa and James (1975) propose that women need to be liberated from capitalism's rationalization of factory labour and from the endless demands of private domestic labour. In the latter case, the forces of production, which operate to privatize domestic labour also serve to constitute it as 'feminine work' and a defining feature of womanhood (ibid.: 33). But this identity is a source of frustration for women, partly because the relation of housework to capital 'runs directly against the factory as regimentation organized in time and space' (ibid.: 22). Domestic work is family-centred and defined in relation to the needs of significant others (Davies, 1990). Conversely, the regimentation of work in the public sphere commands a 'respect for timetables' and disciplined aversion to any 'disruption of the productive flow' (Dalla Costa and James, 1975: 22). Nevertheless, capitalism is at the root of both the privatization of housework and its separation from the chromometric rhythms of the workplace. According to Dalla Costa and James, the advent of capitalism precipitated a transition from a pre-capitalist society of 'co-operative unity in work', to a capitalist system in which 'the unfree patriarch was transformed in the "free" wage earner' (ibid.: 24). Having destroyed the community production of pre-capitalist society, capital set about exacerbating the existing' contradictory experiences of the sexes' and established in the form of the nuclear family 'a more profound estrangement and therefore a more subversive relation between the sexes (ibid.: 24). With the rise of industrial capitalism, the homestead ceases to be a centre of production and women lose their relative power gained from the dependence of family members on their labour, which was seen as socially necessary. The burden of financial responsibility now resides solely with the patriarch and within the family.

> rule of capital through the wage compels every able-bodied person to function, under the law of division of labour, and the function in ways that are if not immediately, then ultimately, profitable to the expansion and extension of the rule of capital. (ibid.: 28)

To the extent that the 'rule of capital' determines the division of labour, then the qualitative rhythms of housework 'function in ways', that are 'ultimately profitable' to the capitalist mode of production. This is because domestic labour is necessary to capital, not merely as a producer of use-values, but also because it 'is essential to the production of surplus value' (ibid.: 33). While previous Marxist feminists stressed the socially necessary role of housework, Dalla Costa and James argue that domestic labour is the necessary condition for the 'reproduction of labour power', from which, in turn, is extracted surplus value. This is precisely because capitalism transfers a vast amount of social services to the privatized nuclear family. Women assume responsibility for these social services 'without a wage and without going on strike' (ibid.: 34). Thus, according to this argument, what is economically productive about housework is that capitalism, by instituting its family structure, guarantees the exploitative bases of domestic labour and in so doing sustains the capitalist organization of work. But herein resides a primary source of contradiction in this Marxist feminist contribution. For Marx, the *raison d'être* of capitalism's organization of work is the expropriation of surplus labour time as a basis for the accumulation of capital. If indeed it is the case that 'the family is the very pillar of the capitalist organization of work', (Dalla Costa and James, 1975: 35), then it would be in the interests of capital to rationalize housework by integrating it with technological innovations, designed to make it more efficient.

The argument is often advanced that Marx considered a primary intention of capitalist production was to eliminate all forms of socially necessary labour and subjugate them to 'the hegemony of capital' (Foreman, 1978: 117). Evidence to support this claim is provided in *Grundrisse* in which

Marx explored the circumstances essential for socially necessary labour to migrate 'into the domain of the works undertaken by capital itself' (Dalla Costa and James, 1973: 531). Marx states that 'there are works and investments which may be necessary without being productive in the capitalist sense, i.e., without the realization of the surplus labour contained in them through circulation, through exchange, as surplus value' (ibid.: 531). In specific circumstances, capital may decide to undertake such works based on the presumption that it will obtain 'out of the general fund of profits – of surplus values – a sufficiently large share to make it the same as if it had created surplus value' (ibid.: 532). Ultimately, capital strives to be capable of transforming the process of social production into commodities produced through exchange relations. Thus Marx argued that:

> The highest development of capital exists when the general conditions of the process of social production are not paid out of deductions from the social revenue, the state's taxes – where revenue and not capital appears as the labour fund, and where the worker, although he is a free wage worker like any other, nevertheless stands economically in a different relation – but rather out of capital as capital. (ibid.: 532)

In other words, Marx anticipated the development of capital to eventually 'subjugate all conditions of social production to itself', thus guaranteeing that all 'social reproductive wealth has been capitalized and all needs are satisfied through the exchange form' (ibid.: 532). Clear parallels exists here between Marx's prophetic analysis and the expansion of commodity markets into the public and private domains. With the rise of industrial capitalism, there occurs a separation of the public sphere from the private sphere and with this a 'transfer of creative activity at home (private domain) to the socially organized workplace (public domain)' (First, 1994: 211). In industrial capitalist society, the production of commodities, within the private sphere, was systematically superseded by the purchase of products in the market. Initially, products produced in the public domain were designed to augment the creative activities within the private sphere. Examples of these products included raw wool, spinning and knitting tools, agricultural appliances and sewing machines. Gradually these products 'have been replaced by their end products' (ibid.: 211). Consumer markets now contain ready-made substitutes for the creative labour that previous generations invested in the production of objects. And this transfer of creative labour from the home to the public sphere has had much to do with the growth of mass production, because it was necessary for capitalists to generate corresponding mass consumer markets (Zaretsky, 1976; Gardiner, 1976; Firat, 1994).

Indeed, it has been suggested that gender segregation in the labour market is a necessary component of mass production, as the household has 'to be populated during the day in order to have continual consumption to absorb the increasing production capabilities in the public domain' (Firat, 1994: 212). So although an increasing array of products now substitute for the creative labour women performed in the private sphere, countervailing forces, within the labour market, encourage women into 'the private domain in order to consume the products' (ibid.: 212). From this perspective it its clear that the relationship between capitalist enterprise and housework has largely failed 'to convert private domestic work … into a public industry' (Engels, 1968: 569). This shortcoming is even more disconcerting when we consider that the restless agitation of capital operating within the industrial process has historically provided the impetus for the transformation of the labour process through the development of new technologies (Seccombe, 1973: 16). Given that labour time is a primary source of value, 'any increase in the productivity of a unit of labour time results in a proportional increase in surplus value' (ibid.: 16). To this extent, it has been the *modus operandi* of capitalist industry to increase the productivity of every unit of salaried labour time. It is this tendency in capitalist accumulation, which has also been a source of confrontation between capital and labour. Indeed, in the history of the working-class struggle, technology has been a valuable means of 'gaining free hours' (Dalla Costa and James, 1975: 29). But this has not been the case for housework. It would appear that 'a high mechanization of domestic chores doesn't free any time for the woman' (ibid.: 29).

Marxist feminists point out that Marx's analysis of 'social reproductive wealth' falls short of explaining why housework has not been 'capitalized' and thus transformed into a system in which 'all needs are satisfied through the exchange form' (*Grundrisse*, 1973: 532). For some feminist writers the problem resides with Marx's gender-blind economic analysis of value and his failure to recognize that the woman 'is always on duty, for the machine doesn't exist that makes and minds children' (Dalla Costa and James, 1975: 29). For other feminist writers the problem is less empirical and more conceptual. Thus, Seccombe (1973) argues that any disjuncture between Marx's analysis of socially necessary labour, and the apparent inability of capitalist society to draw housework into a direct relation to capital, has to be explained in terms of a misinterpretation, by materialist feminists, of Marx's theory of value.

Marxist feminists generally agree that 'women's oppression' in the private sphere is caused by capital. Consensus also exists around the claim that domestic labour creates use-values, which are consumed within the household. Furthermore, there is little contention that 'domestic labour has been socially necessary labour, throughout history and continues to be so under capitalism' (Seccombe, 1973: 10). Significant disagreement does, however, exist as to whether the general attributes of domestic labour 'make the case for it being a productive labour in the specific context of capitalist production' (ibid.: 10). Using Marx's distinction between productive and unproductive labour, Seccombe argues that 'domestic labour is unproductive' (ibid.: 11). In Marx's account of productive and unproductive labour these definitions are:

> not derived from the material characteristics of labour (neither from the nature of its product, nor from the particular character of the labour as concrete labour), but from the definite social form, the social relations of production within which labour is realized. (Marx, 2003: 157, quoted in Seccombe, 1973: 11)

Thus, the attribute which defines productive labour is not the material characteristic of labour, but rather, 'the definite social form, the social relations of production within which labour is realized' (Marx, 2003: 157, quoted in Seccombe, 1973: 11). Furthermore, Marx argues that 'value is determined by objectified labour time' (1973: 532) and 'the labourer alone is productive who produces surplus value for the capitalist' (2003: 477). Marx thus defines productive labour as distinguished by two characteristics: it is performed in direct relation to capital and it produces surplus value (Seccombe, 1973: 11). According to Seccombe, domestic labour, while being 'socially necessary labour' does not meet either of Marx's criteria for discerning productive labour (ibid.: 11). The relation of domestic labour with capital is neither direct (i.e., it is not salaried) nor a source of surplus value (does not create more value than it possesses). To this extent, Seccombe concludes that 'domestic labour is unproductive labour' (in the economic sense) and conforms with Marx's description of an unproductive labour 'exchanged not with capital but with revenue, that is wages or profits' (ibid.: 11). Seccombe's observations concerning the unique duality of productive labour encouraged him to examine an alternative means of expressing the value of domestic labour. To this endeavour Seccombe re-evaluated the relationships between domestic labour and the wage form. He argued that both the husband and wife 'as members of the same consumption unit' have a shared 'common interest in the wage's magnitude, while being sharply differentiated from its form' (ibid.: 12).

But this shared interest is obfuscated by the fact that the 'husband receives a pay cheque while his wife does not'. According to Seccombe, the wage has a 'mystifying quality', which obscures the fact that 'the wage in reality pays for an entirely different labour – the labour that reproduces the labour power of the entire family' (ibid.: 12). And this forms part of the sine qua non of capitalism, i.e., the reproduction of the forces of production (labour power). Domestic labour fulfils this function in its capacity to reproduce labour power on 'a daily basis' and also 'on a generational basis' (ibid.: 14).

But the 'housewife's labour cannot assert itself' as it is 'embodied in another person' and this denies it a 'direct relation with capital' (ibid.: 20). Instead, the housewife's labour in its capacity to convert wage-purchased goods into use-values 'becomes part of the congealed mass of past labour embodied in labour power' (ibid.: 9). Domestic labour, according to this logic, is situated 'beyond the exercise of the law of value' (ibid.: 16). And it is for this reason that, despite developments in the technological complexity of domestic appliances, 'the domestic labour process has stagnated while the industrial labour process has constantly advanced' (ibid.: 17). Labour time embodied in productivity is a source of value, and of vital interest to capital. Nevertheless, Seccombe argues that 'domestic labour is not part of variable capital', it is not an hourly paid salaried wage and thus 'capital has no interest in the productivity of a unit of domestic labour time'. The amount of time required to complete a domestic task is irrelevant to capital as long as this domestic labour time succeeds in its overall task of reproducing the labour force. To this extent it appears unsurprising 'that the household is the least efficient organization of a labour process existent within capitalism' (ibid.: 17). It is certainly the case that while the productivity of labour time expended in housework has increased, it continues to be labour-intensive monotonous work. Nevertheless Seccombe's observations struggle to explain the stagnation of the domestic labour process relative to technological developments in industrial production.

According to Seccombe, the infusion of mass-produced domestic appliances into the home, should not be read as 'a progressive application of technology'. (ibid.: 17) This is because capitalism's history of building into commodities the conditions for their rapid obsolescence means that capital's profit motive can be served 'by the most inefficient product application in order to maximize the quantity of goods consumed per person' (ibid.: 17). And this, according to Seccombe, explains the short product life-cycles of new domestic technologies combined with their erratic development. Because domestic labour time has no direct relation to capital, 'there exists no continual impertus to reorganize domestic labour to improve its efficiency' (ibid.: 17). But this conclusion is unconvincing. Even the most cursory perusal of high street stores reveals the market for domestic technologies to be a fiercely competitive sphere of commodity production. Housework would indeed be made more efficient if it were fully integrated into commodity production, but this transformation in the domestic labour process appears to be tethered by forces which exceed market dynamics. Indeed, it has been suggested that the possibilities of capital, automating domestic work, run up against the combined forces of patriarchy and the discursive constructions of ideal feminine identity (Dalla Costa and James, 1975). Insofar as ideal feminine identity defines womanhood in terms of the maintenance of the home and family, the quest for this ideal engages feminine subjects in practices which encourage 'compulsive perfection in their work (ibid.: 37). We are all familiar with the saying 'a woman's work is never done'. Yet we are less familiar with the conditions which serve to reproduce this construction of feminine identity. Diana Gittins (1994) provides several important observations concerning feminine identity and domestic labour time in the nineteenth-century household. She argues that the demands placed on domestic labour time were invariably linked to discourses that equated cleanliness with both feminine identity and class. To the extent that cleanliness was equated with class, women often distinguished their living standards and themselves 'through the type of accommodation they have, its degree of cleanliness and maintenance' (1994: 121). Indeed, in the nineteenth century, household cleanliness signified 'respectability' and was exclusively defined as women's work (Davidoff,

1976). Thus developments in technology and housework had direct implications for the production of feminine identity. Instead of saving labour time, domesticated appliances became the essential apparatus in the feminine quest for the immaculately furnished and polished home. Arguably advertising promotions operated to sustain this discourse. For example, in the 1890s, the Steel Roll Manufacturing Company widely advertised its newly developed washing machine. The advertising copy was emblematic of advertising's dualistic engagement with both the commodity market, and the promotion of household labour-saving technologies as a source of feminine identity. Thus, the advertising copy states 'Washing Machine for the Residence. Modern and complete with ample capacity to do all the family linen and do it just right' (Advertising Archive, 2006). Within the advertising system the productivity of domestic labour is at one and the same time a marketplace and a site for the production of consumer subjectivities.

The early twentieth century witnessed a further revolution in household gadgets marketed as labour-saving devices. The electrical appliances industry, buttressed by a revolution in advertising, recognized the commercial value of the household as a market for domestic appliances. By the 1950s the blossoming advertising industry had become rapturous in its endeavours to inculcate the 'the ideal of the permanently immaculate home and the need to buy more and more gadgets to keep it that way' (Gittins, 1994: 122).

Thus advertisements directed at the 1950s homemaker depicted ideal femininity as synonymous with an impeccably dressed and coiffured mother (Kates and Shaw-Garlock, 1999). Homes were not just clean, but seen to be *immaculately* clean. Advertising collaborated in an ideology of perfectionism, which contrived to increase, rather than decrease, the amount of time dedicated to domestic chores. Consequently, although advances in domestic appliances required that less time be dedicated to completing a task the levels of quality now required to accomplish the task operated to extend domestic labour time. The advertisement in Figure 4.6 is emblematic of a discourse of womanhood, which ideologically links ideal femininity with domesticity and perfectionism.

Commercialism, consumerism and the growth of mass media

Towards the end of the 1950s, the home had become a privileged site for the individual consumption of mass-produced commodities (Lee, 1993). The physical demarcation of private space, provided by the small family unit, enabled the translation of mass-produced domestic appliances into devices, which promised to increase an individual's discretionary use of time. Indeed, the standardized features and unitary scale of the family unit provided an effective context in which an increase in the discretionary use of domestic labour time could be communicated to consumer markets. Advertisers drew heavily on the labour-saving themes of new consumer durables in their attempts to offer mass-produced products to an

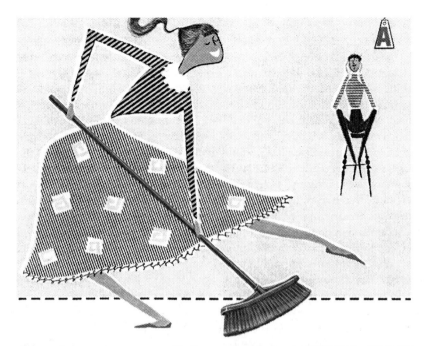

Cleaning goes gay ... light and bright ... WITH ADDIS

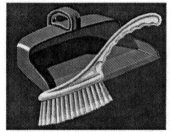

Plastic strongman of a dustpan has a knife-fine edge, and automatic tip-up to keep dust in. 9/6. Easy-grip brush has soft nylon tufts almost magnetic to dirt. 8/11.

Discover the joy of an Addis broom. One has silky-soft nylon tufts almost magnetic to dirt. 23/6. Another has stiff nylon tufts to whizz carpets clean. 21/5. (Prices include handles.)

FOUR CHEERY COLOURS...STAY-CLEAN MATERIALS!
Choose red, green, blue or yellow ... everything Addis make comes in every colour. And the colours *stay* bright. For tufts and quills come up clean-as-new with a swish in sudsy water ... a damp cloth wipes backs and handles spotless.

There are lots of gay Addis products to lighten your work. Look for them in hardware shops or department stores today, or send for illustrated catalogue.

For lighter, brighter housework...

Addis

THE BRUSH PEOPLE
DEPT. A1, BRUSHWORKS, HERTFORD

Figure 4.6   *Engendering time and domestic labour, Addis advert, 1950s*

Source: Reproduced by kind permission of Addis Housewares Ltd. Courtesy of the Advertising Archive.

increasingly urbanized and segmented consumer market. In so doing, advertising capitalized on a cultural paradox of a society seeking to achieve individual distinction through the consumption of mass-produced consumer durables.

Just as the matching of magazine images to everyday life provided motives for consumption, so the emergence of the film medium proved to be a colossal advertisement for consumer goods. Cinema, in the aftermath of the war years, had experienced a boom period, with 1946 achieving 635 million admissions to 4,703 cinemas (Nevett, 1982: 191). The movie was 'a spectacular wedding of the old mechanical technology and the new electronic world' (McLuhan, 1997: 284). And cinema's ability to substitute what James Joyce called the 'reel' world for reality astound audiences (ibid.: 193). But cinema also demanded a level of erudition from its audiences, especially with regards to its construction of time. McLuhan traces our visual experience of cinema to a Western cultural heritage. Narratives provide coherence and continuity to daily experiences. In Western societies, narratives render understanding by connecting (however arcane) parts to a configuration of social networks (Somers, 1992). The positioning of events and happenings is configured into a temporal unity by means of a 'plot'. The 'plot' is the process through which the reader becomes aware of their context and the proximal relation of emergent events. Western movies rely on an unquestioning logic of linearity in film sequence. Characters appear and disappear from view, but coherence is sustained by the capacity of the plot to transform events into episodes. McLuhan (1997: 286) contrasts this visual tradition with non-Western cultures who have had limited contact with phonetic literacy and lineal print. He describes these cultures as less inclined to accept 'the mere movement of the camera eye as it follows or drops a figure from view' (ibid.: 285). Non-Western audiences are similar to Western theatre audiences. Both viewing subjects are inclined to visually trace the movements of the actors on stage. Conversely, film audiences accept the mere sequence of images as forming a logical narrative. The perspective and distancing effects of light and shade evident in Western film denote a peculiarly linear relation to time and space. Axiomatic to the linear sequencing of film narrative is a concept 'of cause and effect as sequential, as if one thing pushed another along by physical force' (ibid.: 287). Conversely, McLuhan identifies non-Western cultures as fascinated by illogical connections between 'hidden forms that produce magical results' (ibid.: 287).

The temporality of Western cinema is also distinguished by its ability to convey vast amounts of information in short amounts of time. 'In an instant' cinema 'presents a scene of landscape with figures that would require several pages of prose to describe' (ibid.: 288). The glossy seductive appeal of Hollywood cinema provided film audiences with an instantaneous source of pecuniary emulation. Advertising agencies eagerly lined up to capitalize on the commercial potential of canned dreams. The Screen Advertising Association, established in 1924, had already helped to cultivate the use of cinema for advertising. By the 1950s, film had accompanied the first great consumer era and was itself a major commodity (ibid.: 291). But it was the popularity of domestically-based television which was to eclipse all other media in the competition for advertising revenue.

In 1955, when commercial television transmissions commenced, the sheer novelty of advertisements had a considerable impact on consumers. Television transformed the dreary spaces of everyday life into novel and glamorous indulgences. It was a vehicle for the circulation of signs and in itself a signifier of status. The acquisition of a television set became a sign of having 'arrived' in affluent society. The social disturbance created by the television image was very distinct from the changes precipitated by film and photography. While TV has the same non-verbal gestalt or bodily postures as film and photography, TV viewing is markedly different. McLuhan famously observed that 'with TV the viewer is the screen' (1997: 313). The TV image is a mosaic mesh of light impulses which bombard the viewer requiring them to ceaselessly form the contour of objects. The viewer is inextricably tied to the production of the image, even to the point of having to select among the millions of dots per second transmitted by the TV. The effect of television, as an extension of the viewer, is also invoked by the low intensity or definition of the TV image. Technically the low definition of TV requires it to operate as a close-up medium. This in itself engenders a high degree of audience involvement. Close-up intimate vantage shots of people's everyday lives, observed from the comfort of one's home, encourage levels of engagement quite distinct from an audience's commitment to film narrative. In the TV image we have an involvement in production which technologically completes the sense of sight. Indeed, McLuhan (1997) observes the iconic mode of representation captured by the TV image to involve a unique sense-mix of touch, sound and sight. The visual sense, when extended to phonetic literacy and the tactual mode of perception, functions collectively to ascribe linear coherence to the millions of light impulses emitted from the TV screen. These advances in television technology provided the basis for a revolution in advertising communication.

Commercial television contractors gain their income (and profits) from advertising. Programme providers are intently aware that in order to attract advertisers they have to achieve high viewing figures. The viewing potential of any programme is in turn tied to production costs and capital investment, generated particularly through advertising. The potential for advertisers to exploit the dependency of programme providers encouraged safeguards to be built into the British 1954 Television Act. Under the terms of the Act, advertisers were prohibited from influencing the content of programmes. Television advertising is therefore restricted to 'spot' announcements which are transmitted during 'natural breaks' in the programme. Advertisers are further restricted to a fixed length of announcement calculated on the basis of time (generally three minutes). While programmers are insulated from the direct influence of commercial promotions, advertisers do know programme schedules in advance and attempt to match commercials to viewing content. The growth of advertising expertise in this respect is quite significant. In its earliest form, advertising research into television viewing involved the use of meters linked to a selected sample of TV sets and monitored in conjunction with special diaries kept by the viewers. This research method soon made it possible for agency planners to map the composition of an audience to specific geographic locations at any given time. In practice, this has meant the harmony of advertising research with commercial interests to produce a remarkably successful educational enterprise predicated on inculcating the ideology of consumerism.

Advertising's huge capacity for gathering, processing and exploiting social data is one of the most edifying aspects of the advertising enterprise. Advertising research constituted a vital apparatus for the annexation of social life as part of corporate capital's insatiable quest to reproduce and expand the commodity-form. McLuhan observes how the forms of advertising aesthetic, emblematic of this era, were characterized by a 'vigorous dramatization of communal experience' (1997: 228). Everyday life became institutionally rationalized and incorporated into an amplifying system of sign values. New arrangements in the circulation of visual imagery in the arts, media and design had already laid the foundation for the maturation of a sign economy. Economic and social prosperity in the aftermath of the war had also released advertising from the task of justifying consumption. The convergence of these aesthetic innovations propelled the commodity-sign into a predominant social form (Baudrillard, 1981). By this stage in the development of consumer culture, the commodity-sign had penetrated into the depth of the community, transforming the ways 'individual consumers articulate, decipher and judge themselves and others as sign constellations' (Goldman, 1994: 188). Advertising was central to these processes especially in its insistence on creating commodity aesthetics which mapped onto the desires, motives and experiences of audiences. 'The product and the public response [had] become a single complex pattern' as advertisers endeavoured to join signs to commodities (McLuhan, 1997: 226).

Dialectics in modern advertising and the emergence of the social/symbolic consumer

Accounts of contemporary advertising history reveal the 1970s and 1980s as the pinnacle era in the philosophical transformation of advertising. During this period advertising became more closely integrated within the marketing concept (Leiss et al., 1990). In essence, the marketing concept refers to a philosophical commitment to ensuring that marketing strategies must be consumer-centred. Marketing managers apply the marketing concept in the selection of products, markets and marketing possibilities (Michman, 1991). The management of the 4Ps, products, promotion, distribution and pricing, is referred to as the marketing mix (ibid.: 8). The inclusion of promotion, in the marketing mix, correspondence to a major transition in the role of advertising. Contemporary advertising is no longer seen as the primary route for promoting consumption (Leiss et al., 1990: 158). As an integral feature of the marketing mix, advertising operates in conjunction with marketing management and its constant pursuit of statistically viable consumer profiles, lifestyles, preferences and behaviour. This mix of consumer profiling and marketing strategy extends beyond advertising's earlier focus on the psychodynamic properties of consumers. While psychology continues to be of interest to advertising design, the philosophy of marketing management encourages a sustained focus on the situational variables that determine the propensity to buy. As an integral component of the marketing mix, advertising is committed to the use of market research to form the basis of design and media decisions. This partly explains the wide adoption of lifestyle segmentation as a strategy for targeting advertising communications. While this development in itself is significant, the incorporation of lifestyle segmentation into advertising communication has heightened marketing interest in time and consumer subjectivity.

In marketing research, the concept of lifestyle refers to 'how individuals spend their time, what they consider important about their immediate surroundings, their opinions on various issues and their interests' (Michman, 1991: 1). Consumer lifestyle is a determinant of behaviour with regards to 'patterns of time, spending and feelings' (Foxall et al., 1998: 147). Consumer lifestyle is also an integral feature of the self-concept as it is assumed to determine the consumer's motives, feelings and beliefs (ibid.: 148). Consequently, lifestyle descriptions have proved immensely popular among marketing managers and advertising practitioners. Moreover, the focus on situational variables in lifestyle descriptions provides a crucial supplement to demographic data and facilitates the operationalization of previously obscure psychological constructs. Psychographics is a widely applied technique used to measure consumer lifestyles (Michman, 1991). Psychographic research uses statistical techniques to quantify certain characteristics of consumers, which can be attributed to distinct lifestyles and can be associated with particular groups of consumers. Psychographic data segment markets into relatively homogeneous clusters of consumers. It is therefore of little surprise that the application of psychographic techniques has encouraged a proliferation of consumer behaviour research studies, all eager to highlight distinctions in consumer lifestyles.

Based on a technical-rational view of knowledge, the dominant discourse of time in consumer lifestyle research assumes a parallelism between the natural and social world. The world, whether natural or social, is conceived of as an objective phenomenon that operates according to strict laws. Deterministic in structure, 'reality' lends itself to accurate observation and measurement by appropriate research instruments. It is axiomatic to this form of knowledge that 'time' and 'space' should be conceptualized as abstract entities existing externally to the individual, in fixed, immutable units. Consequently, when lifestyle research is translated into advertising practice, time is assumed to be an unproblematic resource, which can be manipulated to maximize the attention capacities of consumers. Sean Brierley's *The Advertising Handbook* (2002) provides an interesting account of 'time-based' media advertising. According to Brierley, television and radio are 'time-based media', because they involve duration and the passage of time (ibid.: 112). Commercials intrude into the durational flow of programmes with the aim of affecting desire and memorability. You probably are already aware that advertisers purposely tailor their campaigns to coincide with off-peak and prime-time viewing. But what is less evident is that these practices are designed to map onto changes in consumer behaviour which apparently occur during these times. Thus, direct response advertising is presumed to be more effective at off-peak times as it is less likely to have to compete with big brand advertisers (ibid.: 134). Television viewing during off-peak times is also believed to encourage inattention, so consumers 'have little else to occupy their time than replying to ads' (ibid.: 134). Brierley's account of time-based advertising provides an indication of how lifestyle research attempts to track advertising's adaptation to the multi-media conditions of the modern marketplace. Nevertheless, to study the experience of duration, the estimation of an interval, people's orientation within horizons, or the timing, sequencing and coordinating of behaviour, is to define time as duration, interval, passage, horizon, sequencing and timing (Adam, 1990: 94). Time is not an 'emergent' concept in lifestyle psychographics, but is pre-defined in advance of whatever is being observed (ibid.: 94.). To write of time as objective, external and invariant is to assume a position of neutrality, a consciousness which is capable of being everywhere and nowhere in particular, 'a consciousness at once immobile and omnipresent' (Ingold, 1993: 155).

While it is certainly the case that advertising has spectacularly extended the circulation of signs in modern consumer culture, critical theorists remind us of the pre-eminence of 'political economy at the heart of the sign' (Baudrillard, 1981: 147). Goldman is forthright in this respect, stating that 'it would be a mistake ... to regard advertising as merely a superstructural façade, for advertising not only masks and expresses capitalist logic, it reproduces it' (1994: 185). With advertising there occurs a solicitation and categorization of the social world based on a formula/code linking commodity-objects to the system of production (ibid.: 185). Advertising is pivotal to the processes of commodification and exchange which operate at the heart of the capitalist system. It is central to the economic processes in which exchange-values come to be linked with symbolic usages and cultural associations. Ultimately advertising is an integral part of the process of commodification in which the social times of everyday interaction are transformed into symbolic exchange-value.

The ubiquitous nature of modern advertising functions to create structures of meaning which encode memories, events and desires in terms of ideological discourses linked to the production of exchange-values. Baudrillard demonstrates this relation with regards to the impossibilities of desire. 'In the logic of signs, as in the logic of symbols', material possessions no longer respond to a defined need (Poster, 1998: 44). Rather, objects reciprocate 'a logic of desire, where they serve as a fluid and unconscious field of signification' (ibid.: 44). Advertising discourse clearly operates to arouse desires. It projects onto objects the necessary criterion for social recognition, and it does so forsaking all others. Indeed, in capitalist society, recognition has progressively withdrawn into the complex lexicon of social recognition. Consequently, objects acquire cultural values and signifying elements that bear little resemblance to use-value. In these circumstances, 'a need is not a need for a particular object as much as it is a need for difference' (ibid.: 45). The collective function of advertising is to channel our desires into the system of signification. But our 'flight from one signifier to another is no more than the surface reality of a desire, which is insatiable because it is founded on lack' (ibid.: 45). Given that identity is dependent on the recognition of others, our efforts to confirm a chosen identity through acts of consumption can never be guaranteed. Indeed, the impossibility of satiating the desire for identity is further compounded by contradictions manifest at the level of capitalist ideology.

In rational economic models, consumer behaviour is represented as an individual act driven by the desire to maximize utility value. Reason-why advertising is predicated on the belief that consumption satisfies need and thus ameliorates the tension between an ideal and a present state of being. Conversely, it is evident that even in those instances where consumption appears to be directed at an individual object, it is in fact responding to 'the production of a code of social values through the use of differentiating signs' (Poster, 1998: 46). Consumption is inextricably tied to production and therefore, just as with the production of material objects, it is not an individual process but rather 'one that is directly and totally collective' (ibid.: 46). Consumption regulates the circulation of sign-values and assures the incorporation of individuals into a corresponding system of ideological values. Advertising is complicit in the formation of a system of value signs, which in consumer society is applied to everyone. In Chapter 3 we examined how advertising achieves this by generalizing psychodynamic motivations into institutionalized codes of practice. Advertising's stereotypical evocation of motivations is but a mere alchemy of 'labels' designed to cleanse our desires of moral guilt (ibid.: 46). Consequently a desire for a Gucci bag is (re)presented, in advertising discourse, as an outcome of subconscious motives, rather than avarice. At the same time, advertising endeavours to instantiate circumspection. We are encouraged to reflect on the design of the Gucci bag, its appropriate occasion and contemporaries. Advertising thus mobilizes conflictual connotations, which are perpetually channelled in the phantasmagoria of signs and imagery. Hence the ambiguities of dissonance as consumers never have the opportunity to recognize themselves amidst the frenetic 'flight from one signifier to another' (ibid.: 45). On this basis, Baudrillard argues that consumption is 'exclusive of pleasure' (ibid.: 46). This is not because people are forced to consume. But, rather, the whole system of needs is imbricated into 'a general system of exchange and in the production of coded values' (ibid.: 46). In consumer society, pleasure and desire now exist within a system of consumption where the act of buying is axiomatic to the fashioning of self-identity.

Advertising appears to offer us an abundance of signs, objects and endless opportunities to exploit the possibilities of pleasure. Nevertheless, the dizzy whirl of signs and objects transform the experience of pleasure into an obligation, as identity is increasingly tied to the maximization of existence through consumption. The contradictions of desire and consumption operate to reproduce the internal contradictions of labour power in the process of production. Instead of owning labour power, capitalism's colonization of the means of production ensures that the worker who refuses to sell their labour power will perish. Similarly, constraints on personal needs and well-being are less inclined to manifest as repressive laws or norms of obedience. Rather, modern subjects exist in a system of consumption in which their spontaneous efforts to maximize well-being imbricate them in a process as abstract as the traditional constraint of labour and production (ibid.: 48). Advertising would have us believe that the ideologies of choice and consumer sovereignty are part of a new era of hedonistic pleasure. But 'production and consumption are one and the same grand logical process in the expanded reproduction of the productive forces and their control' (ibid.: 50). Consequently, an understanding of advertising in political economic terms makes transparent the inherent links between commodity-signs, governance and the contradictory relations of capitalist production (Goldman, 1994). By extension, an analysis of the mechanisms by which advertising can 'commodify semiotics for the purpose of reproducing a currency of sign values' (ibid.: 189), reveals the colonialization of social times by advertising to be isomorphic with the internal dynamic of the commodity-form. The following section provides a case study of the cosmetics industry and the advertising of anti-ageing products. The central objective of the case study is to decode the encoding of time in the symbolic appeal of anti-ageing products and to reveal these processes of inscription as inextricably linked to the productive economy.

Case study: gender time and the commodity-sign

According to the market research company Euromonitor, skincare is the largest sector within the cosmetics and toiletries market, worth $50bn worldwide, with a 6.9 per cent annual growth rate (quoted in Matthews, 2005). The market for skincare in the UK is estimated to be worth £5.9bn and has an average annual growth rate of 3.5 per cent (Datamonitor, 2004; Kline & Company, 2004). The women's hand and body sector was valued at £225m in 2004, an impressive 38 per cent increase since 2000 (Mintel, 2005). Nevertheless, facial products account for the largest sector. Facial skincare makes up an estimated 55 per cent of the skincare market and is also the fastest area of growth (Mintel, 2004). Figures show that the rise in facial skincare sales is being sustained by product innovations and a rapid growth in anti-ageing products (Kline & Company, 2004). Euromonitor International identify sales of anti-ageing products to have increased by nearly 200 per cent between 1997 and 2003 (quoted in Girard and Mulard, 2004). In 2004, the anti-ageing market was estimated to be worth $7.5bn worldwide. The pre-eminent brands in the UK anti-ageing product market include RoC, L'Oréal Nivea, Neutrogena, Lancôme, Olay, Chanel, No 7 and Clinique. The technical bio-medical language of advertising in this sector is self-evidently intent on convincing us that these companies have revolutionized the quantum mechanics of ageing. Products with names like 'Time Resisting Day Cream' (No 7), 'Retin-Ox Multi-Correxion' (RoC), 'Activa-Cell' (L'Oréal) and 'Ultra Correction' (Chanel) appear relevant to a science of human rejuvenation. Olay's advertisements for its anti-ageing product, Regenerist, provides a novel parody of this practice. It states that: 'The beauty buzzword on every celebrity's lips at the moment is Pentapeptide KTTKS. Don't worry if you can't pronounce it; at least now you can afford it. Olay, 2006.'

In May 2005, the Advertising Standards Authority (ASA) raised significant doubts about the efficacy of the bio-medical claims used in the promotion of anti-ageing products. It branded advertisements for L'Oréal's Wrinkle De-crease cream 'misleading' (Gibson, 2005). L'Oréal's television advertisement for its Wrinkle De-crease cream featured model Claudia Schiffer contorting her facial expressions and thus, according to the ASA, 'giving the impression that the product worked on human face lines' (quoted in bbc.co.uk 2005). The advertisement had claimed that 76 per cent of the 50 women sampled positively self-evaluated the effects of the cream after three weeks and 'reported visible reduction on expression lines' (quoted in bbc.co.uk 2005). L'Oréal also claimed that the product was 'the first anti-creasing cream with Boswelox to counteract skin micro contractions' and that this bio-medical innovation could 'rapidly reduce wrinkles' (quoted in bbc.co.uk 2005). But the ASA was less convinced, as it ruled 'The ASA's expert considered that there was insufficient evidence to allow such a claim about the effect of the product on the human face' (quoted in bbc.co.uk 2005). L'Oréal disagreed with the verdict but was seen to comply with the ASA when it later amended the advertisement as directed. While this event has interesting implications for the anti-ageing skincare sector, the purpose of this case study is not to question whether these products work. Rather, it is the intention of this case study to understand better the ideological processes whereby advertising translates the ageing of the body through time into a particular commodity. How does the time of ageing come to be transformed into a commodity-sign? Goldman (1995) describes the commodity-sign as a signifying unit, constituted by a signifier (word, image) and signified (meaning). The relationship between signifier and signified is arbitrary, determined only in terms of the positioning of each element within a sign-system. Commodity-signs arise when 'images are allied to particular products and the images are then deployed as signifiers of particular relations or experiences' (ibid.: 18). Similarly, the advertising of anti-ageing products operates to attach specific meanings or attributes of ageing to commodities as part of the process of creating symbolic exchange-values.

The effect of anti-ageing promotions is to constitute ageing as a process of depletion requiring supplementation. For instance, Chanel's Precision anti-ageing cream contains the label 'Ultra Correction', which Chanel describes as an 'Ultra firming skincare. Restore the foundations, firmness and tone of youthful skin.' Ageing is here and elsewhere inextricably linked to time. While this may be unsurprising, the construction of time in anti-ageing product promotions is distinct in its form and function. Our experience of ageing is essentially a social construct, for it embodies the beliefs, attitudes and practices of a given cultural and historical context. The meaning of ageing reflects wider inequalities of race, class and gender.

Of particular relevance is the encoding of gender difference in the advertising of anti-ageing products. L'Oréal has recently launched a new range of anti-ageing products aimed specifically at the male market. Clear distinctions exist in the aesthetic style and linguistic appeal of this campaign. First, the product range is called 'L'Oréal Paris Men Expert' as opposed to L'Oréal's 'ReFinish' and 'Plenitude' product ranges for women. The signifier expertise is clearly designed to connotate the mastery of science over the passage of time. The specific product is called Hydra Energetic and is described as a 'Daily anti-fatigue moisturising lotion'. The advertisement confronts the reader with a series of questions: 'Looking tired and worn out? Not getting enough sleep? Fight back!'. In bold type the advertisement then presents the 'Hydra energetic, moisturising lotion with vitamin C' as the solution. The cult of vitamins is clearly being trading upon here. Dichter identifies the signifying meaning of vitamin supplements to connotate 'the basic motivation of self-love' (1964: 234). The genuine bio-medical basis for vitamin supplements is a contested arena of claims and counter claims. But this is irrespective to the fetishized meaning of vitamins in the health food industry. The reference to vitamin C in the L'Oréal advertisement clearly attempts to link the energizing capabilities of vitamin C to a notion of male grooming as a legitimate indulgence. In the centre of the advertisement is located a series of vividly coloured orange symbols, one clearly detonating a battery and the other a 24-hour clock dial. Adjacent to the battery symbol is stated, 'Your skin feels recharged with energy. Healthy look. Revived skin.' And adjacent to the clock dial symbol is written, '24hr hydration, non-greasy, non-sticky formula. Used daily after shaving, it soothes razor burn.' The appeal to a culture of work and productive efficiency suggests a specifically gendered encoding of time and the meaning of ageing. This is evident if we compare the advertising copy for Hydra Energetic with L'Oréal's female anti-ageing product Plenitude. The advertisement includes a product endorsement by the actress Judith Godrèche. The advertising copy immediately after the brand name reads 'Innovation: Activa-Cell. In 8 days my skin is reborn.' In the far-left corner is incorporated a spiral helix with a label describing it as a 'Activia Cell'. Immediately beneath this image the advertisement states 'Technological breakthrough. The Activa-Cell to help reactivate the skin's natural defence and repair process.' While the rhetoric of technological breakthrough and the mastery of ageing is also evident in this advertisement, the description of the body makes no appeal to time and work or even productivity.

This gender distinction in the social meaning of ageing evident in L'Oréal's Plenitude and Hydra Energetic advertising campaigns attends to socio-biological discourses of gender difference. Socio-biological discourses of gender distinction are concerned with the effects of biology on social behaviour. They set out to demonstrate how 'natural' genetic and hormonal differences between the sexes result in different 'natural' forms of behaviour (Weedon, 1992). Natural femininity and masculinity incline men and women to different occupations, social and familial roles (ibid.: 130). Given the inherent inequalities in the gender division of domestic labour, socio-biological discourses sustain rather then challenge gendered relations of power. The effect of the advertising campaign's socio-biological discourse is to determine in advance what constitutes normal femininity and masculinity, to fix subjectivity, by insisting that the experience of ageing is determined by natural forces which have intrinsic gender distinction. The idea of natural physiological processes is a powerful discourse, which in bio-medical discourse assumes knowledge to be guaranteed by neutral empirical observations (ibid.: 130). In this sense, bio-medical accounts of ageing gain status because they are assumed to have been ascertained by the accumulation of objective, true facts, which are independent of particular social, moral or political interests. Any bio-medical claim to the existence of gendered human processes, which are universal in the sense that they determine male and female lives, irrespective of historical circumstance, constitutes a formidable regime of truth. And deviation from these factual impressions is thus deemed 'un-natural', 'against nature' and 'un-scientific'. Thus socio-biological theory attempts to convince us that any attempts to organize society in contradiction with natural processes 'will not only in the long run be self-defeating, they may also lead to problems of social order and social control' (Grimshaw, 1993: 106). The advertising campaign's trajectory in socio-biological discourse ascribes it with scientific legitimacy, which sustains the claim that gender differences propel men and women into dissimilar patterns of ageing. Men and masculinity are associated with the public sphere of work and activity. Thus, the Hydra Energetic is a product designed to overcome the signs of 'Daily anti-fatigue' for men who 'Look overworked'. Conversely, feminine identity is associated with the private sphere of reproductive activities. Thus, Plenitude is designed to make skin 'Reborn'. The imaginary of natural gender distinction in the socio-biological conditions of ageing functions to obscure the intervention of cultural practices in determining gender roles. In this sense, advertising operates to encode the process of ageing through time, with gender-specific connotations and in so doing create symbolic exchange-values linked to the acquisition of commercial profit. Segmenting the market for anti-ageing products has effectively multiplied the potential for consumer demand.

At a further level of analysis the reference to birth in the L'Oréal advertisement for Plenitude appears resonant with psychoanalytical discourses which define feminine subjectivity as tied to a fixed signifier of sexual differences, 'the phallus' (Weedon, 1992). Indeed, the name 'Activa-Cell' and the symbol of a spiralling helix nested in a small enclosure (womb?) appear to make subjective appeal to the psycho-sexual development of the female subject. Additional signs of psycho-sexual development are evident with regards to the inscriptions placed on the model's face. The model's face is partitioned into three areas, each ascribed a separate label indicating the daily process of improvement that the consumer might expect. The first label reads 'Day 1 Instant velvety skin'. The second label reads 'Day 5 Skin texture refined'. The third label reads 'Day 8 Lines and wrinkles visibly reduced'. Time emerges here as a process of gestation towards the rebirth or rejuvenation of the consumer. Feminist psychoanalytic theory is of some relevance to this analysis. Freud traced the determination of masculine and feminine identity to the psychic structures of sexual identity located within the early years of childhood (Weedon, 1992). Freud argued that the acquisition of masculine and feminine identity in adulthood involved repressing those aspects of childhood sexual identity which are in contradistinction with the normative order (ibid.: 46). Freud emphasized that it was the precarious psychic nature of childhood and not biological determinism, which encouraged individuals to adopt gender specific adult roles. He located the psychic development of the child within the social organization of the nuclear familiar, which in 'normal' circumstances leads to the acquisition of heterosexual identities. In Freudian analysis, the development of gendered subjectivity involves the unconscious and conscious mind, as it endeavours to decipher the gendered coding of the Oedipus complexes. The perplexities of sexual identity are resolved differently for the male and female child. Given that in Freudian analysis 'masculinity ... , is taken as the norm against which difference is measured, the process of psycho-sexual development is clearest in the male child' (ibid.: 47). Conversely, the acquisition of female sexuality is a more precarious process. Freud's narrative of female psycho-sexual development locates the female within a maelstrom of rejected and re-directed affiliations which culminate in the transference of desire. Having recognized her anatomical difference from the male, the female subject identifies both herself and mother as castrated. Psycho-sexual development is at this point driven by desire and envy for that which the female subject lacks. This provokes the rejection of the mother as an initial love object. Desire is transferred onto the father with the 'promise of satisfaction at some future point through bearing a male child' (ibid.: 48). In Freudian analysis, the resolution of the Oedipus complex, for the female subject, is driven by a desire for completeness in a psycho-sexual order in which the masculine is the principal signifier. Returning to the advertisement for L'Oréal's Plenitude, the signifiers 'reborn' and 'Activa-Cell' reinforce a notion of biological womanhood which is tied to a Freudian reading of female psycho-sexual development. The primacy of birth as a principal signifier can be read in symbolic terms as a definition of femininity in terms of lack defined against the masculine ideal. This recognition provokes a disregard for the older woman (mother) and transference of desire to heterosexual love engineered by the rebirth of the body. As with socio-biological symbolism, the phallocentric symbolism attempts to tie gender distinction to a fixed sexual order. The assumption that the ageing of the body through time is a transparent medium with natural distinctions implies that gender relations are expressed rather than constituted though discourses. The product is used to label and reinforce gender-specific forms of ageing and this has significance for the reproduction of wider forms of gender inequality.

An additional feature of anti-ageing product promotions relates to the reification of time and the transformation of time into an object with exchange-value. For instance, Clinique in an advertisement for their 'Preventive Cream SPF 15' has an image of a stopwatch which has a broken case and is leaning (defeated) against a small jar of anti-ageing cream. Across the jar is large black type which reads 'advanced stop signs eye'. Time and ageing are represented in this advert as embattled relics defeated by the appliance of science. A similar theme is evident in an advertisement for Dior's Capture Totale. The advertisement declares this product to be 'The latest breakthrough against time'. This claim is followed by statistics and endorsements leading to the ultimate claim that 'After using Capture Totale, the perceived age of the face is significantly less than the actual age.' The self-acclaimed 'Anti-ageing expert', Dr Pierre Ricaud advertises its Illuminez-moi using similar references to the value of 'Science to fight the effects of time'.

Elsewhere, an advertisement for RoC's 'New Retin-Ox Multi-Correxion' contains an image of a model and the statement 'I'm 55, I've just fallen in love'. Time is constituted here as an enchanted experience and the product is a key to desire. In an advertisement for L'Oréal's Solar, the caption reads 'Yes to summer, no to the signs of skin ageing.' The appeal here is to reverse the negative associations of time, ageing and the sun. Thus, time is depicted as leisure reclaimed through bio-medical innovation. In an advertisement for Lancôme's High Résolution Collaser-48™, the advertising copy reads 'Fight wrinkles! Feel new dramatic power, inspired by laser therapy.' Time is constituted here as a nemesis to be overcome in the scientific battle against ageing. The product design reinforces this with its sci-fi chrome lacquered cover and precision applicator. NIVEA, in an advertisement for their product Q10 plus, appeals to the consumer:

> Make NIVEA body firming lotion your new daily routine for firmer skin. With dual action of Co-Enzymes Q10 plus R, it not only cares for your skin, but will significantly improve its firmness in just two weeks. NIVEA 2005

This advertisement is particularly interesting as it constitutes anti-ageing as a project to be laboured over time. The consumer is encouraged to expend labour time to complete the production process and enable the anti-ageing product to work. The responsibility for producing use-value belongs to the consumer and their labour-time, in producing the desired effect/product, is expropriated by the company as profit. A similar example is evident in No 7's campaign for its Time Resisting Cream. This advertisement is themed on a forthcoming class reunion and the advertising copy provides 'Seven essentials for your class reunion'. The first essential states 'No 1 don't panic, you've got two weeks to prepare.' The sixth essential states 'No 6 make sure you don't look your age.' And the seventh essential contains no statement but instead seductively positions the No 7 product. Thus we are expected to assume that the seventh essential for the perfect (re)presentation of the self is No 7. The NIVEA and No 7 advertisements both focus on anti-ageing as a project to invest the self over time. This contrasts with Lancôme advertising for its product Primordial Optimum. In Lancôme's advertisement, anti-ageing is a rapid process in which consumers can have 'Super skin in seconds'. This audacious statement features above an image of the product speeding off the page leaving a jet stream in its midst. *Tempus fugit* is no idle imaginary but real and accessible at the right price. Elsewhere an advertisement for NIVEA's Age Reversal Intense Rejuvenating Cream is intent on reversing Newtonian physics as it beckons consumers to 'Grow young gracefully' and thus reverse time's arrow.

A recent advertising campaign for L'Oréal's ReFinish is particularly interesting in terms of its reification of time into an object with exchange-value. The advertisement projects a stylized image of scientific innovation manifest at the level of product design and advertising aesthetic. ReFinish appears removed from the visceral matter of ageing. It has become a sign of rejuvenation. Indeed, the advertisement's self-endorsement announces ReFinish as a 'Resurfacing skin renovator'. But ReFinish, as a sign of rejuvenation, has no referent in the material world. We all know that the biological passage of the body through time is unidirectional. Nevertheless, 'In just 2 minutes' ReFinish can 'renovate your skin'. ReFinish achieves its symbolic meaning from an abstract and systematic relation to other object-signs. For it exists within a product category, which in recent years has constituted a multi-million pound industry predicated on selling to women the dream of controlling the ageing process. The conversion of ageing into a vast commercial industry has in itself become a sign. It symbolizes modern scientific ingenuity. The wealth and prosperity of the anti-ageing industry signify scientific success in controlling the irrational processes of the body. Scientific alchemy represents, here, a definitive taxonomy of the body in which the fluidity of time is at last channelled into the calculable and quantifiable patterns of a scientific order. The object-symbol ReFinish is detached from the natural qualitative rhythms of the visceral body and deployed as a signifier of rejuvenation. When we think of rejuvenation, we now think of ReFinish. The relation of product to image becomes indissoluble, as 'the product gives rise to the image' (Goldman, 1995: 19). We can observe that what is consumed is not the product but the image it gives rise to. Just as the true nature of the product is obscured, so too the conversion of the product into a systematized status of signs disguises the labour process involved in its production.

The capacity for consumption practices to convert economic exchange-value into sign-value and vice versa is 'because the logic of the commodity and of political economy is at the heart of the sign' (Baudrillard, 1981: 146). The commodity is therefore, not merely asserting itself as a thing but rather mapping onto a specific logic. Critical theorists identify capital accumulation and the patterns by which this process of accumulation is regulated as assuming a definitive logic. The logic is a framework within which capitalist social practices are defined and enacted (Goldman, 1995: 19). This logic is evident in the form and function of the 'formally rationalised contractual and juridical codes of capitalist society' (ibid.: 19). And its principal features determine the processes deployed in advertising's production of commodity-signs.

Given the centrality of time to the commodity-form, it is of little surprise that time is crucial to the process of linking commodity objects to socially valorized meanings. We can observe this process at work in the advertisement for ReFinish. While the advertisement makes frequent reference to time, '2 steps, 2 minutes, 2 times a week', time is no longer a lived duration. Time has become transfigured into an object-sign where it is consumed (Baudrillard, 1981). In order to be integrated into the order of production, the commodity-form detaches human characteristics from temporal relations and transforms them into exchangeable entities. These entities are ascribed the appearance of independent constructs separate from the lived and contradictory relations of their original context. The process of dislocating social relations from their original organic context is defined as 'abstraction' (Goldman, 1995: 21). Abstraction has definitive trajectories in the separation of use-value and exchange-value as both condition and consequence of the extension of the commodity-form (ibid.: 21). Abstraction is also evident in the labour process with the separation of useful labour and abstract labour. Indeed, abstraction is apparent on any occasion in which 'social relations have been split into quality and quantity, form and content' (ibid.: 21). In the operation of the commodity-sign, abstraction materializes in the emptying out of meaningful content and the separation of means and ends (ibid.: 24). In order for a social relation to be transformed into sign currency, it needs to be stripped of all characteristics which might disrupt the mechanistic order of production (Baudrillard, 1981). We can observe evidence of abstraction in the ReFinish advertisement. Age rejuvenation is separated from the total context of nutrition, biology, environment, income, genetics, etc., of which it is inextricably part, and relocated within a new context constituted by the commodity. As a function of scientific ingenuity, rejuvenation now belongs to the realm of science and quantitative rationality and the consumption of ReFinish is a logical means of defying ageing.

If we look more closely at the ReFinish advertisement, our attention is drawn to the relevance of reification in the making of subjectivity through time. The advertising copy contains an intriguing endorsement from a L'Oréal Paris Skincare Adviser. Of particular significance is the statement that 'in my practice I see a lot of women who from the age of 30, see the surface of their skin changing, losing its radiance and youth'. This statement functions to reify time into an entity constituted by discrete commodifable units. Thus, the age of 30 is transformed into an objective thing, bestowed with specific connotations and implications for subjective happiness. Reification is a process of forgetting in which human beings can no longer recognize their part in the creation of social reality (Goldman, 1995: 31). In the advertisement for ReFinish we are seduced by the fantastic form of a newly invigorated landmark age. Irrespective of our own lived experience of being 30, we are persuaded to live this time again in its newly renovated form. In this respect, 'the goods acquire a life history, while humans lose theirs' (ibid.: 32). This defines consumption as a peculiar moment in the making of subjectivity. For the ultimate task becomes the consumption of objects in order to erase the making of the self through time.

In an advertisement for RoC's Retinol Body Modelling, time is reified into an object of memory. The advertisement contains a model trying on a pair of tight-fitting jeans, followed by the statement '10 years back to skin firmness'. This statement encourages the spectator to comprehend the past as a present reality. We are pushed back into the past to retrieve idealized memories of when, as female adults we once wore tight-fitting jeans. The image of the female model provides the spectator with a spatial context in which to perform the advertisement's nostalgic flight of fantasy. Our real historicity is denied and appropriated by a memory that is neither shared nor lived in material existence. As Williamson puts it, 'our real past, history, is appropriated by the advertisement to be filled by the product, or to become represented by a single subject' (2000: 155). We are enticed by the advertisement to move out of our reality into the metaphysical past of the advertisement.

Reification occurs in the many occasions when advertising conflates the consumption of a product with an actual experience of event-based time. We need only reflect on the commercial success of the invention of 'Mother's Day', 'Father's Day' and its numerous derivatives to comprehend the more general role of advertising in reifying time. This reification of time in advertising discourse directly links to the process of abstraction. Goldman observes how 'advertisements ... separate the intrinsic qualities of being human from actual living humans' (1995: 31). The formal logic of the commodity-sign, analysed by Goldman, is efficacious in the fashioning of a meaningful continuity between discrete moments in time. For instance in the ReFinish advertisement, objects are purposely positioned in such a way, so as to establish a narrative of time unfolding. The model's (Natalie Imbruglia) face dominates the left-hand side of the advertisement. Adjacent to this is a column of bio-medical claims. We are encouraged to make a narrational link between Natalie Imbruglia and the possibilities of anti-ageing products. Advertising analysts have long since drawn attention to how the distancing and lighting of objects in advertisements signify specific relations to the past and future (Williamson, 2000). In the Re-finish advertisement, the actual product is located in the foreground on the right-hand side. It has a patch of light falling upon its sleeve which, in conjunction with the narrative sequence of object positioning, appears to signify the future. Similarly, the gaze of the female model is indicative of a future horizon, which we are encouraged to apprehend as we follow her eye line. Collectively these images position the potential consumer within a contrived narrative time, in which the past is idealized and the future transformed into an inspirational ideal. The present becomes a mere intersection to a time less mundane and divorced from the unsatisfactory realities of everyday existence. The semiotics of the advertisement assumes a chronological and sequential articulation of time, in which individual moments of time (i.e., past, present, future) function as signs. In order for the exchange of temporal signs to have currency, they need to be integrated into the order of production and mobilized as a productive force with a definite commercial outcome (Lee, 1993). The narrational properties of the commodity-sign are therefore indexed to a productive system in which signs are rendered meaningful by first being 'framed discursively within the text in order to establish a recognisable temporal distance between each of them' (ibid.: 155).

Conclusion

The symbolic construction of time in the commodity-sign is predicated on the existence of a discursive frame to render the flow of time meaningful and 'achieve the necessary closure around the commodity it promotes' (Lee, 1993: 155). The latter issue of 'closure' in the context of time and advertising practice is effectively detailed by Williamson (2000). As a starting point, Williamson (ibid.: 152) argues that the time of the advertisements is always already past, 'since the picture is finished and the future events are never open, but specifically directed'. The spectator is situated, by the advertisement, in a position of closure, whereby the narrative sequence and its apparitional future have been determined in advance by the logic of the commodity-form. The narrative instantiates a social meaning of time in which the present is a state of lack and the product signifies a connection to a more satisfied state of being. This narrative of time is in contrast to the flow of time in everyday social relations. In *Being and Time* (1962), Heidegger's account of *Dasein* informs our comprehension of human identity as stretched across time (Thomas, 1996: 51). *Being* is dispersed through the chronicles of time. The existential time of *Dasein* possesses an intense immediacy, uniquely relevant to the person. And yet, *Dasein* as a concept also draws attention to the way subjectivity is always lived in embodied form (Thomas, 1996). Subjects live time–space events as well as being constituted by them. Time is, therefore, inextricably bound up with places, spaces and the body. For people 'do not so much think real time but actually live it sensuously, qualitatively' (Urry, 1995: 6). The identity, which emerges in the process of the self, stretches across time as 'the person one is now has a historical connection with the person whom one was yesterday' (Thomas, 1996: 45). By reflecting upon previous experience, present contingencies and future desires the self is consistently bringing itself into existence (ibid.: 52). Narrativity is thus axiomatic to modern self-identity. Indeed, Giddens (1993: 76) describes how the production of an interpretative self-history is central to self-identity in modern social life. The 'reflexive monitoring' of self 'forms a trajectory of development from the past to the anticipated future' (ibid.: 75). Giddens describes the future as resonant with possibilities, 'yet not left open to the full play of contingency' (ibid.: 77). Foucault (1979), in particular, demonstrates the profound historicity of modern subjectivity. Society and culture provide specific 'technologies of the self' through which identities are constituted. The self is a developing site of cultural inscription (Thomas, 1996: 47). Our existential experiences of time are re-inscriptive of society's social rhythms rather than mere representations. The modern self as a narrative text is always lived in an embodied form so that 'subjects are dialogical, bringing specific personas, discourses and voices to contexts of negotiation, and domination' (Thrift, quoted in Thomas, 1996: 47). But what becomes of narrative time in advertising discourse?

Williamson observes how in time and advertising narrative, the open future of everyday interaction is transformed into 'a deterministic and unalterable present' (2000: 152). The closed future of advertising narrative has a demonstrable ideological function. It operates to disengage subjects from the natural flow of time and ascribes their being a 'synchronic status' in which events unfold within a kind of 'eternal moment (ibid.: 152). The 'ideology of the synchronic' misrepresents history as a horizon of events which occur simultaneously when observed from 'the vantage view point of the present' (ibid.: 154). It might help to think again of the ReFinish advertisement. The statement, '2 steps, 2 minutes, 2 times a week' constructs time as a continuum in which events are inseparable and merge together in the present. In place of a diachronic flow of time, the time of the advertisement has a given beginning and determined end which we can observe from the vantage point of the present. The narrative time of '2 steps, 2 minutes, 2 times a week' begins in the present as a response to a situation of lack and culminates in the present as this lack is defined and satisfied by a guaranteed solution i.e,. the product ReFinish. By extension, Williamson argues that the ideology of the synchronic operates to deny the possibilities of our present as it contrives to map a sense of need onto our experience of the advertisement. As she puts it, 'no present pleasure exists because in the actual present you are looking at the *ad* anticipating but not enjoying' (2000: 155). The advertisement substitutes our lived embodied present with a 'false' present. Within this context we are encouraged to decipher the advertisement's chronological and sequential articulation of time. Thus the material existence of synchronicity 'must be outside of real time, since all time is available to us at once as we stand in real time, in front of the ad' (ibid.: 155). The advertisement in this sense attempts to capture time both in regard to the re-constructed present and the dislocation of the spectator from the natural flow of time. But time is ephemeral:

Time of course is not something that can be owned; it is common to us all, and cannot be divided. It is the extreme spatiality of our consciousness that leads us to assume that we can partition time and make it our own, through material objects. (ibid.: 156)

Part Three

Advertising in Postmodern Time(s)

Figure Part III *Advertising and time (space) disruptions in postmodern virtual worlds, Toshiba, 2005*

Source: Reproduced by permission of Toshiba.

5

'The Times They Are A-Changin''

Transformations of work and leisure in the time/space economies of modern and postmodern advertising

The signifying properties of advertising practices provide fascinating revelations into the commodification of leisure time as a precondition for capitalist production. The transition to monopoly capitalism in the early twentieth century precipitated a movement from absolute surplus-value to relative surplus-value extraction and an emphasis on the social conditions of wage labour (Goldman, 1995: 16). The appropriation of relative surplus-value involves an intensification of the productive process (Lee, 1993). And the resulting accumulation of surplus products requires a 'qualitative reconfiguration of consumption' if capital is to avoid a crisis in accumulation (ibid.: 123). This chapter examines leisure as an extension of social transformations under capitalism. In critical theory, leisure time is revealed as functionally dependent on the labour market system. Theorists variously describe industrialism as precipitating radical transformations in the sanctioning, definition and organization of recreation. As a counterpart to the commodification of labour, leisure time became a precious commodity and subject to the laws of exchange-value (Baudrillard, 2003: 152). Leisure is a product of capitalist culture and its specific mode of production. It is 'time-as-object' and ascribed equivalent status to all commodities produced within the system of capitalist production (ibid.: 152). Time conceived in linear dimensions can be transformed into an object of temporal calculation and exchanged against other commodities. In so doing, it is homologous with the exchange-value system (ibid.: 153).

Critical theorists draw attention to the colonization of free-time, by economic logic, as evidence of advertising's role in the reproduction of time as a productive force. Leisure time is earned; it is capital on which productive value can be returned. Under conditions of modern capitalism, the market is ascribed the capacity to satisfy all needs. The centrality of markets to the productive process promotes the cultural and economic conditions necessary for the commodification of leisure. Workers go to the market for paid labour and have neither the time nor skills for the domestic production of leisure activities (Slater, 1998: 398). Capitalism's insatiable desire for ever more commercial opportunities to sell commodities invites the transformation of leisure into an activity, which can be sold in the form of an object (ibid.: 398). Money functions as an expression of value, thus making leisure comparable and measurable to other commodities. In this sense, leisure time is most successfully ingratiated into the system of production as chronometric capital, capable of being exchanged against any other commodity (Baudrillard, 2003). Indeed, the abstraction of leisure is effectively accomplished when the exchange-value has detached it from any specific social context (Haug, 1986). From the point of exchange-value, each leisure activity, regardless of its particular form, matters only as an 'abstract form of wealth' (Baudrillard, 2003). Money facilitates the exchange-value of leisure, but the conditions which partake in the reification of leisure exist also at the level of advertising practice.

In this chapter, motor car advertising provides a continuous source of empirical reflection. Early twentieth-century car advertising concentrated principally on the use-value of the product. This materialized in the primacy given to science and technology, in the concern to quantify, calculate and ensure efficiency in mobility. For instance, the 1960s DamienChrysler advertisement in Figure 5.1 describes DamienChrysler's premium craftsmanship and links this to the utility-value of leisure. In so doing, the advertisement attempts to transform qualitative experiences of leisure into a quantifiable, abstract utility compatible with the exchange system of value.

As a means of transportation, the motor car constitutes a distinct relationship between the owner and product. Unlike previous forms of locomotion (e.g., bicycle, horse and carriage), the owner of the motor car is forever dependent on fuel supply, specialist equipment and engineers for its operation. The motorist's relation to their car is 'that of user and consumer – and not owner and master' (Gorz, 1983: 71). In the early twentieth century, advertising equated the utility value of the motor car with a meritocratic ideal which linked time-disciplined leisure and economic productivity, but this corporate ideal neglected to take into account how the time spent earning the money for the motor car's purchase and maintenance reproduced social inequalities. Because the 'freedom' and 'democracy' offered by the mass-produced motor car stopped short of addressing endemic disparities in the distribution of financial resources in both the public and private spheres. What was meant rather, by the blessing of 'freedom' and 'democracy' promised to the industrial worker, was the freedom to 'cultivate themselves among the incontestable fruits of the new industrial cornucopia' (Ewen, 1977: 27). Not only was this alleged freedom designed to redefine the worker as a consumer of mass-produced motor cars. It also secured lucrative revenue from a wealth of auxiliary expenditures. For possession of the motor car committed the owner to consume a host of commercial services and industrial products that could only be provided by a third party (Gorz, 1983: 71). The rational utility-maximizing agent of early twentieth-century motor car advertising sought 'freedom' through the efficient use of time, but instead gained dependency, for their locomotion, on a commercial source of energy (ibid.: 72). The first section of this chapter examines the objectification of leisure

Presenting the completely new

1960 CHRYSLER

The car of your life
for the time of your life!

There have never been so many new advances in Chrysler, for any single year, as you'll see in the new Chrysler for 1960. Bold strides in styling . . . in ride and room . . . in reliability and convenience.

New ideas in styling. Shaped for the *spirited sixties*, that new and adventurous and eager decade ahead. Bold, strong grille. Graceful rear deck. Flying wedge taillight design. Clean lines sheathed in color-bright Lustre-Bond, the hardest automotive finish known.

New ideas in convenience. Every Chrysler offers automatic Swivel Seats. Open the door . . . they turn out. Leave the car . . . they turn in. Automatically! Inside, your fingertips span a nest of pushbutton controls. Instruments are housed in a new three-dimensional AstraDome control center. And at night, new Panelescent lighting bathes them in a soft, glare-free glow.

New ideas in comfort. With all that's new, there's a return to comfort, too. Seats have been raised . . . padded with extra foam rubber . . . reinforced with a new spring design. There's

more leg, knee, hip and head room front and back! Door openings are wider . . . with no knee-knocking projections. New interiors are clothed in sturdy, color-bright designer fabrics.

New ideas in reliability. For 1960, Chrysler features a new body and frame built in a single, rattle-free unit. Stronger. Quieter. Yields more room inside. Chrysler calls it *Unibody*. It's rugged . . . with a velvet road touch. A new protective dipping process locks rust out of vital areas.

Get touching close to this new Chrysler soon. Compare its fresh, clean beauty with the look of any other car. Swing inside and see how Chrysler has actually built in *more* room while other cars continue to be cramped. Then take it out on the road and have the time of your life!

This is Chrysler's greatest . . .

the lion-hearted 1960 CHRYSLER

Figure 5.1   Utility and leisure in car advertising, Chrysler, 1960

Source: Copyright DaimlerChrysler Corporation. Reproduced with permission.

147

time in motor car advertising. It describes how an ideological focus on technical rationality permeated early twentieth-century advertising discourses, and created the conditions through which a new world of leisure could be integrated into the new world of technified work.

The second section of this chapter describes how the neo-classical utilitarian models of demand were being significantly challenged in the early decades of the twentieth century. In 1909, Veblen, in his writings on the limitations of marginal utility, insisted that consumer behaviour was characterized by 'unhedonistic, irrationalistic pecuniary traffic' (quoted in Mason, 1995: 874). Elsewhere, writers began to challenge the legitimacy of 'rational' utilitarian demand theory (Pigou, 1925; Maynard, 1936). By the mid-1920s writers within the emerging discipline of marketing increasingly took issue with the assumption that aggregate demand could be derived from compounding individual demand schedules (Mason, 1995: 871). Neo-classical interpretations of consumer demand were variously identified as understating 'the importance of product symbolism and status' (ibid.: 878). Consumer behaviour specialists were increasingly turning to the social sciences to provide alternatives to the asocial, neo-classical economic interpretations of consumer demand. This would have profound consequences for the role of leisure advertising as 'the very ideology of alienated labour' (Baudrillard, 2003: 155). But general appreciation of these transformations is often obscured by the marked tendency, in Marxist analysis, towards a definition of leisure time merely as an objective expression of the exchange-value system. The commodification of leisure is observed in historical terms, by critical theorists, to have been the outcome of 'applying to it an instrumental rationality which increasingly narrowed the range of social roles available within leisure practices' (Hemingway, 1996: 30). In this sense, leisure time in capitalist society is irredeemably degraded. As Hemingway puts it, 'culture consuming leisure is instrumental, making use of subjects and objects encountered in leisure without engaging them as other than partners in temporary exchange relationships' (ibid.: 36). Critical leisure theory is constrained in so far as it focuses solely on 'time-as-object'. The potential already exists for alternative conceptions of leisure time. Analysis of advertising aesthetics in the production of the commodity-sign appeals to forms of temporality, which emerge out of social practice (see Chapter 4). The production of the commodity-assign in advertising discourse appears less inclined to the construction of time-as-object, as it invokes inter-subjective non-linear temporalities. For the commodity-sign operates to ally particular products and images and deploy these as signifiers of social relations embedded in time–space events (Goldman, 1995: 18). This conception of time provides a means of mapping advertising onto crucial transformations in work and leisure in the late modern era.

The third section of this chapter has as its focus post-Fordism and the transformations of work and leisure, which have arisen as a result of new ways of organizing the labour process. The postmodern condition suggests that we are experiencing an intense phase of time–space compression and their fragmentation both globally and locally (Harvey, 1990). Unparalleled advances in communication technology have intensified, fragmented and dramatically delineated complex value-chains, inducing a 'systemic perturbation in the sequential' ordering of time/space (Castells, 2000: 464). Advertising in the twentieth century was characterized by a belief that a relatively fixed system of human needs could be discovered for different segments of the consumer market. In its more sophisticated renditions and especially within innovative advertising, these needs are seen as socially constructed and thereby open to being formed and furnished by those seeking to sell their products and services (see Chapter 4). From this perspective, products and services can be seen as solutions looking for a problem to solve. Advertisers who have moved this far within the framework of modernism have less difficulty in confronting the challenge of postmodern markets, where consumption involves the exchange of signs (Baudrillard, 1981) that are 'free floating' – not tied to an object of signification but simply circulating in a space of signifiers. These transformations in signifying practices attest to radical changes in the commodity-form. For the increased productivity of lean manufacturers has speeded up the pace of commodity production to unprecedented levels. At the same time, work and leisure have become less fixed and less differentiated by definitive boundaries and frontiers. The third section identifies how motor car advertising provides an example through which to analyse the intensity of time/space compression in Western capitalism since the 1960s with all its emergent features of excessive ephemerality and fragmentation in work and leisure times.

Rational utility in the time and space economies of mass-produced leisure

The turn of the twentieth century witnessed the development of the internal combustion engine and the motor car. It was an invention which was to revolutionize leisure respectability and rational recreation. While the earlier prototypes of the motor vehicle originated in Europe, the industry was to develop in the United States (Montgomery, 1968). Indeed, the US-based Ford Motor Company is frequently cited as initiating large-scale mass production. 'I will build a motor car for the great multitude', said Henry Ford in 1910. Less than a decade later, he delivered his promise by producing what was advertised as the 'universal car', the Model T. This achievement laid the foundations for revolutionary transformations in the entire motor vehicle industry. The Model T was designed as a practical and reliable means of travel for what Henry Ford called 'the great multitude'. The key to its mass production was the idea of accurately timing manufacturing operations. Frederick Winslow Taylor (1856–1915) had earlier formulated the principles of 'scientific management'. Taylor's technological interventions into the 'natural' flow of work events were geared towards achieving the wholesale rationalization of the labour process. Taylor's famous tract, *The Principles of Scientific Management* (1911), describes how labour productivity can be dramatically increased by 'breaking down each labour process' into narrowly specialized, unskilled tasks performed according to 'rigorous standards of time and motion study' (Harvey, 1990: 123). Time was translated into economic terms 'it became the medium in which human activities, especially economic activities, could be stepped up to a previously unimagined rate of growth' (Nowotny, 1976: 330). Built into Taylor's approach was a notion that 'progress', defined as both material and moral advancement, is a positively natural force guiding the destiny of mankind (Rose, 1975: 57). Ford applied Taylor's scientific management principles in an attempt to achieve complete and consistent interchangeability of parts and ultimate simplicity in assembly. Tasks were broken down into hundreds of small individualized production processes performed on long assembly lines designed for the production of standardized products. Machines regulated the rate of production, as they substituted skilled labour for standardized mass production. Braverman (1974) describes how Fordism entailed the concentration of utilized labour power in minimal units of time, which maximized the extraction of surplus value in its most rational economic form.

Ford's Model T was designed as a universal car and produced in high volumes to attract customers keen to purchase mass-produced, low-cost, sturdy vehicles. By emphasizing a marketing strategy dominated primarily by price, Ford advocated the prevalence of neo-classical utilitarian models to marketing analyses of consumer demand. Neo-classical analysis marginalizes the significance of wider social influences on consumer choice, focusing instead on the ideas and principles of value and intentioned consumer rationality (Mason, 1995: 875). Thus, for example, in 1924, Ford published the following advertising statement: 'By stimulating good health and efficiency, owning a Ford increases your earning power' (quoted in Stern and Stern, 1978: 15). Simple and unmistakable, Ford's earlier advertising merely sought to appeal to the rational utilitarian mind-set, which informed the logic of mass assembly line production.

These early developments in Ford's marketing strategy perceived consumption as exclusively about 'economic exchange' and therefore not about other kinds of human behaviour and emphasized the capability of the marketer to influence or control consumer behaviour. Figure 5.2 is an advertisement which illustrates Ford's utility-maximizing approach to consumer behaviour. Axiomatic to this concept of economic exchange is a notion of transactions as 'one-time exchanges of values between two parties who have no prior or subsequent interaction' (Easton and Araujo, 1994: 74). The identities of parties are of limited significance as 'transactions are assumed to be perfectly replaceable across parties with similar utility functions' (ibid.: 74). Further examples of this conception of consumer subjectivity include the following magazine advertisement by Ford Motor cars in 1937:

> Worthy to serve the most exalted, upon occasions of the utmost circumstance, yet marked by a chaste restraint of line never suggestive of opulence, or arrogance, the Ford V-8 '22' has performance of a measure and refinement making it handsomely worth twice its price of £210. As economical, as efficient in its infinite range of duty. It is the car for Britons, the world over, in Coronation Year. There is No Comparison! (quoted in Advertising Archive, 2006)

Figure 5.2   *The Ford Times, August 1926, Ford Motor Company Limited*

Source: Robert (1976), by kind permission of the publishers. Reproduced with kind permission of Ford Motor Company Limited.

This famous advertisement attempts to simulate a sense of individualized urgency in its appeal to the temporal logic of desire. Its creation of a need projected into the future (Coronation Year) is a function of the simulacra of duration as an object of consumption (Appadurai, 1996). Consumption creates the simulacra of time as a period absent ('upon occasions of the utmost circumstance'); an opportunity potentially lost ('As economical, as efficient in its infinite range of duty') and an opportunity gained ('It is the car for Britons, in the world over, in Coronation Year. There is No Comparison!'). But the 'man of distinction' to whom this advertisement is directed is also mere illusion as the mass production of standardized goods seeks to produce the complete opposite of individual distinction. Indeed, the utilitarianism of reason-why advertising offered the promise of distinguished efficiency as a ruse to obviate the stultifying homogeneity of mass production. It is clear, therefore, that the concept of economic exchange seductively contrives to detach the exchange relationship from its embeddedness in a plethora of densely woven power/knowledge relations. The 'pure' economic exchange has no historical context as the 'history of past relations is immaterial and all elements of exchange are contained in sharply defined time frames' (Easton and Araujo, 1994: 74). Rational agents are represented as engaging in a de-contextualized, game of self-seeking opportunism. Marketing, Ford insisted, had to recognize that 'the work and the work alone controls us' (quoted in Ewen, 1977: 24). Efficiency and reliability were advertised as distinguishing Ford motor cars and the self-reliant consumer of its goods. Efficiency and reliability equate with time conceived as a unit that is readily given to monetary value (Becker and Michael, 1973). So, for example, time can be used to price products in relation to the labour cost of their production or simply to measure the opportunity cost of leisure time spent on consumption.

Time in Fordist production is a controllable scarce resource; a 'pressure' in decision-making, and a unit for measuring performance and a 'fair day's work'. Ford's establishment of the 'five dollar day' became a powerful symbol of how the perfectly trained worker is supposed to function as predictably and precisely as clockwork (Pietrykowski, 1999). Indeed, Ford strenuously believed that the proper application of corporate power could instil labourers with the moral and mental discipline required to work the highly productive assembly-line system (Harvey, 1990: 126). His preoccupation with exactitude and control appears, therefore, to have been only partially motivated by the technical imperatives of mass production.

The introduction of time and motion studies into the wholesale rationalization of labour had instigated dramatic changes in domestic and social rhythms. Time-disciplined labour was delineated from other forms of activity, and labour relations were redefined by the principles of exchange. The alienation of the producers (wage earners) in the labour process affects not only their relation to the products of their labour, but also their social relations in the public and private sphere. For the extension of economic rationality into all spheres of social life is integral to the development of capitalism (Gorz, 1994). A key to the inter-relations between mass assembly-line production, leisure and advertising is evident in the specific form of social managerialism, which emerged in the early twentieth century.

Ford's innovations meant huge savings over earlier production techniques. It is estimated that by the early 1920s approximately half of the eight million motor cars on US roads were Model Ts (Stern and Stern, 1978). The growth of goods offered a context in which workers could be considered as potential 'citizens of a new industrial civilisation' (Ewen, 1977: 14). Such a development, once again, attempted to tie the identity of the wage labourer to the broadly equivalent values embodied in the realm of consumption (Lee, 1993). Indeed, Ford equated mass motoring with a version of social equality, as evidenced in the following excerpt: 'If they manage to adjust to exemplary machines, then their pay will go up, and the time will not be far when our own workers will buy automobiles from us' (quoted in Wolf, 1996: 72). Ford's desire to iron out social difference, to transform diverse groups into acceptably socialized mass consumers, echoed the intellectual context of marketing and advertising research in the 1920s and 1930s. By emphasizing a marketing strategy dominated primarily by price, Ford advocated the neo-classical utilitarian models to marketing analyses of consumer demand.

Mass production pointed towards the need for markets which transcended the traditional supply and demand models of industrial goods consumption (Ewen, 1977). The consolidation of the productive system required by mass production necessitated a redefinition of labourers into consumers. This entailed a movement away from defining workers merely by their productive capacity. 'Progressive' managerialists were increasingly motivated to transcend the question of organizing the factory and move towards an understanding of the arenas in which workers might be self-disciplined to commit themselves to the industrial process (ibid.: 15). In other words, the transformation of the labour force into consumers necessitated the redefinition of both working and non-working times in terms of the logic of economic rationality. As Gorz states, 'economic rationality has no room for authentically free time which neither produces nor consumes commercial wealth' (1976: 174–5). In this respect, Gorz echoes E.P. Thompson's (1967) identification of how new opportunities for leisure in the twentieth century posed specific problems of social control over the industrial labour force. Capitalism's response to the dilemmas of controlling working-class leisure and the need to absorb excess goods was 'consumerism'. The process of capitalist industrialization transformed leisure from a collective activity, embedded in occupational communities into market-based activities compatible with the dictates of the workplace. With the advent of mature capitalism society, wage incentives accompany expanding consumer drives as 'palpable rewards for the productive consumption of time' (ibid.: 91). 'Time is money', it is marked by time thrift and binds a clear demarcation between 'work' and 'life'. Indeed, 'in mature capitalist society all time must be consumed, marketed, put to use;

it is offensive for the labour force merely to "pass the time"' (ibid.: 91). With the realization of profitability from the production of needs advertising presented an attractive vehicle for the mass production of consumer markets.

The first section of this chapter was keen to illustrate the objectification of leisure time in specific modes of motor car advertising. It described how an ideological focus on technical rationality permeated early twentieth-century advertising discourses, and created the conditions through which a new world of leisure could be integrated into the new world of technified work. But spectacular advances in advertising knowledges and practices were (and still are) radically disrupting the linear reality of rationalist models of consumer subjectivity and the rationalization of social relations, which they encourage. Church (1993), for example, describes how after the retail slump of British motor cars in the 1930s, a condition for survival was the adoption of marketing-orientated strategies. Promotion campaigns sought to expand consumer markets and 'accommodate public taste for variations in demand for different types of cars' (ibid.: 43). Britain's major car producers were increasingly employing 'intensive selling methods' including promotional campaigns emphasizing the basis of successful selling as 'the right model, in the right place, at the right time' (ibid.: 45). Elsewhere, critical theorists have similarly identified rationalist utility models of consumption as radically undermined in the 1930s and the 1940s, as advertising began to develop an identity distinct from macro-economic analysis (Goldman, 1995). Given the apparent ideological and structural 'fit' between utilitarian advertising models and the commodification of labour, it is surprising that they attracted significant resistance from alternative paradigms. The following section discusses the challenge presented by advertising techniques, which promote commodities as 'personified expressions of human characteristics and relationships' (Kline and Leiss, 1978: 17). It will suggest that the challenge presented by advertising's promotion of the commodity-sign suggests a more complicated relationship between advertising, leisure and the economic base than is often assumed in Marxist cultural theory.

Leisure and the commodity-sign

Technical innovations adopted by the British motor car industry in the mid-1920s provided for the evolution of a new approach to design, styling and accessories (Church, 1993). These developments contributed to the formation of a distinctively modernist aesthetic in car advertising. Some of the very earliest attempts to entice the public into abandoning the horse and cart for the car were modelled on propriety, sobriety and the nostalgic aesthetic of art nouveau (Roberts, 1976). The meticulously designed engravings of late nineteenth-century and early twentieth-century advertising imagery mirrored the wilful asymmetry and swirling convolvulus of art nouveau iconography (Montgomery, 1968). Late nineteenth-century car advertising often shared with art nouveau a nonchalant disinclination for matters of form, function and practicality (Roberts, 1976). It was emblematic of art nouveau's appeal to the natural fecundity and botanical world of English cultural heritage.

Art nouveau is a *fin-de-siècle* art tending towards phantasmagoria, decadence and the exquisite (Dunlop, 1994: 14). This iconography appears in juxtaposition to the solemnity of late nineteenth-century and early twentieth-century reason-why advertising. Although by the 1900 the motor car had scarcely begun to affect public life, it had already acquired cultural distinction among the middle classes. The aristocracy drove the first motor cars; nonetheless, the tendency of the burgeoning middle classes towards 'pecuniary emulation' (Veblen, [1879] 1994) generated an eagerness to secure social status through the conspicuous consumption of the car. The semiotic appeal of the car was its ability to convey a sense of identification with the ostentatious wastefulness and languid idleness of the leisured classes. Prestigious cars symbolized refined tastes, cultural distinction and were 'a sign of continuity and dependability' (Dymock, 1993: 8). The art nouveau forms in motor car advertising were particularly evocative of a vehicle tailored to symbolize a distinctive character, culture and way of life. They evoked an image of an idyllic style of life divorced from the technocratic imperatives of the productive economy and work. One might suggest that the form of aesthetic experience suggested by art nouveau appears at odds with the ideals of saving and investment fundamental to the Protestant work ethic (Bell, 1976; Harvey, 1990). Indeed, the commodity aesthetic embodied in art nouveau appears to subvert the conversion of use-value into the expenditure of quantifiable labour time. Nevertheless, to a newly emerging middle class, luxury cars conveyed the idyllic charm, good taste, staunch tradition and erstwhile style of the aristocratic leisured classes. The luxury car advertising of the early twentieth century seemed also to embody a heady nostalgia for a cultural legacy and aesthetic appeal, which appeared to be passing away (Dymock, 1993: 17).

The commodification of market relations under the new conditions of mass production, circulation and consumption pioneered radically new forms of modernist cultural aesthetics (Harvey, 1990: 23). Technological advances in production, transport and communication appeared to reify the possibilities of linear progress, absolute truths, rational planning and objective knowledge (ibid.: 23). While art nouveau had pursued the aesthetic experience as an end in itself, mass production demystified the uniqueness of artistic craftsmanship and thus required a redefinition of aesthetic design to embrace a context of reproductive copy (Benjamin, 1969; Harvey, 1990). The advent of the mass-produced motor car intersected with this new era of radically changing aesthetic design and cultural meaning. In car advertisements this was epitomized by streamlining. Inspired by the thrilling innovations in aviation design and epitomized by the teardrop organic shape that symbolized rationalized modernity, streamlining was more than a visual experience. The airplane, with its combination of speed, freedom and modern configuration, motivated Fordist industrial designers to construct a form which would enhance both the perception of speed and also enhance speed itself (Brandon, 2002). Enquiry into the relation of shape to speed was not new to intellectual curiosity. What was new was the elevation of streamlining to the position of philosophical dictate, as design engineers began to envisage its place in a whole world-view (ibid.: 266). The technical precision and efficiency emblematic of streamlining came to symbolize an optimistic vision of an integrated, smoothly functioning future (ibid.: 276). Rationalization and teleological linearity were axiomatic to the construction of a newly designed social existence which would 'ensure the organisation of people, work, wealth and leisure' (Geddes, 1934: 4–5). Indeed, streamlining epitomized a rationalization of temporal consciousness, which was projected to the future in an unbroken trajectory of innovative design and progress.

The streamline modernist aesthetic of the motor car sought to symbolize social progress through the seemingly irreconcilable forces of functional mass reproduction and aesthetic pleasure. Streamlined modernity commanded belief in the existence of uniform time and space and in return promised a dynamic technological society of joy and endless movement. The aeronautic design of the car absolutely encapsulated the streamlined view of the world and the role of modernist design within it. The mass-produced streamlined car would make the enhanced experience of speed, economic efficiency and durability available to everyone. As product ranges diversified and discretionary spending power increased, the aesthetic appeal and design features of the car were increasingly emphasized. Indeed, advertising started to have a visible impact upon the motor car as a commodity, creating the potential for real material changes in wider social relations. The advertisement in Figure 5.3 exemplifies the streamlined aesthetic appeal of the new mass-produced motor car. But what is particularly interesting about this advertisement is the transformation in leisure from a time of utility to a signifier of symbolic status.

The overall effect of the positioning of the Armstrong-Siddeley Sapphire motor car within the screen frame is to simulate the existence of a uniform space, in which mutually informative measurements can be made between past, present and future. One might argue that the past is signified by the rural backdrop and the present the streamlined motor car. The female character is positioned as both object and subject of the masculine gaze. As an object of the gaze, the female passenger is constituted as an acquisition. But the driver's seat is unoccupied, thus as a potential driver she assumes a non-traditional role and signifies cultural distinction. Changing times perhaps? In this sense, the advertisement involves the 'incorporation of time into space' (Williamson, 2000: 153). The streamform design of the motor car connotes an economy of scale indistinguishable from the sprawling acres of natural habitat. Indeed, the semiotics of the advertisement is replete with narrational devices intent on generating a seamless blend of mass-produced

Figure 5.3 *Armstrong-Siddeley Sapphire, 1955*

Source: Copyright The British Motor Industry Heritage Trust.

functionality and aristocratic lifestyle. The motor car offered owners an opportunity to communicate distinction, wealth and status. It achieved this not only through its role as an object of conspicuous consumption, but also because the motor car provided a means of translating social space, between classes, into geographic space (O'Connell, 1998: 79). The motor car provided its owners with a degree of independence unparalleled by public forms of transport. These attributes were also in accord with the values of middle-class society as evident in the following extract from *Autocar*, published in 1929: 'Public transport, no matter how fast and comfortable, inflicts a sensation of serfdom which is intolerable to a free Briton. It dictates the time of starting, the route, the speed and the stoppages' (quoted in ibid.: 79). The motor car bestowed on its owner a freedom from the regulated uniformity of public transport. It was customary to criticize the railway system as transforming travellers into a mass of 'living parcels' with indistinguishable social status (ibid.: 79). Conversely, the motor car offered symbolic capital tied to space and the geographic distances which the privileged classes could afford to exploit. The individual's ability to gain distance from the mediocrity of mass population was a sign of wealth and status. It was in this sense that the motor car came to be linked with the rise of the 'romantic gaze' in the early twentieth century (Urry, 1990). The car's capacity for speed and distance enabled its owners to access remote aspects of English heritage (O'Connell, 1998). These spaces were romanticized in advertising iconography and transformed into objects of status and distinction. Figure 5.3 is indicative of the use of rural and suburban scenes to provide the car with symbolic appeal. Homes, when depicted, were more often than not mansions with sprawling lawns, radiant flora and iridescent blue skies. Such vivid imagery of natural geographical pastures became inextricably intertwined with an ideology of the 'small escape'. Weekend outings to the countryside during holidays or even the pleasant relaxation to be gained from bank holidays by the sea provided for an escape from the alienation of mundane work (Wolf, 1996: 195). In motor car advertising, escape, excitement and healthy living were combined to conjure up the required association of the car with outdoor leisure. This is evident in the following advertisement:

> Built also for the good of your health – to carry you 'jarlessly' over any kind of half decent roads, to refresh your brains with the luxury of much 'out-doorness' and your lungs with the 'tonic of tonics' – the right kind of atmosphere. (Ford, 1910: 55)

The spread of the car radically transformed the whole ecology of everyday living; it also ushered in dramatic changes to road systems and unparalleled transformations to cities. Indeed, the increased use of the car conferred a disturbing paradox as city planning and housing were altered such as to transfer functions to the car, which its own massification had made necessary (Gorz, 1980: 70). Nevertheless, mass production necessitated its mirror image, mass consumption, and a guaranteed certainty over transaction costs, supply and demand. Advertising played a significant role in acclimatizing workers to 'the idea of shopping as a productive, culturally legitimate leisure-time activity' (Pietrykowski, 1999: 182). But this functionality was to be radically challenged by the structural transformation of the post-war capitalist system which produced seismic supply-side shocks, crippling Fordist production and precipitating its breakdown (ibid.: 181). For instance, Harvey argues that it was mainly through 'spatial and temporal displacement' that Fordism survived its major overaccumulation crisis in the period immediately after the Second World War (1990: 185). Temporal displacement defines the switching of resources from immediate to 'future uses' or 'an acceleration in turnover time' (ibid.: 182). Conversely, spatial displacement involves 'the absorption of excess capital and labour in geographical expansion' (ibid.: 183). Harvey argues that by the 1970s accelerated production was triggering high inflation and undermining the value of fixed capital assets (ibid.: 182). And intensified competition between geographically distinct markets had the unintended consequence of increasing the level of international competition (within the mass-produced sector) over a wider geographic area (Pietrykowski, 1999: 181). The outcome of this left domestic markets struggling to compete with the lower labour costs of their international competitors. These market developments effectively set the stage for 'systemic perturbation in the sequential' ordering of time and space in Fordist production systems (Castells, 2000: 464). Deficient levels of aggregate demand and uncertainty over transaction costs left Fordist production systems unable to sustain long production runs and undertake the continued investment in fixed-cost specialist machinery dedicated to the production of a single product (Pietrykowski, 1999: 181). These historical developments set the scene for the decline of Fordist production. The following section describes how, in the micro-electronic world of post-Fordist production, time is constituted as a local definition, a dimension of an event rather than as an unproblematic medium whose neutrality permits comparison and communication across diverse boundaries. The increased productivity of 'lean manufacturers' has speeded up the pace of work to unprecedented levels. And leisure times are less often rationally defined and ordered by definitive boundaries and frontiers. Motor car advertising provides an instance through which to analyse consumer subjectivity and the intensity of time–space compression in Western capitalism since the 1960s with all of its emergent features of excessive ephemerality and fragmentation in work and leisure time.

Advertising leisure in the time/space economies of post-Fordist production

In *Liquid Modernity*, Bauman (2001: 145) describes early modernity as characterized by a mutual dependency of capital and labour, which serve to fix their pursuits in bounded spatial locations. With the advent of 'software capitalism' and 'light modernity', capital became unshackled from its dependency on the physicality of place (ibid.: 145). Capital is now 'free-floating capitalism' distinguished by the 'disengagement and loosening of ties linking capital and labour' (ibid.: 149). The flexibly organized space of post-Fordist inter-firm networks also invokes dramatic changes in labour time and the expropriation of surplus value. The streamlining of automation facilitates the invocation of flexible production systems and the ability to eliminate waste, both of materials and workers' time (Hayter 1994: 49). While vertically integrated production operated according to objective linear time, outsourcing 'makes possible the just-in-time delivery of intermediate goods and materials' (Lash and Urry, 1994: 56). In a 'just-in-time' system, parts are delivered to meet immediate production needs, thus eliminating the use of buffers and reserves. The rationalization and simplification of production flows in just-in-time systems operate through the intensification of work time. Labour tasks are broken down into precisely defined units, which can be reallocated to workers so as to ensure that they operate continuously (Hayter, 1994: 49). Similarities exist here with the 'time-study vengeance' of Fordist production (Parker and Slaughter, 1988). The rationalization of labour in just-in-time systems entails the transformation of tasks into 'transferable work components', which are repeatable by all workers performing that task. 'Idle time' is eliminated as job rotation between teams induces constant and continuous movement. Indeed, motion study in 'lean manufacturing' systems seeks to achieve an intensification of both Taylorism and Fordism (Parker and Slaughter, 1988). And the reduction of buffer stock accentuates the intensification of work as production becomes more 'tightly coupled in terms of time, space and levels of quality' (Jenkins, 1994: 24).

Productivity in just-in-time systems entails an acute time/space compression geared at producing more in less time. And the sine qua non of just-in-time systems is the transformation of organizational cultures into team-based 'learning cultures', in which workers are self-disciplined into achieving the optimum standardized task performance (ibid.: 24). Indeed, the classical Fordist model of management, which sought to separate cognition from physical labour, is abandoned in the lean management processes of post-Fordist production (Rifkin, 1996: 97). In contrast to classical Fordism, post-Fordism's implementation of cooperative managerial approaches (e.g., production teams) is designed to harness the mental capabilities and communicative skills of everyone involved in the labour process (ibid.: 97). This is because language has gained a key role in every facet of the production process (Gorz, 1999: 41). Under the broad rubric of re-engineering, corporations are transformed from pyramidal incommunicative structures into horizontal networks transferring flows of activity. And new information technologies, coupled with digitization increase the emphasis placed on abstract cognition in production (Rifkin, 1996). This denotes a specific instance in the subjectivization of labour to capital. For language is put to work in the time-compressed culture of post-Fordist production and the worker's communicational capacities have become valuable resources for capitalist production (Gorz, 1999: 41). Indeed, the deliberate engagement with the worker's personality, as it becomes woven into the 'learning culture', triumphs in linking the social background of labourers with the behavioural codes of corporate capitalism. It would appear that recent developments in marketing discourse have trajectories in this post-Fordist pursuit of self-actualization in work. Of particular relevance is the transformation of the brand into a high involvement component of corporate culture. Jesper Kunde, in his book *Corporate Religion*, expresses this new imperative as follows: 'In the future, building strong market positions will be about building companies with a strong personality and corporate soul' (2000). Traditionally brand values were merely 'the expressions, attitudes and abstract attributes that companies ascribe to their products beyond their functional qualities' (ibid.: 8). The brand in this traditional sense communicates 'the non-material and emotional values which give a product its brand status' (ibid.: 8). At the heart of the brand reside the core values and identity of the product provider. Some convergence therefore exists between the brand's identity and the product provider's image. Traditionally the brand operates to create sales, by engaging consumers with the company's external non-material values. In recent years marketing gurus have accentuated the qualitative nature of brand identity, often dismissing technical advantage as criteria for market dominance. Language and symbolism 'are replacing physical attributes as the fundamental marketing influence' (ibid.: 2). In other words, the identity of the company is being continually manufactured in the attempt to ascribe products with emotional values.

The insubstantiality of the brand concept has the effect of producing the ideological and cultural conditions which legitimate its proliferation. Consequently, it is of little surprise that marketing gurus have begun to preach the imperatives of 'corporate religion'. This philosophy converges brand identity with both the company's external image and its intrinsic central belief system. Thus, Kunde argues that, 'When external positioning and internal culture come into harmony, the easier it is for the company to consolidate its chosen market position' (ibid.: 4). Against this background is projected the need for companies 'to describe themselves – both internally and externally – because they are no longer adequately defined simply by the products they make' (ibid.: 3). In this sense, the corporate religion is 'a description of the company's personality' (ibid.: 3). By extension, 'the better the personality description is, the easier it becomes for the whole company to understand it – and rally around it' (ibid.: 3). The ideological appeal of this rhetoric places the worker's identity at the core of corporate culture. Social integration of each and everyone is imperative 'for the market to assess whether it likes the company or not' (ibid.: 3). Gorz argues that 'mass intellectuality' has become a defining feature of the entire labour force in post-Fordist production (1999: 41). Mass intellectuality refers to a context 'in which information and communication play a key role in every facet of the production process' (ibid.: 41). Direct parallels exist here between mass intellectuality and the new marketing religiosity of corporate branding. An essential component of corporate religion is the inculcation of the worker's personality, identity and self-concept. Thus, Kunde states that: 'People are usually employed for their professional skills, and of course their abilities must be appropriate ones. But it is just as important that the employees' attitudes and values are compatible with those of the company' (2000: 11). In this sense, it is no longer primarily labour time which is expropriated in the productive process. The new corporate ideal of brand management mobilizes the worker's body and soul as raw materials in the process of brand production. According to Kunde, this synergy is crucial 'in the battle among brands ... for positions of strength in the eyes of the consumer' (ibid.: 3). Indeed, the worker's personality is axiomatic to a corporate brand's success, thus it is 'Only when these attitudes and values go hand in hand with skills ... will the company be equipped to attain the ultimate position of Brand Religion' (ibid.: 11). Kunde is clearly proposing that workers attach an intense level of commitment to the company, such that 'perhaps an employee's best qualification is their belief in the company' (ibid.: 11). In exchange, the corporation offers its employees the possibilities of securing a form of identity embedded in the symbolism of the corporate culture (Gorz, 1999: 36). For instance, Kunde details the importance for companies to implement 'spiritual management', as a strategy for sustaining a competitive brand position. As he puts it, 'The companies that have ground to a halt are those that persist with mechanical control systems' (ibid.: 30). Such systems are based on forecast sales and technical mechanisms which are rooted in the past. Conversely, successful international companies need to 'possess the will and ability to keep people on track and to lead the way, regardless of where in the company they work' (ibid.: 30). Spiritual management attempts to integrate the worker into a corporate religiosity which might – for some workers – provide a refuge from the isolating individuality of modern society (Gorz, 1999). The production of work-based identity envisaged here differs from the socializing endeavours of previous managerial orders. In the Human Relations tradition, the worker is constituted as an inherently social creature driven by the pursuit of social meaning through group relations in the workplace (Du Gay, 1996: 60). Conversely, Kunde's account of corporate branding constitutes the quest for identity as derived from the individualized autonomy of spiritual management. Spiritual management is effective because it refrains from operating 'highly function-divided hierarchies' (2000: 31). Thus companies are staffed by autonomous individuals, self-directed in the pursuit of the company's ideals. According to Kunde, this operational structure is essential 'because it provides the only protection against the complexity of new products and the speed of market change' (ibid.: 30).

One of the crucial demands on the workers is their use of initiative and internal determination in adapting to the flexible environment of post-Fordist production. As Kunde puts it, 'Strength is about having a courageous and innovative core to the company' (ibid.: 31). This suggests a shift in capital's domination of labour from hierarchical observation to the spontaneous production of subjectivities which are compliant with the needs of post-Fordist production. The space of the factory and the workplace ceases to be the main arena of capitalist domination now that 'selling oneself and particularly, selling the whole of oneself' has become a condition of work (Gorz, 1999: 43). This process exceeds the traditional demarcation of work and leisure. This is because the centrality of co-operative and relational communicational capacities to the labour process transforms every experience, place and time into raw materials for the manufacturing of identity (ibid.: 42). Thus, the emphasis on corporate innovation both 'internally' and 'externally' in the pursuit of competitive branding is not achieved through coercive surveillance and manipulation. Rather, competitive corporate brands entice the best from their workers by harnessing 'the psychological striving of individuals for autonomy and creativity and channelling them into the search of the firm for excellence and success' (Miller and Rose, 1990: 26, quoted in Du Gay, 1996: 60). It is important to recognize that the integration of personality as an attribute of labour power is not a new condition of work. Writers have long since observed the methods used to harness identity, personality and even lifestyle to the service of the professional organization (Blau and Schoenherr, 1971), but these conditions were limited to the culture of the professional classes. In post-Fordist enterprise, the linguistic and cultural capacities of every worker have become integral features of labour power. Thus, Kunde argues that 'A Corporate Religion ensures that all employees in a company share the same qualitative values' (2000: 98), the imperative being to harness these values to the corporate concept as part of the development of brand culture. Axiomatic to this value chain is the consumer and their propensity to attribute belief and instinct about a brand's excellence. Within Kunde's discourse of corporate branding, consumers are constituted as discerning subjects, driven by the desire to maximize individuality through the conspicuous consumption of branded goods. He states that:

> When confronted with proliferation and diversity, choice becomes increasingly informed by belief. It is belief and instinct about a brand's excellence that matters. [Consumers] ... want to know who is behind the products that they buy. They want to know what you think. And the better your company communicates its attitudes, the stronger you will become. (Kunde, 2000: 8)

Thus, at the heart of effective corporate branding resides a consumer-centred focus. The consumer is sovereign and it is the duty of corporate branding to subordinate its procedures to the preferences of individual consumers. Indeed, the process of evaluating brand performance is increasingly predicated on ascertaining consumer involvement with the brand. This is evident when we consider that traditionally the value of the brand was calculated by using quantitative measures such as market share and the degree of distribution. Conversely, the diminishing role of the product's physical properties in determining brand positioning has encouraged a shift towards measuring both the quantitative and 'non-material' aspects of a brand's value (ibid.: 49). For example, brands can be said to have achieved the status of 'brand culture' only when they 'are so strong in the eyes of the consumers that they become equivalent to the function they represent' (ibid.: 9). Thus, consumers are an active component of the enterprising culture of the brand. And the success or failure of a particular brand is predicated on the extent to which it induces involvement from the consumer. The ultimate accolade is to extract 'high involvement' as this involves the consumers' commitment of themselves to the brand and its values (ibid.: 52). According to Kunde, the achievement of a 'brand religion' epitomizes the highest level of consumer involvement that a brand can acquire. At this level of brand recognition, 'The brand is a must – a belief – for consumers. They swear by it, and are very reluctant to have other brands in the categories where a Brand Religion is present' (ibid.: 63). The imperative to satisfy consumer needs and thus achieve the highest position of branding is a powerful driving force in determining business enterprise. It also assumes a peculiar morality as the brand becomes 'so much more than a generic product property' (ibid.: 63). Branding assumes the status of a virtuous system in its endeavours to convince us that brands give 'customers an optimal solution and ultimate self-worth' (ibid.: 63). By extension, it can and has been argued that it is the company's moral obligation to ensure consumer-centric management (Du Gay, 1996: 77), and axiomatic to this intention is the achievement of a consistent Corporate Concept 'where the brand's mission controls the company' (Kunde, 2000: 66). This involves a shift from a utility definition of the product to a value definition and the need to 'pull everything around the brand and get the company to follow the mission' (ibid.: 66). Thus, the mission framework transforms both workers and consumers into enterprising subjects driven by the quest for self-identity and subject to their own desires to maximize quality of life. The effect of all this revolution upon advertising is manifest at both the level of advertising aesthetic and communication channels.

The subjectivization of labour and advertising aesthetics

The advertisement in Figure 5.4 provides an illustration of how the subjectivization of labour in post-Fordist work combines with advertising aesthetics in the regulation of leisure time. The main text of the advertisement states, 'There are places in this world where you are not a CEO, a mogul, a player or even a hotshot. Places where all you are is a human being.' One gains a sense here of the accentuated demands on the autonomy of self, consistent with post-Fordist flexibility. Certainly the distinguishing features of modern flexibility are not new; 'flexitime' and flexible hours have long been a feature of work and organization. But what is new is the re-application of flexibility to redefine the worker. Indeed, the concepts 'players', 'moguls' and 'hotshots' trades upon commercial iconography, which denotes modern work as a highly individualized, frenetic corporate existence, and suggests a form of time/space compression, which no longer seeks profitability through 'extracting more time from labor or more labor from time under the clock imperative' (Castells, 2000: 437). Rather, the isolated figure of the Range Rover set against a turbulent naturalistic background appears resonant with the isolated pliant self of Bauman's *Liquid Modernity* (2001). Indeed, Bauman describes how with the advent of 'liquid modernity' the modern romance with progress loses its allure as it becomes 'individualised … deregulated and privatized' (ibid.: 135). It is now 'individual men and women on their own who are expected to use, individually, their own wits, resources and industry to lift themselves to a more satisfactory condition' (ibid.: 135).

At a further level of analysis, the advertisement makes explicit the commodification of counter-cultural ideals as part of the production of a new 'capitalist mythology' (Frank, 1997). The advertisement defiantly declares 'Work hard. Be successful. Go someplace where none of that matters'. In his book

Figure 5.4 *'Work hard. Be successful. Go someplace where none of that matters',*
Range Rover, 2001

Source: Courtesy of Land Rover.

entitled *The Conquest of Cool,* Thomas Frank (1997) identifies how corporate
management theories and advertising practises 'commodify dissent'. He is particularly agitated by corporate 'hipsters' and advertising moguls who disguise

consumer capitalist intentions with images of left-wing ideals drawn from the counter-culture revolutions of the 1960s. Such practices are a 'sort of corporate antinomianism', according to which 'commercial fantasies of rebellion' have become a spiritual cathexis against the stultifying demands of capitalist society (ibid.: 4). Frank is deeply sceptical of the liberatory zeal evident in contemporary advertising, especially as it is indebted to the counter-culture radicalism of the 1960s. That era epitomized a transition, in cultural values, from an emphasis on family, community and work to the irresolute epicurism of consumption (King, 2000). With its colourful nonconformity against grey-flannelled middle-class organizations, the 1960s counter-culture was a vehicle for the unceasing pursuit of hedonistic pleasures (ibid.: 16). But corporate capitalism began co-opting these ideals almost as fast as the counter-culture movement could create them. From its earliest beginnings, business overwhelmed the counter-culture 'with a fake counterculture, a commercial replica that seemed to ape its every move for the titillation of the TV-watching millions and the nation's corporate sponsors' (Thomas, 1997: 7). Rather than presenting a challenge to the core values of consumer capitalism, counter-culture was revolutionary as a vehicle for a new ideology of business (ibid.: 30). Its rebellious agenda addressed inherent contradictions between the individual's role as consumer and their role as producer. Counter-cultural rebellion ameliorated this perplexity as it transformed 'all the complaints about conformity, oppression, bureaucracy and individualism … into rationales for consuming' (ibid.: 31).

Capitalism's rediscovery of the counter-culture revolution in post-Fordist times operates similarly to foster the discontents of capitalist oppression and harness these sentiments to consumer capitalist lifestyles. In this sense, products exist to facilitate our rebellion against the inhibited world of mass production. Moreover, cultural radicalism entices us to gain knowledge of our authentic selves and 'to express our outrage at the stifling world of economic necessity' (ibid.: 22). The fundamental cultural rationale of business's appropriation of the counter-cultural is geared towards convincing us that however we may deplore the intensity of work, we can be rebels in our leisure-time activities of consuming. The text of the Land Rover advertisement is clearly indebted to a form of liberatory marketing, in which consuming conjoins with a conscientious resistance to the alienation of capitalist existence. The setting up of 'moguls' against dissidents has trajectories in the counter-cultural revolutions of the 1960s with their emphasis on humanism, self-expression and self-actualization. This post-Fordist advertising rhetoric lives on the playful and self-reflexive nature of the 1960s counter-culture movements. Advertisers attach counter-culture signifiers to objects and just as quickly detach them, all in the name of novelty and play. But the outcome of advertising's frivolity is to 'transform alienation and despair into consent' as the de-politicization of counter-cultural ideals becomes part of the relentless expansion of consumer culture (ibid.: 235). Indeed, the Range Rover advertisement's strong association between freedom, choice, creativity, self-determination and leisure time is far removed from left-wing emancipatory politics. Instead, these features of the autonomous self (Gorz, 1999) are transformed into mere commodities in the synchronous ideology of advertising discourse. Thus, the 'moment of truth' in the realization of discontent with post-Fordist corporatism is converted into the desire for a Range Rover ... just-in-time.

Leisure, post-Fordism and the 'value for time' revolution in advertising channels

> Money is the currency of commerce. Time is the currency of life. In the end, what people buy is value for time, and that's where the focus of competition under Right Side Up marketing moves to. (Mitchell, 2002: 146)

The 'value-for-time' revolution denotes a specific form of religiosity in post-Fordist advertising. Alan Mitchell provides a creative and wildly enthusiastic account of 'value-for-time' marketing in his book entitled *Right Side Up: Building Brands in the Age of the Organized Consumer* (2002). According to Mitchell, 'value-for-time' marketing advances beyond a previous era of industrial age marketing predicated on quality and money. The utilitarian model of consumer needs evident in the industrial age was 'vendor-centric' and therefore failed to focus attention on the consumer's value system (ibid.: 156). Conversely, value-for-time marketing proposes to be consumer-centric with its focus on time and 'the value of each minute and each hour to that human' (ibid.: 147). Marketing academics increasingly identify contemporary work intensification and modern-day living as having heightened the value of time to consumers. Time is a valuable resource for modern day consumer markets; indeed, it is 'the currency of life' (ibid.: 146). Value-for-time marketing seeks to respond to the differentiated needs of the 'time-squeezed' consumer.

Convenience and 'streamlining' have been popular features in the value-for-time revolution. The Henley Centre (2001) describes streamlining as the process of achieving value-for-time through the provision of products and services geared at establishing convenience. Value-for-time marketing also seeks to enrich our experiences of time through the provision of rewarding consumption opportunities. This feature of value-for-time marketing is particularly salient in that it presupposes a distinct rationalization of personal time. Carla Hendra, of the marketing group OgilvyOne, provides an account of 'precision timing', which is characteristic of how time is rationalized in post-Fordist marketing discourse:

> Because the average person is feeling time-pressured, communications and interactions which do not add value are a nuisance ... Emerging technology requires a firm strategic and creative handle to initiate the type of engaging customer interactions which lead to actionable Moments of Truth and positive brand experience. (Hendra, 2003: 53)

Central to this account is the supposition that the need for consumer durables is instantiated at specifiable points in time ('moments of truth'). The desire in marketing discourse to constitute need as 'moments of truth' is emblematic of an 'ideology of the synchronic', which pervades marketing knowledges (Williamson, 2000: 155). The concept of need in marketing discourse is a construct, which seamlessly links past and future so that these temporal horizons happen at once from the vantage point of the present. Marketing constructions of desire rely upon linking our experiences before consumption (the past) with the satiation of desire (the future) through their positioning within an unbroken stream of events, a total sequence of time (ibid.: 154). Synchronicity is evidenced by the representation of past and future experience into the present context. The present is constituted as 'the moment' in time before consumption. But the marketing intention to sell constitutes the present moment as 'closed' in its possibilities and thus unlike the 'open' present of lived experience. The subject is constructed through the synchronic present of marketing discourse. While this is not a new feature of marketing discourse, value-for-time marketing heralds a technological revolution in the commodification of work and leisure time.

The key to value-for-time marketing is identifying the specifiable time and place in which the consumer is most likely to respond to the brand. This presents huge operational challenges for marketing research. Advances in market segmentation knowledges have provided effective responses to these operational demands. And the combination of marketing knowledges with the Internet and wireless communication applications has enabled a revolution in digital marketing techniques (Hendra, 2003). As Blair puts it, when mobile communication applications are combined with Internet services, the brand is able to penetrate into the 'brand world of the consumer' (2003: 9). The move to real-time or even just-in-time advertising communications ultimately seeks to link 'the offer to an engagement point' (Hendra, 2003: 51). In so doing, value-for-time marketing attempts to transform the qualitative flow of time into optimum times in which specific products can be made to fit a need. Value-for-time also attempts to maximize the commodification of time in consumption. Mitchell, for instance, states that:

A just-in-time product or service is convenient for me: it fits into my life as I happen to be living it. It does not demand that I stop what I am doing to go out hunting and gathering the products and services I need. It adds value 'in my life'. Instead of my having to plan and organize my time around the convenience of the supplier, the supplier has to plan and organize his time and operations around my convenience. (2002: 155)

But the convenience to which Mitchell refers is merely the rationalized commodified leisure time of post-Fordist marketing discourse. To the degree that post-Fordism entails the colonization of more and more spheres of human activity by time/space compression, value-for-time marketing offers a means by which leisure can be made manageable by linking it with the dictates of post-Fordist production. This is clearly apparent in the technological advances in location-based advertising.

The motor car has featured quite significantly in value-for-time marketing especially with regards to 'telematics'. Hendra defines 'telematics' as the convergence of Internet connectivity with telecommunications, situated within a location-specific context (2003: 52). Visual wireless navigation systems and vehicle diagnostic devices provide ideal interfaces for telematic communications. Indeed, the motor car is identified, in value-for-time marketing discourses, as a gateway to new opportunities for real-time engagement with consumers. As Hendra puts it 'telematics provides new opportunities ... to create new services tailored for increased personal enjoyment and/or business productivity in the vehicle environment' (ibid.: 52). Telematics aims to provide a communicative environment in which firms can engage consumer interactions with brands in real-time context. What is particularly significant here is the expansion of marketing influence, to embrace any instance in the consumer's real-time experiences. As Hendra reveals, 'moments of truth occur any time there is an interaction, at any touch point, between a brand and the consumer' (ibid.: 50). Advances in communication technologies have facilitated the honing of marketing efficiency to bring the effects of its rationalization of time, into the minutest elements of everyday activity.

Value-for-time marketing is clearly resonant with the transformations of time/space in post-Fordist productive systems. The instability, volatility and flexibility which post-Fordism generates combine with value-for-time marketing, to produce a form of subjectivity unlimited in its openness to adjustment change and the unforeseen. The re-definition of leisure time, in the $24 \times 7 \times 365$ matrix of value-for-time marketing, coincides with a wider flexibility and multi-skilling of the workforce in order to match the 24×7 production times of post-Fordism. As consumers are working longer hours, it becomes increasingly difficult to delineate leisure into rationally defined spaces/places. Value-for-time marketing seeks to capitalize on the complexity of modern day living through the use of real-time communications in the delivery of advertising messages at any time in any location. Advertising in this sense actively engages in the cultural legitimation of consumption as an appropriate leisure activity. Indeed, in the complex multi-layering of modern day times we can shop for leisure 24×7. In so doing, advertising actively reproduces the time/space compression of post-Fordist production.

Conclusion

This chapter has been concerned to identify the signifying properties of modern advertising as providing incisive revelations into the commodification of work and leisure as a precondition for capitalist production. Modernity, among other things, is about the creation of truth, the universality of reason, the disciplining of the soul, mastery and control. Where work and leisure once were integrated in a communal life, the advent of modernist production systems invoked the emergence of a delineated form of rational recreation (Hemingway, 1996: 34). Rational recreation is the corollary to the processes of commodification discussed with regards to Fordist production systems. Ford's systems identified leisure time as an opportunity to extend the parameters of managerial control as part of the reproduction of existing patterns of social, political and cultural dominance. Advertising's eagerness to endorse instrumental-rational models of consumer demand supported wider power/knowledge relations keen to define legitimate leisure according to rational and commercial enterprises. Indeed, advertising was a crucial element in the rendering of ever increasing amounts of cultural activities amenable to commodification. Critical theorists draw attention to the analogy between leisure and money as evidence of advertising's role in the reproduction of time as a productive force. Leisure time is earned; it is capital on which productive value can be returned. There is a marked tendency here towards a definition of leisure time as an objective expression of the exchange-value system. Critical theory is constrained in so far as leisure time is conceptualized in purely chronometric form. Conversely, this chapter explores the significance of advertising knowledges to the constitution of leisure as a productive source of quantitative and qualitative value. Early advertising constructions of consumer subjectivity emphasized the pursuit of utility value as motivating rational linear decision-making processes. Leisure time is constituted in these early – and present-day – representations as an objective unit homologous with the commodified form of work time. The valorization of objective leisure time as a fixed utility fits efficiently with the logic of capitalism's exchange system of value. The structural transformations which precipitated the breakdown of Fordism ensued dramatic transformations in work, leisure and the commodity-form. These historical developments reinforced the significance of advertising to the wider processes of 'cultural work' (Clarke and Critcher, 1985), involved in defining appropriate leisure. It has been the aim of this chapter to illustrate how an examination of transformations in advertising can provide a basis from which to trace developments in the rationalization of time, work and leisure in capitalist society.

6

Mapping the Subject of Postmodern Advertising Technology

Figuer 6.1 *Advertising and modern technologies of power, Business Insights, 2005*

Source: Reproduced by permission of Business Insights Inc.

Chapter 5 examines the intensity of time/space compression in Western capitalism since the 1960s with its emergent features of post-Fordist advertising and its excessive focus on enhancing consumer welfare. This chapter extends these themes into the analysis of advertising and consumer surveillance. The central aim of this chapter is to engage with key literatures that identify advertising research as a powerful site for consumer surveillance in the twenty-first century (Goss, 1995; Leslie, 1998; Hackley, 2002; Andrejevic, 2003). Within academic circles and in the media, consumer surveillance has often been described in distinctly Orwellian terms. Orwell's vision of a centralized panoptic system anticipated a schema of control in which the body is made subject to an insidious regime of surveillance. Advances in advertising research, particularly with regards to Geographic Information Systems (GIS), provide the technology for marketers to locate and graphically delineate the time/space distribution of consumer characteristics (Goss, 1995: 171). Advertising's dedication to these electronic databases conjoins Orwell's vision of a panoptic system with the decentralized, rhizomatic networks of electronic information processing (Lyon, 2002: 348). The strategic implication of these developments has been to provide advertisers with access to massive electronic databases containing aggregated records on consumer characteristics, behaviour and residential location. Marketing research companies extol the virtues of this vast expansion in the scope and capacity for mapping distributions of consumer characteristics. For instance, MapInfo (2005) describes its TargetPro as the 'Geo-demographic analysis solution', which 'enables customers to use location to transform information into business advantage'. Electronic databases provide new techniques and technologies for 'tracking the customer's every move and purchase, building up an ever more detailed profile' (Mitchell, 2002: 66). Database marketing is hailed to have filled 'the information hole at the heart of marketing' and promises to 'liberate marketing from its many constraints' (ibid.: 65).

Elsewhere, critical theorists have been highly sceptical about the technological 'revolution' in marketing research (Goss, 1995; Leslie, 1998; Lyon, 2002; Andrejevic, 2003). Of particular concern have been developments in the practice of geodemographics and the monitoring of the time/space paths followed by consumers. Goss defines geodemographics as 'a detailed knowledge of consumer behaviour obtained through systematic surveillance of social life, the elaboration of reductionist models of consumer identity, and the inference of unobserved behaviour from residential location' (1995: 172). Goss persuasively argues that this mode of market segmentation 'represents a strategy to exercise rational knowledge-power over everyday life' (ibid.: 171). Goss's theoretical framework provides an effective combination of Marxist analysis with Foucauldian analytics. Consequently, emphasis is placed on linking capitalist production and consumer subjectivity with powerful regimes of knowledge controlled and mobilized by contemporary advertising technologies. Geodemographics is thus revealed to be 'based upon an instrumental rationality that desires to bring the processes of consumption further under the control of the regime of production' (ibid.: 172).

Similar conclusions are evident in Andrejevic's (2003) examination of mobile commerce. New techniques and technologies such as bar code scanners, loyalty cards, and computer cookies provide advertisers with valuable information on the real-time paths followed by consumers. Andrejevic observes an increased use of mobile commerce in advertising design and communication. A disturbing consequence of these developments has been an accumulation of information which digitally tracks the public and private activities of individuals. Companies justify these developments as important advancements in the efficient application of marketing strategy. The rhetoric of efficiency is frequently cloaked in ecological inferences. For example, Mitchell argues that the bygone era of the mass marketing communications represented a potential 'environmental hazard'. Conversely, database marketing 'turns anonymous entities called consumers into identified named customers' and thus enables the precise and effective distribution of advertising communications (2002: 65). Critical theorists have been less convinced by this environmentalist rhetoric and pseudo-individualistic appeals to the consumer. Andrejevic (2003) observes the accumulation of electronic databases on consumer behaviour to be motivated by a desire to extend commodified relations into ever more areas of private life. As he puts it, 'spaces associated with leisure and domesticity can become increasingly economically productive insofar as consumers are subjected to comprehensive monitoring in exchange for the promise of customization and individuation' (ibid.: 132). These issues have relevance to Lyon's (2002) claim that consumer surveillance has become axiomatic to the 'network society'. Of particularly interest are the concerns he raises about the exchange of data between networked agencies and the reduction of individuals aggregates of information. Lyon convincingly details networked surveillance to involve the abstraction of personal data 'from bodies to be re-constituted as data images, about which automated decisions are routinely made' (ibid.: 349). He persuasively claims that 'it is now information flows that are under scrutiny' and individuals are mere artefacts in the information network (ibid.: 349).

For a generation of sociologists, advances in marketing technologies provide a near-perfect analogy of Michel Foucault's principle of discipline. The incessant dedication to electronic performance monitoring and ubiquitous accumulation of coded information, evident in marketing research, is often cited as typifying disciplinary modes of regulating activities in time/space (Goss, 1995; Lyon, 2002). There is a tendency in these accounts to read Foucault's conception of subjectivity 'as a product of controlling and dominating social bonds … of the person as simply responding to disciplinary power' (Ezzy, 1997: 428). Foucault's account of disciplinary technologies is (mis)read as hyper-rational tempo-spatial systems capable of 'electronically tagging', tracing, and regulating passive bodies within insidiously coercive 'information panopticons'.

Axiomatic to this techno-determinist reading of Foucault (1979) is an absolutist conception of linear time/space (Knights and Odih, 2002), whereby marketing technologies place the human subject in linguistic and semiotic systems which have the effect of dividing the subject according to the coding of disciplinary space. Some support for this supposition is evident in Foucault's account of the objective conditions which enable the efficient application of discipline to the body. The elementary portioning of subjects into spatial grids provides for an impressive economy of means in which 'Each individual has a place and each place has its individual' (quoted in Dreyfus and Rabinow, 1982: 155). And this breaking up and rearrangement of activities in space 'must also be understood as machinery for adding up and capitalizing time' (Foucault, 1977: 157). It is this disciplinary time which authors observe to be imposed on marketing technologies, in their efforts to code and delineate the time/space paths of individual consumers. Nevertheless, Foucault also observed that disciplinary technology 'has as its correlative an individuality that is not only analytical and "cellular", but also natural and "organic"' (1977: 156). Thus, although marketing technologies are similar to the disciplinary modalities which effect changes on 'mute and docile bodies', one feature overrides such comparison, 'the modern subject is not mute; he must talk' (Dreyfus and Rabinow, 1982: 155). In short, a reading of marketing technologies as hyper-rationalist electronic panopticons designed to enact a monolithic regime of control fails to recognize the distinction between subjects being constituted *through* rather than *by* a variety of disciplinary technologies. Foucault argued that 'power is exercised not only subject to, but through and by means of conditions of possibility' (Gordon, 1980: 246). Consequently, the seriation of activities in linear time is made possible by acting upon the existing actions of thinking subjects. Power is exercised upon free subjects who have the capacity to imbue each moment of time with social meaning. Thus, Foucault's *Discipline and Punish* details modern subjectivity as constituted through technologies and techniques which operate in consequence of the co-operation of linear and subjective social times. As he puts it:

> The disciplinary methods reveal a linear time whose moments are integrated, one upon another, and which is orientated towards a terminal, stable point; in short, an 'evolutive time'. But it must be recalled that, at the same moment, the administrative and economic techniques of control reveal a social time of a serial, orientated cumulative type: the discovery of an evolution in terms of 'progress'. (1977: 160)

Foucault's account of discipline is clearly not limited to the quantitative dimensions of abstract technological systems capable of mapping the activities of individuals according to the linear dimensions of clock time. Rather, social times involve a 'discovery of an evolution in terms of genesis' (ibid.: 160). Individuals have the ability to attribute meaning to duration and thus imbue the quantitative dimensions of abstract electronic surveillance systems with symbolic meaning. Thus, marketing technologies can be observed in Foucauldian terms as 'a new way of administering time and making it useful, by segmentation, seriation, synthesis and totalization' (ibid.: 160). Nevertheless, this objectification of subjects in linear time relies on the co-existence of social times which enable their subjectification. Without the spontaneous identification of subjects with the products of marketing practice, the motivations for consumers to buy products and services would require a more overt renunciation of freedom. Conversely, advertising incites, it induces, and it seduces our compliance. It achieves this though a 'macro–and a micro-physics of power' (ibid.: 160), in which marketing technologies exercise control by the seriation of time and the discovery of the genesis of subjectivity in the temporal continuum of social time. It is at this interface that 'power is articulated directly into time' (ibid.: 160). The following sections examine advances in marketing research with particular emphasis on market segmentation. The central intention of this enquiry is to reveal the objectifying propensity of these technologies and the effect of advertising in conditioning the spontaneous identification of consumers with disciplinary modes of subjectivity.

Advertising modern technologies of disciplinary power

Market segmentation involves the precise classification of groups in order to facilitate the achievement of the marketing concept. Marketing practitioners identify market segmentation as a vital competitive business strategy in modern times. It is generally recognized that social and economic life in the West is experiencing dramatic change. Of particular relevance are the changing character of numerous institutions such as the household, employment, welfare, the public sector and the market. Alongside these institutional changes and closely associated with them is the weakening, if not disintegration, of many 'traditional' values relating to the family, gender, class, leisure, morality and work. At a personal level, the decline in traditional collective solidarity's (e.g., social class, community, nationality) has resulted in a shift away from identities secured through such relationships towards identities that depend more on a particularly distinctive or differentiated lifestyle and mode of consumption. In short, many Western societies are experiencing an intensification of the instability and disruptive growth characterized by de-massification. Marketing firms often cite de-massification as a primary motivation for the development of market segmentation technologies. For example, the strategic marketing company SMART (2005) state that 'to compete successfully in today's volatile and competitive business markets, mass marketing is no longer a viable option for most companies. Marketers must attack niche markets that exhibit unique needs and wants.' Segmentation typically uses the statistical technique of cluster analysis, which enables a market to be partitioned into mutually exclusive groups of individuals with relatively similar profiles. In marketing rhetoric, the overall benefit of segmentation is 'to improve your company's competitive position and better serve the needs of your customers' (ibid.). Indeed, segmentation enables the fine-tuning of a company's marketing strategies to ensure the delivery of 'effective and cost-efficient promotional tactics and campaigns' (ibid.). In order to achieve the most efficient and productive operation, it is necessary a priori to construct/inscribe the nature

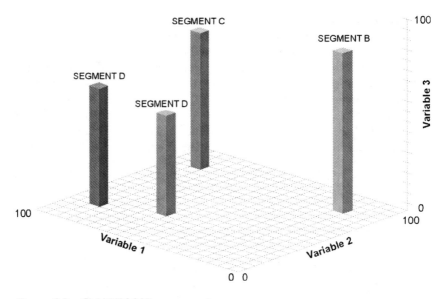

Figure 6.2   SMART 2005 *segmentation*

Source: Reproduced by permission of Strategic Marketing and Research
Techniques®, www.S-M-A-R-T.com.

of the classification categories; to 'identify' – through surveys and quantitative
techniques – the individuals who fit the definitions proposed and to place
the segmented into the ordered space and to parallel the distribution of
functions in the structure of space in which they will operate. The marketing practitioner channels resources efficiently by ensuring that all of the
space/population within a confined area must be ordered; there should be
no gaps, no free margins, nothing should escape the classificatory criteria of
the practitioner. The spatialization of markets into 'mosaic fields' is illustrated in Figure 6.2 and articulated as follows: 'Segment identification –
determining a given number of homogenous market segments based on
selected segmentation variables and criteria. Segments should be customer-
focused, a justifiable size, distinguishable, accessible, accountable and profitable' (SMART, 2005).

In recent years, technological advances in market segmentation have
elaborated a whole range of techniques and practices designed to make
possible the regular intervention of the marketing concept into everyday life.
For example, geodemographics is an information technology that provides
marketers with predictive information about consumer behaviour based on
residential location (Goss, 1995: 171). It is invariably used to exploit new
markets for promotional literatures and other advertising communications.
Geodemographics operates by collecting 'spatially referenced data on consumers, constructing statistical models of identity, and mapping distributions

of consumer characteristics or types' (ibid.: 171). The UK-based company MapInfo (2006) is a software technology leader in geodemographics. MapInfo describes its service as providing location-based solutions. More specifically, MapInfo's promotional literature states that its 'predictive analytics provide market-leading solutions for spatial analysis and geographical visualisation so that your organization can anticipate your customers' needs and make better informed decisions' (2005a: 1). As is customary with geodemographic system providers, MapInfo operates through the use of vast electronic databases that contain demographic information and aggregated patterns of consumer behaviour. This form of Geographic Information System (GIS) enables the marketer to index records of consumer behaviour to locations and distributions across spatial territories. Thus, MapInfo's GIS software, TargetPro, provides a selection of 'individual customised Data Powerpacks' providing demographic and lifestyle data. The demographic data enable companies to analyse areas in terms of consumer profiles, visualize and target the most profitable locations. The lifestyle/behavioural data include information about car ownership, health, computer/Internet and personal finance. The combined capability of this information enables business to accurately identify the location of customers. As MapInfo's product literature states, 'MapInfo's capabilities allow you to clean and standardise customer addresses and other location information, add spatial coordinates that let you place these locations on maps and manage this spatial information along with attribute data about your customers' (2001). The publicity literature provides technically advanced 3-D impressions of location-based information. Indeed, the layering of customer profile data appears intent on producing a form of mimesis in which the aggregated lifestyles and demographic profiles of individual consumers constitute replicas or electronic imitations of their real selves. Subjectification is transformed into 'the dynamics of continuous evolutions' that 'replaces the dynastics of solemn events' (Foucault, 1977: 161). Thus, the process of mimesis develops through time as each software interface incorporates more and more aspects of the consumer's individuality into the creation of a 3-D electronic replicant.

MapInfo's Geocoding Data Management enables business to manage spatialized customer profiles in conjunction with their existing corporate data to ensure 'the seamless integration of spatial data with attribute data for improved performance, access and broad deployment' (2001). The extent of centralization is really quite significant. Most especially when one considers the claim that 'Hundreds of organisations world-wide use MapInfo's server and developer products to deploy mapping applications' (ibid.). Most companies access this information through Internet applications 'that give an organisation's employees access to timely, map-based information and analysis features' (ibid.). Such practices are correlative with what Foucault observes as the seriation of activities in space, which 'makes possible a whole investment of duration by power' (1977: 160). Figure 6.3 contains publicity material advertising MapInfo's TargetPro and provides some visual indication of the scale and sophistication of this GIS software.

Use
TargetPro to:

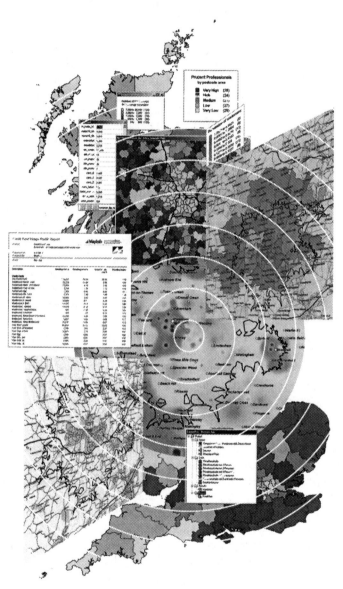

Figure 6.3 *TargetPro GIS, MapInfo, 2005*

Source: Reproduced by permission of MapInfo Ltd.

MapInfo (2005b) promotes its GIS software TargetPro as helping 'you profile, analyse and understand customers and markets to predict buying behaviour for virtually any business or consumer product or service'. The sales rhetoric evident in MapInfo's promotional literatures emphasizes the capability of geodemographics to provide predictive data 'for making informed decisions about potential or existing locations' to direct marketing campaigns (ibid.). Geodemographics is therefore an important technology of normalization. It has the effect of reducing the complexities of human behaviour into measurable constructs defined by secondary data analysis, unobtrusive observation and marketing research attitude surveys (Goss, 1995). In the writings of Foucault, discipline can be observed to operate similarly as its technologies are applied differentially and precisely on 'bodies' (Dreyfus and Rabinow, 1982: 156). 'Discipline "makes" individuals: it is the specific technique of a power that regards individuals both as objects and as instruments of its exercise' (Foucault, 1977: 170). It achieves this not by overwhelming subjects, 'the individual is not to be conceived as a sort of elementary nucleus, a primitive atom, a multiple and inert material on which power comes to fasten or against which it happens to strike, and in so doing subdues or crushes individuals' (Gordon, 1980: 98). Discipline is 'not a triumphant power' but a more modest 'permanent economy' of influence (Foucault, 1977: 170). The permanent economy to which Foucault refers, relates to the incessant coding and classification of subjects in disciplinary regimes, which operates through combining hierarchical surveillance and 'normalising judgements'. Foucault characterizes normalizing judgements as a penalty of power in which more and more aspects of social life become encoded into a grid of differentiation (Dreyfus and Rabinow, 1982: 156). Normalizing judgements provide the premise upon which consumer behaviour is defined in geodemographic segmentation. The motivational constructs which initiate consumption are assumed in geodemographic logic to exist as objective facts, external to the meanings systems of the individual consumer. They are thought of as structures, which are composed of determinate relationships between constitutive parts. It is therefore assumed that explanations of human behaviour can be gained through exploring these constitutive parts of social reality. For example, a marketing analyst examining buying behaviour would aim to elicit objective aspects of our social world which can then be said to determine buying behaviour, e.g., social class, ethnicity, age, etc. Each of these social structures, as objective facts, lends itself to detached observation. Moreover, as an objective fact the social world lends itself to quantification and prediction and thus the methods of investigation of the natural sciences. Consequently, segmentation analysis unproblematically uses psychographic variables, in conjunction with secondary data analysis, in 'an attempt to reduce the complex nature of consumer motivations and predispositions to patterns in digital data' (Goss, 1995: 187).

Goss identifies geodemographics to be predicated on a 'conception of consumer identity as synchronically and diachronically coherent' (ibid.: 188).

Consumers are presumed to exhibit predictive behaviours, which map onto identifiable spaces and have desires for goods which seem more in tune with marketing expectation than the inconsistencies of everyday life. Moreover, consumer identity is presumed to unfold into a 'coherent narrativity characterised by functional developments over time, with the consumption of an increasing quantity and diversity of complementary goods' (ibid.: 188). This reading of GIS is indicative of attempts to conceptualize GIS as a hyper-rationalist system linked to other technologies intent on producing a monolithic regime of oppression. Such interpretations appear less cognizant of Foucault's accounts of 'discontinuity' in the development of disciplinary regimes. Indeed, Foucault argued that the development of discipline is marked by 'the appearance of elementary techniques belonging to a quite different economy; mechanisms of power which, instead of proceeding by deduction are integrated into the productive efficiency of the apparatus' (1977: 219). In this sense, the analyst of discipline should be less inclined to trace a perfect correspondence between the orders of discourse (Gordon, 1980: 247). Rather, the analyst should be motivated to uncover the effect of non-correspondence between practice and effects. For it is the propensity of disciplinary regimes to repair such discontinuities, which make 'it possible to adjust the multiplicity of men and the multiplication of the apparatuses of production' (Foucault, 1977: 219). Foucault's analysis of discontinuity has relevance here particularly in determining the process of transformation by which objective market segments metamorphose into spaces for the construction of consumer subjectivity. Ideally technological advances in marketing practice should affect programmes which guarantee consumption patterns and ensure a perfect fit between demand and supply. But, in reality, marketing science is beset by the impossibilities of perfect correspondence. This is because consumers are simultaneously both object and subject of marketing analyses. Knowing the consumer can never really be accomplished by accumulating objective information detailing the time/space paths, attributes and profiles of consumers. The objects of marketing discourse are continuously engaged in the production of first-order representations of their world. They are not speechless docile bodies. Consumers are creative discursive beings. Consequently, the development of marketing knowledges can only ever be arbitrary impositions onto the first-order representations of everyday life.

The application of marketing knowledges in the production of market segments, therefore, produces a 'double hermeneutic' in that the topics and subjects of marketing inquiry can use the findings of marketing research to restructure the nature of their universe (Giddens, 1979). Advertising is axiomatic to these signifying processes. Advertisers are constantly involved in complex processes of meaning transfer. As key cultural intermediaries, advertisers are ceaselessly ransacking various traditions and cultures in order to produce new symbolic goods and, in addition, provide the necessary interpretations of their use (Featherstone, 1991). In this endeavour, consumer lifestyles and subjectivity have become resources in the processes whereby commodities come to be imbued with cultural meanings only arbitrarily linked to the referent that they originally signified. Indeed, as a key component of the marketing mix, advertising agencies must forage into the cultural knowledge of consumers in order to design advertisements which link marketing categories to particular consumer cultural communities (Hackley, 2002: 211). These categories can only become reference points when advertising has successfully quarried into the cultural meaning and practices of the cultural communities to which a campaign is targeted (ibid.: 214). And having done so, there is limited guarantee that these representations of everyday life will form the basis upon which consumers restructure their universe. The following material is drawn from an empirically informed study of gender, consumption and the personal financial services market in the 1990s (Odih, 1999a). The study was particularly keen to examine advertising as a primary source of cultural meaning linking marketed financial products to social categories, which form part of the consumer's gendered repertoires of self-identity (Odih, 1998).

Case study the women's market marketing, fact or Apparition?

> When God created woman He may not have realised that it would take so long for her to be discovered by the financial services sector.
>
> (Observer, 29 October 1995)

With minor exceptions, traditional selling practices in the financial services industry have been deeply rooted in gendered perceptions about male 'breadwinners' as their target market. Consequently, one half of the population – women – are neglected as direct, rather than indirect, potential customers. Apparently encouraged by recognition of increasing patterns of female economic activity, the industry in the early 1990s became highly sensitive to this 'untapped' market. Accordingly, numerous financial services companies focused attention on the potential of marketing specifically to women (e.g., the National and Provincial Building Society, the Royal Bank of Scotland, the Halifax Building Society, the Bradford and Bingley Building Society and the National Westminster Bank). Typical of the activity in this area is a Halifax Building Society study, conducted by Andrew Irving Associates, which argues that an 'increasing understanding of women's needs enables product offerings, customer services and promotional activities to be tailored appropriately ... to make them more convenient, appealing and relevant to the female market' (1992: 4). Of particular interest has been the marketing campaigns intent on encouraging women to buy long-term contractual products. Part of my study's empirical research involved an examination of the financial contribution structures of selected contractual products (namely, insurance, investment and personal pensions). These commitment structures were tested against a set of predetermined 'employment scenarios' that reflected dominant national patterns of female employment. The findings demonstrated that these patterns of female employment were incompatible with the contribution structures of long-term contractual products, most especially in those instances where the product's chronological structuring imposes the need for regular contractual financial contributions, any interruption of which is severely penalized. Some explanation for these incongruences between patterns of female employment and the payment structure of long-term contractual products is evident in wider patterns of gender segregation at work and the domestic division of labour within the private sphere.

The organization of the workplace, as of the home, reflects and reinforces a hierarchy of time control; the time of subordinates is largely controlled by superiors whereas senior people have 'gatekeepers' to protect them from the pressures of others' time demands. Since women are disproportionately represented in the subordinate ranks of organizations, their time is more regulated by others than by themselves. The combination of this subordination and the pressure of domestic responsibilities which women readily assume frequently results in broken or part-time patterns of employment. Yet even when working full-time, women are disadvantaged in the career stakes because of their family commitments, whereas men may manage excessive time demands at work through this labour being serviced domestically by a woman. This problem suggests a fundamental incongruence between the embedded temporality of long-term contractual products and the lived experience, of time, of female consumers.

Significantly the advertising of personal financial services to women during the 1990s often traded upon gender difference in the domestic division of labour. In 1995, for example, PPP Health Care, Pinnacle Insurance, Zurich Life and Legal & General all launched female-specific Permanent Health Insurance (PHI) products. PHI provides cover if the person insured has a serious accident or serious illness which renders them unable to work or relatively immobile. In these circumstances the PHI provider will pay the claimant a monthly income up to the age of 60 or 65. PHI is disproportionably more expensive for women because the actuarial tables used by companies build into their calculation gender differences in life-expectancy, employment and critical illness claims (Bourke, 1991). The production of actuarial tables is based on actuarial science which is dedicated to the statistical calculation of risk. It is the art of maintaining insurance as 'the losses of the few [are] paid for by the contributions of the many' (Pawley et al., 1991: 77). Axiomatic to the actuarial supervision of life insurance is the aggregation of statistical data determining the risk profile of given populations. In establishing premium rates for PHIs, providers plot the consumer's previous health and present lifestyle against the aggregate risk profiles of their given population. This level of actuarial intervention into the ebb and flow of everyday life has clear parallels with the concerns raised early about geodemographics. Both systems are predicated on the ubiquitous accumulation of coded information as part of the application of disciplinary modes of regulating subjects in time and space.

We need only reflect on the lifestyle codes inscribed into the complex format of health insurance applications to recognize the normalizing and disciplinary effect of PHI. Not surprisingly, marketing PHIs to women presents advertising creatives with a particularly challenging task. An analysis of the PHI market in the 1990s reveals that advertisers often attempted to address these difficulties by appealing to stages in the female lifecycle and attaching these to PHI product attributes. Of particular interest were those advertisements which employed socio-biological discourses of gender distinction and were concerned with the effects of biology on social behaviour. These advertisements set out to demonstrate how 'natural' genetic and hormonal differences between the sexes result in different PHI needs. Figure 6.4 contains promotional material from AXA PPP Healthcare, published in 1997. The image of the mother and child provides an illustration of how advertisers reach into the cultural lives of consumers by expropriating the symbolic meaning of events and re-forming these cultural meanings into product associations.

Motherhood is not a unitary experience, nor is it a simple one. To be a mother demands that a woman takes on a complex identity (Richardson, 1993). She is still herself but she is also a mother, with the incumbent roles, responsibilities and relationships which this entails. While women define their own expectations about mothering, they are also guided in this by cultural ideas about motherhood about what a 'good' mother is supposed to do and to be. In the potential myriad of social prescriptions for motherhood, certain claims to knowledge are given priority over others, pass into popular discourse and come to represent our everyday understandings of motherhood. For example, significant shifts and transformations in motherhood practices during the 1950s, 1970s, 1980s and 1990s (see Richardson, 1993) suggest the existence of discursive struggles to attach meaning to the signifier 'motherhood' and establish responsibility for childrearing. While it is axiomatic that understandings of motherhood may shift over time, over the lifetime of individuals and in differing spatial and cultural contexts it is possible to recognize in Figure 6.4 some of its contemporary discursive constructs.

The advertisement represents motherhood in accordance with familiar symbolism relating to self-sacrifice and the subordination of self to the needs of the infant. This conception of motherhood suggests a particular relation to time and the spatial setting of the event. This is because the social time of motherhood is 'relational'; it exists in relation to the time demands of significant others (Davies, 1990). This is captured by the phrase 'a woman's time is never her own'. Issues of time ownership have been articulated by Hernes, who has stated that 'time disposal is partly determined by the individual, partly by social and legal coercion and partly through negotiation with others' (1987: 104). Social and legal coercion as well as negotiation with others, however, relate to issues of power. Women's subordinate position in the public sphere, as well as their ascribed domestic role in the private sphere, significantly inhibit their power to decide over their own time and that of others (Davies, 1990).

The advertisement is keen to link this discourse of motherhood to AXA PPP Healthcare. Consequently, the female figure is seen cradling an infant

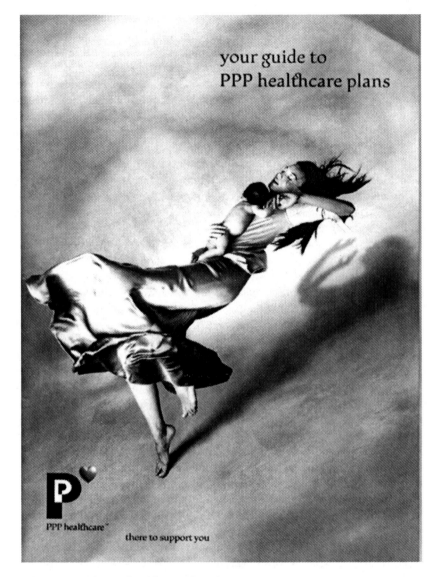

your guide to
PPP healthcare plans

P

PPP healthcare™

there to support you

Figure 6.4 *Women's healthcare plan, 1997*

Source: Reproduced by permission of AXA PPP Healthcare.

while floating in the ambient textual space of the advertisement. When we gaze more intently at the silhouette we recognize another female figure whose arms are positioned so as to signify a gesture of support. Indeed, the text of the advertisement states 'PPP healthcare there to support you' At this instance the product assumes human qualities as we re-interpret the narrative voice as female and are encouraged to envisage a sisterhood of reciprocal support. But the ability of advertising to transfer these meanings onto the product relies upon the identification of another subject, the reader. Consequently, this symbolic representation of motherhood derives its political affectivity only through the meaningful constructions of subjects who identify with the forms of subjectivity it advances and act upon them (Weedon, 1992). It is therefore necessary to understand the advertisement's symbolic meaning system in terms of the existence of complex discursive forces within which female subjects situate themselves, and are situated, and come to identify with a mode of existence which has at its centrality the subordination of self to the needs of an infant. For many women the motherhood ideal finds expression in the subordination of self to the 'needs', demands and desires of significant others, be they family members, friends, super-ordinates, etc. Motherhood, then, is an ideal that in emphasizing acquiescence leaves little space or time for an active and autonomous subject who can place equal demands upon those whose labour and identity are serviced by contemporary heterosexual arrangements (1999b). The advertisement is clearly cognizant of this motherhood ideal. Nevertheless this transfer of cultural meaning realizes its ambition in the motivation to buy the PHI, only when subjects position themselves, and are positioned, in the desire to achieve a sense of meaning and direction through identifying with the advertisement's particular construction of the motherhood ideal. But why might an individual position themselves within this discursive representation of motherhood? The precariousness and uncertainty which are both condition and consequence of increased individualization since late modernity, provide a form of society where it is appropriate to turn the self into an object to be managed (Foucault, 1977; Miller and Rose, 1997). The task of self-management and self-discipline is, however, impeded by the very conditions upon which it trades. It is dependent on the acknowledgement and recognition of others and yet the individualization of society in modern times means that individuals are separate from each other (Knights, 1997: 224). Through processes of (re)signification, advertising discourses centred on the women's market offer female subjects a source of securing both self-identity and the recognition of others. While security products provide a means of sustaining present well-being, they can also be stored or invested to secure subjective well-being into the future (ibid.: 225). In a materialist society such as our own, this suggestion is seductive in that it simultaneously offers both future security and the aberration of others 'through the conformity to the material and symbolic values of success' (ibid.: 225). This sense of security is, however, transient, having to be continually renewed through engaging (indeed being committed to) social practices that are the outcome of particular exercises of power. Consequently, the female subject, through her identification with modes of subjectivity which are the product of discourses centred around the women's market, becomes self-disciplined in sustaining practices that are supportive of a meaning or identity that promises more stability. In this sense, marketing constitutes social relations as it becomes applied. The discourse and practices of advertising are productive of, as well as constituted by, a particular form of modern society, one that is dominated by mass consumption of individualized subjects desperate for a sense of collective meaning and identity both as distinctive and embedded within a recognizable culture.

Conclusion

Marketing research is a formidable site for consumer surveillance in the twenty-first century. Nevertheless, an excessive insistence on the panoptic effect of marketing surveillance leads to the risk of overlooking all the mechanisms and effects of power, which do not pass directly via commercial markets, and yet often sustain these markets more effectively than its own institutions. In fact, commercial markets can only function on the basis of other already existing power networks such as gender relations, the family, kinship, knowledge, and so forth. It has been the central objective of this chapter to draw attention to advances in the production, accumulation and circulation of consumer data. Authors have tended to liken the vast databases of marketing agencies to Orwell's vision of a centralized panoptic system. In so doing, these authors fail to recognize that the objectification of groups and their transformation into market constructs require a series of subjectifying methods and procedures to interpret their underlying meaning, albeit in the guise of 'needs', values and desires. Advertising is a prominent feature in the process of cultural meaning transfer in which subjects become self-disciplined into identifying with the marketed appeal of a product. But this transfer of meaning is never really guaranteed in time.

Sign of the Times

Postmodern disruptions in advertising times

The postmodern condition entails the treatment of time and space as finite or tied to the social context of their use. They are, from a postmodern perspective, no longer unproblematic media whose neutrality permits comparison and communications across diverse boundaries. There are no longer common times and spaces 'in' which we all live in more or less mutual relevance. On the contrary, time and space are constituted as a local definition, a dimension of an event, a unique and unrepeatable location or period (Adam, 1990). The hyper-real spaces of postmodern consumer culture (e.g., shopping precincts, themeparks, gaming arcades) radically challenge modernist demarcations predicated on boundaries which delimit the real from the unreal, inside from outside. These postmodern hyper-spaces transcend 'the capacities of the individual human body to locate itself, to organize its immediate surroundings perceptually and cognitively to map its position in a mappable external world' (Jameson, 1992: 44). Morse uses the concept of 'distraction' to describe the 'de-realized' spaces of shopping precincts (1990: 193). The shopping precinct is a rootless re-ordering of the urban landscape. Its timeless capacious buildings and vivid media implosion denote 'a loss of referential anchorage to the world' (ibid.: 196). While retaining elements of the milling crowd, the spatial condensation of shopping precincts 'are the locus of an attenuated fiction effect' (ibid.: 191). Displaced and separated from the outside world, shopping precincts constitute a non-space 'of both experience and representation, an elsewhere which inhabits the everyday' (ibid.: 195). Similarities exist between these de-realized spaces and the diaphanous expanses of multi-media culture. In the micro-electronic world of virtual communication, places are no longer rationally defined and ordered by their boundaries and frontiers (Robins and Webster, 1999). Rather, new media precipitate a disconnection of localities from their historical geographic meaning and a reintegration 'into functional networks, or into image collages, inducing a space of flows that substitutes for the space of places' (Castells, 2000: 375). Thus, the boundaries of modernist existence are in disarray as we begin to realize that every communication is a prosthesis or projection of a unique identity (Burrell, 2005). Indeed, Baudrillard identifies hyper-reality as ensuing dramatic discontinuities in the contextual link between the subject and its specific world. In the 'third order of representation', technologies gain their own momentum, providing a simulacra of actual events effacing any access to a 'real', which itself is an effect of the code system (Sarup, 1998: 111). Direct parallels exist between the dissolution of narrative time in Baudrillard's 'third order of representation' and postmodern advertising aesthetics. This chapter identifies the dual effects of the demise of the centred subject and the collapse of universal historical narratives, in postmodern advertising imagery, to radically disrupt conventional experiences of temporality.

Of particular concern is the representation of advertising reality as a hyper-reality of fragmented images. Modernity entails the rational ordering and control of time and space, which are founded on instrumental rationality, progressive history and the suppression of difference. Time in modernity is not only a narrative temporality but also axiomatic to the reflexive construction of modern subjectivity (Giddens, 1993). For 'self-identity is not a distinctive trait possessed by the individual. It is a self as reflexively understood by the person in terms of her/his biography' (ibid.: 53). A crucial effect then of modern narrativity is the 'handing down of possibilities from the self to the self', which has the effect of 'stretching' our 'Being across time' (Thomas, 1997: 45). This is to say that 'the movement of self-stretching across time is the source of a person's self-identity, in that the person one is now has a historical connection with the person whom one was yesterday' (1997: 45). Identity in modern times relies on 'the capacity to keep a particular narrative going' (Giddens, 1993: 54). What this signifies is that every person is only as 'good' as his or her last 'claim' to a particular identity. In pre-modern societies where identities were primarily ascribed at birth through kinship and blood lineage or acquired through affinal ties of marriage, this precarious and unending process of achieving and sustaining one's identity through social activity was unknown. However, in modern society, identity becomes ever more absorbing as it is precarious and it begins to be the measure of life – a fluid, reflexive process instantiated through the time–space events, which it also serves to constitute (Lefebvre, 1991; Giddens, 1993). Contrived to forge its own identity, the modern subject is presented with the ironic proposition of having 'no choice but to choose' (Giddens, 1994: 75). Thus, in modern times identity becomes a 'personalized problem, the solution of which lay in the future' (Clarke, 2000: 220). Marketing in the modern era reproduced this conception of subjectivity in its belief that a relatively fixed system of human needs could be discovered by tracing the development of consumers through time–space events (see Chapter 4). And advertising embraced a modernist aesthetic, which ascribes human beings with 'a unique personality and individuality' (Jameson, 1985: 114).

In this modernist sensibility, the object of advertising 'can be expected to generate its own unique vision of the world and to forge its own unique, unmistakable style' (ibid.: 114). Advertising lives symbiotically on the audiences' reservoir of social and cultural meaning (Proctor et al., 2002). Advertisers rummage through everyday culture in the relentless search for symbolic meanings to augment the utility value of commodities. The informal symbolic productions of social relations, in time and space, are a particularly attractive source of raw material for the creation of commodity values. Advertising congruity allies commodities with culturally constituted representations of everyday life. Advertising achieves this by separating 'the intrinsic qualities of being human from actual living humans' and this 'reification imparts a time-lessness to the manufactured product' (Goldman, 1995: 32). The ebb and flow of everyday interaction is an integral feature of capitalist commodity circuits, as advertisers endeavour to transform the symbolic meaning of informal productions into currency. But the transfer of meaning is only achieved by the creative ingenuity of consumers 'whose interpretations reflect their own experience, social situations and concerns' (Proctor et al., 2002: 35). Consumption is an active and productive cultural practice, which requires the accomplishment of 'symbolic work' (Willis, 2000: 69). Symbolic work involves 'symbolic understanding' deployed in the interpretation of sign-values (ibid.: 69). It can be seen as 'sensuous cultural practices' in which socio-symbolic meanings are produced and adapted dialectically to the situated and personal context of consumption (ibid.: 70). Advertising trades upon these contextual meanings turning them into fetishized human qualities which 'become time-bound, contingent on possessing the product's properties' (Goldman, 1995: 32). Thus, modernist advertising requires a 'remembering subject' (Williamson, 2000: 158) as a source of meaning production. It also depends on the consumer's interpretative skills and their ability to invest symbolic work in making coherent 'the fragments and flows of commodity culture' (Willis, 2000: 69).

Conversely, the postmodern world of simulacra and 'hyper-reality' is a world without 'fixed' references of meaning. The extraordinary time/space compression of the postmodern era disrupts the modernist segmentation of culture and the segmentation of life into separate value spheres. In so doing, the postmodern condition presents a radical challenge to the linearity that modernist advertising aesthetic takes for granted. In response, postmodern advertising imagery presupposes that identities have become 'eminently contingent and continually reproduced in specific discursive contexts' (Tribe, 1993: 4). The fleeting presence of subjects, objects, sounds and sensations in postmodern advertising imagery is evidence of new times in the expropriation of consumer subjectivity as a condition of capitalist accumulation.

Advertising consumer subjectivity in postmodern times

Postmodern writers identify multi-media culture as producing a surfeit of images and signs that give rise to a world of simulations, which efface the distinction between the real and the imaginary. Postmodern advertising is allied to visual media and its ability to provide the viewer with a world of glittering media surfaces. In the hyper-real world of postmodern advertising, everything mutates into everything else, all is image, appearance and simulation. Nevertheless, amidst this cacophony of sights and sounds can be discerned several consistent styles. Postmodern advertising employs 'eclecticism' to generate 'parody', 'pastiche' and the inter-textual effect of 'allegory' (Wheale, 1995). The word eclecticism can be traced back to the Classical era, where it was used to denounce a school of Greek philosophers whose ideas were entirely drawn from a variety of existing schools (ibid.: 43). Thus, the eclectic mixing of styles, ideas and methods is not a new cultural practice but what is distinct about this practice in postmodern advertising is that multi-media based culture enables creatives to exercise a radical eclectic mode of sign production. Advertising creatives exploit vast repertoires of multi-media materials for the purpose of producing commodity aesthetics, which spectacularly eclipse the imagery abilities of previous times (ibid.: 44). Figure 7.1 illustrates the use of eclecticism to generate the postmodern advertising aesthetic of parody.

The concept of parody derives from Classical Greek where it was used to describe a form of mimesis in which a copy of an original was produced with the intention of provoking sceptical reflection. By the sixteenth century, in English culture, the concept of parody had adopted a burlesque version associated with ridicule and mimicry (ibid.: 44). In the finest examples of postmodern advertising, the use of parody reverts back to its pre-modern allegorical forms 'where one part comments upon another' (ibid.: 44). Hermeneutics has long since identified the dialectics of textual meaning to be embedded in social cultural practices. Moreover, the task of uncovering the author's contextual location is itself an act of interpretation. The reader of the text thus enters into a negotiated or dialectical *Verstehen* in which he/she attempts to align with an interpretation of the author's intentions. Constructivist accounts of advertising have also, long since, identified the meaning of advertising symbolism to be indexed to 'a common cultural pool that exists in society at particular points in time' (Proctor et al., 2002: 34). Parody in postmodern advertising extends beyond both of these accounts of the dialectics of textual reading. In its more mediocre form, postmodern parody can merely 'ironize to no purpose, in a frantic picking-and-mixing' (Wheale, 1995: 44). Conversely, the more sophisticated forms of postmodern parody are intent on combining divergent cultural artifacts to provoke scepticism and circumspection. The advertisement in Figure 7.1 fits into this latter category of expertise. The text is flirtatiously inter-textual in its endeavour to seduce the reader into entering its encoded meaning system and decoding its mystery. The text percolates with the creative effervescence of other textual structures both past and present. Each reading of the text is creative, as interpretations become cross-fertilized with discourses 'drawn from the reader's own socially, culturally and historically situated experiences' (Proctor et al., 2002: 34). The text is therefore convergent as it is 'shaped by the repetition and transformation of other textual structures' (ibid.: 34). Let's examine these elements of parody more closely.

The text of the advertisement in Figure 7.1 states, 'Like time, I wait pour non homme' (Like time, I wait for no man). The advertisement denotes an intentioned combination of text-and-image. The signifiers 'time' and 'man'

Figure 7.1 *'Like time, I wait pour non homme', FCUK, 2006*

Source: Reproduced by permission of FCUK.

narrated by the female subject implicitly invoke questions of derivation and re-presentation. We are immediately aware of the advertisement as the derivation of a more famous phrase, but we instinctively feel that some convention and or iconography is being subverted. This is even more apparent when we trace the past and contemporary references of the text. Within the relatively isolated worlds of early modern Europe, space and time were comprehended as part of a mysterious cosmology determined by some remote authority, heavenly host, or more sinister figures of myth and imagination' (Harvey, 1991: 241). An example of this relation to time is evident in the poetry of Robert Burns (1759–1796). Robert Burns' poetic splendour enthused with a passion for his native Scottish culture. His poems are also renowned for 'capturing the realised moment of experience' (Hepburn and Daiches, 1959: xiii). Drawing upon the prophetic prudence of Scottish folk legend, Burns' poetry echoed a sense of time's all-consuming power. For Robert Burns, the 'natural processes' of change contains vivid social truth; humans exist within the flow of time and cease to exist with the passage of time (Quinones, 1972). Indeed, it has been suggested that the phrase 'Time and tide wait for no Man' derives from Robert Burns, and in its original form states 'Nae man can tether time or tide'. This phrase appears in Robert Burn's quintessential narrative poem called 'Tam O'Shanter', the specific context of the phrase is as follows:

But pleasures are like poppies spread:
You seize the flow'r, its bloom is shed;
Or like the snow falls in the river,
A moment white – then melts for ever;
Or like the rainbow's lovely form
Evanishing amid the storm.
Nae man can tether time or tide

(quoted in Hepburn and Daiches, 1959: 350).

In this extract from Robert Burn's 'Tam O'Shanter', time is represented as embroiling man (*sic*) in the natural order of things. Throughout the pre-Classical and much of the Classical era, the predominant iconography of nature was that of a vestal, generative symbol, Mother Earth. In this era the interpretation of signs and the capacity to recognize signs relied upon a system of erudite and metaphysical knowledges which established resemblances between the sign and that which it signified (see Chapter 2). In this system of resemblances, Mother Nature's all-embracing cycles provide an understanding of man's (*sic*) relation to the earth, the universe and time. For example, Ovid (43BC–7AD) – using an image that Dante and Shakespeare would imitate–compares man's (*sic*) relation to time in terms of the movement of the waves:

The tyme itself continually is fleeting like a brooke.
For neyther brooke nor lygthsomme tyme can tarrye still. But looke
As every wave dryves other foorth, and that that commes behynd
Bothe thrusteth and is thrust itself; Even so the tymes by kind
Doo flyy and follow bothe at once, and evermore renew.

For that that was before is left, and streyght there dooth ensew
Anoother that was never erst.

(Ovid, 1904: 199)

In Ovid's analogy, time, like Mother Nature's movement of the waves and unlike the life of man (*sic*), is infinite. In this sense, neither change nor the future is critical to an existence, which is at one with God; his (*sic*) universe and Mother Earth. Conversely, Classical Greek mythology displaces the female iconography of time and change. In Greek mythology, Cronus, the son of Gaea (earth) and Uranus (sky) ruled the earth until his son Zeus dethroned him. While the account of Cronus differs in the various traditions of Greek mythology, Cronus invariably displaces Gaea (Mother Earth) as the personification of time (Forman, 1989: 4). Hence the Classical basis for the word chronology.

In Medieval and Renaissance art there exists a recurrent allegorical link between time and death (ibid.). This iconography of time depicts a cannibalistic image of Father Time, directly linked to Classical Greek mythology. According to Greek legend, Cronus is linked directly to time because he is the god of the harvest who ripens produce and 'matured every form of life' (Murray, 1998: 27). Cronus is also a devourer of human existence. In order to prevent the fulfilment of a prophecy, that he too would be dethroned by his youngest born, Cronus devours whole each of his first five newborn children. Rhea, his wife, tries to prevent her sixth child (Zeus) succumbing to this fate. According to Greek legend, Rhea wraps a stone in swaddling clothes and succeeds in duping Cronus as he swallows the decoy whole. Cronus thus believes that he has subverted the prophecy and continues to reign. Meanwhile, the newly-born child Zeus flees to the island of Crete, and upon adulthood returns to Greece to slay his father and establish his rule for all time (ibid.: 30). In Classical Greek mythology, time is the devourer of human existence … it waits for no man. In the sixteenth century, this cannibalistic iconography of time gives way to a more benign image of Father Time (Forman, 1989: 4). With the passing of time is revealed the truth and thus Father Time conveys to man (*sic*) knowledge and wisdom. It is only through a familial relation that the female is linked to the making of time. Thus, we see in the sixteenth century, the notion of 'Veritas filia temporis'– Truth the daughter of time (Forman, 1989: 4).

This chronology in the iconography of time appears to be what Riffaterre (1990) describes as the 'intertext'. That is the other text(s), which a reader requires knowledge of, so as to decode an advertisement. On further analysis, the advertisement in Figure 7.1 appears to be situated at a discursive interface between the Classical Greek iconography of Father Time and populist feminism. Indeed, the precarious positioning of the advertisement between these camps prevents the reader from ever really achieving a conclusive interpretation of the text. This is because both texts are a derivation of myth and populist sentiment. In this sense the use of parody is subversive in that it challenges both the original (masculine basis of time) and the facsimile (FCUK's appropriation of populist feminism). This has the transformative effect of a 'deviant simulacrum', which de-realizes both the original and the copy (Wheale, 1995: 44). Consequently, the advertisement provides an illustration of postmodern parody as a mode of mimesis, which consciously seeks to generate questions of derivation and re-presentation.

Pastiche

Reflect on the indiscriminate pillaging of the past in the shape of retro-advertisements and the more recent tendency to re-incarnate Hollywood idols for the purpose of selling products, the likes of which are, at best, arbitrarily associated with their lifetime. Jameson (1985) delights in labeling this new advertising form 'pastiche'. This consists of a playful self-referential medley of styles, materials and symbolic codes. Pastiche is like parody in that it involves 'imitation of a peculiar or unique style, the wearing of a stylistic mask, speech in dead language' (ibid.: 114). But pastiche is devoid of parody's dialectical mimesis of text and sub-text for it merely represents the aleatory coalescence of cultural fragments devoid of their historicity. Thus, the fabrication of fantasy through pastiche dismisses the existence of a 'unique self and private identity', which has the effect of inducing a latent feeling that there no longer 'exists something normal compared to which what is being imitated is rather comic' (ibid.: 114). Pastiche exists within the world of free-floating signifiers whose signifieds have long since dissimulated. Figure 7.2 contains an advertisement for the insurance product Sheila's Wheels. The advertisement's playful self-referentiality illustrates the particular practice of pastiche in postmodern advertisements.

The use of pastiche in Figure 7.2 is truly postmodern as it isolates the product from its utility function and displays it almost as a self-referential mixing of codes. In characteristically ironic mode the advertisement references a tongue-in-cheek stylization of women drivers. This is ironic because it 'is ungrounded, not appealing for validation from truths or mandates which are external to the work, such as a real world' (Wheale, 1995: 45). Actuarial observations have consistently identified women drivers as a statistically lower risk category than their male counterparts. This fact is playfully obviated in the advertisement's ironic medley of 1960s female youth culture and antipodean machismo. In postmodern consumer culture, the practice of pastiche invariably incorporates an element of nostalgia. Jameson (1985) observes this form of nostalgia to be distinct from its conventional connotation i.e., a yearning for the return of a past experience. Some suggestion of this distinction is evident in Figure 7.2. Nostalgia is clearly evident in this advertisement but this seems far removed from a desire for the return of the past. The advertisement is indeed metonymically nostalgic, in that it incorporates signifiers of the past. Nevertheless the creative motivation of the advertisement appears disinclined to reinvent an image of the past in its lived entirety. Rather, nostalgia operates in the advertisement by 'reinventing the

Figure 7.2 *Pastiche in postmodern advertisements, Sheila's Wheels, 2005*

Source: Reproduced under licence © 2005 Esure Services Limited.

feel and shape of characteristic art objects of an older period ... it seeks to reawaken a sense of the past associated with those objects' (1985: 116). Thus, the advertisement in Figure 7.2 appears referenced to its own satirical characterization of history, gender difference and masculine antipodean culture. It is in this sense that the advertisement assumes self-referentiality. Each signifier relates to the advertisement's sign-system as opposed to the lived experience of the past. Jameson argues that the colonization of nostalgia as an aesthetic in popular imagery mirrors a particular conjuncture in consumer capitalism. Cultural production in postmodernity is driven by the desire 'to seek the historical past through our own pop images and stereotypes about the past, which itself remains forever out of reach' (ibid.: 118).

Hyper-reality

Baudrillard (1975) argues that in postmodern consumer culture the commodity assumes its importance as a sign rather than something that is inherently 'useful'. In so doing, Baudrillard directly challenges Marx's distinction between the use-value and exchange-value. For the use-value itself is revealed as a 'construct of the system of exchange value which produces a rationalized system of needs and objects that integrate individuals into the capitalist order' (Best and Kellner, 1991: 114). This transformation in the system of needs is located within a particular genealogy of simulation. Baudrillard argues that with the transition from pre-capitalist to capitalist society, objects begin to function like signs. The object is abstracted from its concrete relationship between people. It now 'assumes its meaning in its differential relation to other signs' (quoted in Lane, 2000: 75). Like the Saussurean sign, this understanding of representation goes beyond the reductive notion of the sign as a vehicle of meaning and signification. In the postmodern era, the components of the sign are differentially and arbitrarily ordered. Baudrillard maps this form of signification onto three orders of signification: 'counterfeit, production and simulation' (Rodaway, 1996: 245). Each of these orders is grounded in stages of capitalist production. In the first order of simulacra, a representation of the real (e.g., a map) is a counterfeit of an exterior reality. Baudrillard (1983) describes how the map is not an identical copy of reality. Nevertheless it suffices as a cultural representation of an independent reality. In modern industrial capitalism, we observe a second order of simulacra, which blurs the distinction between reality and representation. Baudrillard (1983) illustrates this order of simulacra by recounting Borges' fable of the cartographers who constructed a map of the Empire, which was so exact that it virtually covered the entire territory. Axiomatic to this exactitude of science is 'a rational and creative agent individually orientated and critically willing to challenge accepted conventions through the application of reason and science' (Rodaway, 1996: 248). But this relation of subject and object is radically transformed in the third order of simulacra. In the postmodern stages of capitalism, cultural representations are no longer linked to an independent reality. Baudrillard describes how cybernetics, media and computerization have produced a 'quotidian reality in its entirety – political, social, historical and economic' (1983: 147). One that 'from now on incorporates the simulatory dimension of hyperrealism' (ibid.: 147). Representation no longer blurs the distinction between real and copy, rather, there is a detachment from both of these as multi-media simulations become realer-than-real, 'a hallucinatory resemblance' of its own existence (ibid.: 142). In the 'third order of representation', technologies gain their own momentum providing a simulacra of actual events effacing any access to a 'real', which itself is an effect of the code system (Sarup, 1998: 111). As Baudrillard puts it:

> abstraction today is no longer that of the map, the double, the mirror or the concept. Simulation is no longer that of territory, a referential being or a substance. It is the generation of models of a real without origin or reality; a hyperreal. The territory no longer precedes the map nor survives it. Henceforth, it is the map that precedes the territory – PRECESSION OF SIMULACRA – it is the map that engenders. (original emphasis, 1983: 2).

The extreme eclecticism of postmodern advertising collage is similarly detached from the concept of representation, mimesis and any relation to an original, which 'is lost in a continuous play of signs' (Rodaway, 1996: 248). Firat and Venkatesh describe how in Nike advertisements 'the need for a context seems to be increasingly transcended' (1993: 234). Similar aesthetics are in evidence in Figure 7.3. Baudrillard argues that in postmodernity the relation between sign and referent is completely arbitrary 'determined by its [their] position in a self-referential system of [floating] signifiers' (Featherstone, 1991: 85). In this sense, signification means simply difference and nothing else. For Baudrillard (1968), the only meaning that signs retain is their difference from other sign. Signs are entirely self-referential, making no attempt at signification or classification, their only point being to make a temporary impact on our consciousness.

The advertisement in Figure 7.3 is distinct in its aesthetic as 'it is no longer a question of imitation, nor of reduplication, nor even of parody. It is rather a question of substituting signs of the real for the real itself' (Baudrillard, 1983: 4). Devoid of specific referentiality, the signifiers in Figure 7.3 assume a materiality of unparalleled intensity as they explode into our consciousness. Jameson describes how, in the absence of a 'meaning effect' or even the illusion of mirage, 'the signifier in isolation becomes ever more material – or better still, literal – ever more vivid in sensory ways' (1985: 120). The isolated disconnected signifiers resist any attempt to weave meaning into a coherent narrative sequence or signifying chain. Rather, time is a function of each isolated position, a dimension of each self-referential event. It is fractured, multiple and discontinuous. Since 'our feeling of identity depends on our sense of the persistence of the "I" over the "me" over time', the subject of postmodern advertising loses the ability to thread 'certain paths' through the image (Jameson, 1985: 119). The search for an authentic narrative is disrupted by the 'pure' sign, which resides within a self-referential context and almost coincidentally, collides with 'products' (which are themselves mere signs). In postmodern consumer culture, goods no longer provide a basis for the construction of fixed identities, but rather 'make people seem different through a collage of fragmentary images' (Proctor et al., 2002: 34).

Figure 7.3 *Multiphrenic intensity of postmodern signs, Harvey Nichols, 2005*
Source: Reproduced by permission of Harvey Nichols

Seduction

In postmodern imagery, meaning is perpetually deferred, constantly slip-ping beyond our reach. Baudrillard argues that the third order of simulacra coincides with a loss of a private sphere in which 'the dramatic interiority of the subject, engaged with its objects as with its image, is played out' (1985: 128), whereby the incessant saturation of communication networks in the private sphere effaces its erstwhile distinction from the public arena 'in a sort of obscenity where the most intimate processes of our life become the virtual feeding ground of the media' (ibid.: 130). Axiomatic to the modernist separation of economy and culture, public from private is a subject 'situated within the world and able to make sense of that world through application of its powers of self-awareness' (Rodaway, 1996: 249). This modernist narrative assumes that the subject 'acts upon an object' and thus is an active agent in relation to the world (ibid.: 249). Moreover, the self has an interior a private universe 'invested as a protective enclosure, an imaginary protector, a defense system' (Baudrillard, 1985: 130). Conversely, in the media-saturated world of postmodernity, the 'self is nowhere and everywhere at the same time, totally abstracted, rapidly flitting before us in myriad versions unanchored to concrete experience' (Holstein and Gubrium, 2000: 66). The self is constantly on display as both a trophy and signifier of commodity culture.

The cavalcade of the self in postmodern advertising has been raised to new levels of spectacle by the growing convergence of media entertainment with advertising content. Often described as 'branded entertainment', this innovation gives rise to the creation of entertainment as a vehicle for the promotion of brands (Raney et al., 2003). In 2006, the advertising agency Saatchi & Saatchi UK manufactured a pop group for the sole purpose of providing sponsors with a vehicle to promote their brands. The corporate brands, which hire the manufactured group, will decide on its name and lyrics as well as what the group will eat, drink and wear in public. The association between brands and popular music has long been established, but the creation of a pop group for the sole purpose of selling branded goods is a disconcerting trend. For it takes the hyper-real staging of the self to new extremes. Baudrillard (1983) argues that hyper-reality is a condition of excess, which undermines the self-determining world of the historically and geographically anchored subject. The modernist episteme positions the Cartesian subject at the fulcrum of existence, for the 'knowing agent [is] contextualised and a locus of power' (Rodaway, 1996: 251). The metaphysics of presence which explicates this notion of knowledge orientates the subject within the context of experiential time and space (Holstein and Gubrium, 2000). The self is able to evaluate experience by linking the social meaning of time–space events into signifying chains. Although this knowledge is never flawless, the subject sought reassurance in the belief that it possessed access to an object with which to compare representation (King, 1998: 51). Conversely there is no reverent with which to compare Saatchi & Saatchi's virtual band. Instead we receive the sights and sounds of any number of brands metamorphosing into a hyper-real object independent from human subjects. Consequently, its 'representations are totally free-floating, they have no object but themselves; they are self-determining' (King, 1998: 51). In its defence, Saatchi and Saatchi have stated that the phenomena 'could be as simple as sponsorship of a tour through to clothing that could be worn, drinks, cosmetics' (quoted in Davis and Elliot, 2006: 4). Rather than alleviate our concerns, such assurance suggests that we will actually be witnessing a proliferation of self-presentation. The aesthetic populism of postmodern advertising already provides us with a proliferation of 'accounts and images of possible selves, especially of our inner worlds' (Holstein and Gubrium, 2000: 67). Nevertheless the brand-new band has no object with which to compare. The observer, therefore, 'becomes entirely dependent on the simulacra of hyperreality' (King, 1998: 51).

The public will be introduced to the brand-new band in a reality TV documentary called a 'mobisoap' which fans can download onto their mobile phones (Davis and Elliot, 2006: 4), thus providing the consumer with 'the absolute proximity of the total instantaneity of things' (Baudrillard, 1985: 133). No longer is there any distantiation between subject and object, spectator and spectated, 'all becomes transparence and immediate visibility' (ibid.: 130). The brand-new band is transformed and manipulated into a downloadable mobile artifact. It has reached new heights in its significance as an object. It is now free to represent the world in anyway it chooses, wherever and whenever. It is capable of subverting any direct challenge to its authenticity as no one has access to a comparable real world by which the hyper-reality can be compared (King, 1998: 51). And so the object causes mischief as it disrupts the experiential time of meaning, language and agency. The object's foundationless representations ingratiate experiential time, driven by the intention of seducing some semblance of identification with its 'ready-made packages of meaning' (Rodaway, 1996: 252). In this instance there occurs, 'a sort of contraction in each other, a fantastic telescoping, a collapsing of the two traditional poles into one' (Sarup, 1998: 113).

Baudrillard's concept of 'seduction' engages objects and subjects in an intense metaphysical attraction, with the capacity to 'turn appearances in on themselves, to play on the body's appearances, rather than with the depths of desire' (1990: 8). In the enchanted simulation (*trompe-l'œil*), objects seduce subjects by the 'pure play of appearance' (ibid.: 8). Seduction pronounces a relation between subject and object diametrically distinct from the immense capacity of the modernist subject. In modernist representation, the subject has superiority over the unknown object, which it has the power to represent. In the third order of simulcra objects efface the subject, seducing the latter to abandon its claims to sovereignty over the object world (Best and Kellner, 1991: 129).

Interactivity: 'The medium is the message'

> The Extent to which the barrage of stimuli that reach our senses can be turned into digital information, has a direct bearing on the influence of a medium and thus its commercial function. (Postma, 1999: 74)

In the 'software universe' of modern communication, space can be traversed literally in 'no time' (Bauman, 2001: 117). Previously distant spatial relativities now form part of our daily lives as demarcated boundaries become 'permeable' membranes saturated by unceasing tidal waves of information, imagery and text (Morley and Robins, 1995: 75). Indeed, the 'creators' of the Internet were initially interested in solving the single problem of 'how to connect isolated computers in a universal network', enabling electronic communication between computers regardless of type or location (Sherman and Price, 2001: 17). The interactive capacities of the Web have since exceeded the expectations of earlier innovations. Web users soon had available to them customized operating systems in which to unfold their unique lifestyles, desires and identities without leaving the confines of their home (Andrejevic, 2003). Central to these innovations has been the development of convergent technologies. This concept refers to the integration of two or more information teleologies into a combined system (Hellmund, 2001). Domestic applications of convergence connectivity typically include mobile phones, personal computers and personal digital assistants (PDAs). The vast numbers of wireless devices now in circulation constitute a brand new marketplace for advertising communication. Industry experts generally identify wireless communication technologies as providing 'many opportunities for marketers and advertisers to reach consumers no matter where they are' (Wright, 2000: 149). Indeed, advances in location positioning technology have combined with technological innovations in wireless communication to enable marketers to 'reach consumers when they are most likely to make a purchase, accept an offer, or use a service' (ibid.: 149).

The applications of short-range wireless communication for travel have brought into being a new multi-million pound market for mobile advertising. Mobile commerce 'refers to any activities related to a (potential) commercial transaction conducted through communication networks that interface with mobile devices' (Yuan and Tsao, 2003: 399). Mobile advertising is a field of application for mobile commerce. Mobile advertising can complement wireless devices and Internet-based e-commerce, making it possible for 'advertisers to create tailor-made campaigns targeting users according to where they are, their needs of the moment and the device they are using (i.e., contextualized mobile advertising)' (2003: 399). The commercial attractiveness of wireless devices is summed up in two words, 'ubiquitous interactivity' (Kannan et al., 2001). Location-based services enable firms to target consumers when they are in close proximity. According to the rhetoric of location-based marketing, 'applications can be used to enhance a consumer's daily activities through a number of value-added services' (Wright, 2000: 152). For example, Barnes describes how location-based marketing can enable 'the roaming phone user ... to be provided with information, alerts or even advertisements based on their location' (2002: 173). Research and development into 'smart' vehicles continues apace to develop a seamless connectivity between wireless voice control and data transfer capability (Barnes, 2002). Advertising opportunities are targeted here at the businessperson's 'considerable amount of time in-transit' (ibid.: 170). Developments in this area include in-vehicle networks of wireless connectivity automated via voice control, enabling motorists to connect to the Internet and receive interactive advertising communications.

Innovations in portable interactive devices have now taken the metaphor of cyberspace full circle, even when away from our homes we can remain plugged into our time/space paths in cyberspace. Thus, our paths through cyberspace now map onto our physical motion in the real world. As Andrejevic puts it: 'To the extent that the elastic boundaries of cyberspace stretch beyond the confines of the home or office to contain the physical motion of the mobile consumer, this motion becomes the real-world, physical analog of "surfing the Web"' (2003: 134). Advertising commerce has been quick to respond to the promise of wireless networked technology. The interactive overlay of real-time spatial paths followed by users and advertising communication has fuelled the revolution in mobile commerce. In a retail context, mobile commerce seeks to track consumers' motions through space so as to 'open up new information dimensions that can be used to further facilitate the consumption of space and the spatialisation of consumption' (ibid.: 134). For instance, Microsoft's Matchmaking software combines proximity data with customer profile data and is able to send customized shopping information to a consumer's mobile device (Litchford, 2001). Microsoft describe mobile commerce as 'enabling people to get information and data they want anywhere any time, and on any device' (ibid.). Elsewhere social theorists have been deservedly sanguine about the benefits of mobile commerce. Time–space path mapping seemingly offers a strategy of heightened customization in which advertising appeals can be directed at customers with optimum relevance. In this sense, 'the invitation of m-commerce is to specify one's individuality through motion' (Andrejevic, 2003: 135). For example, Kannan et al. state that 'the fact that it [wireless device] is available at all times to interact with users suggests that it can be used to obtain instant feedback from customers at usage context for market research purposes' (2001: 2). Mobile commerce thus accentuates the tracing of bodies in time/space, which functions to reinforce the portrayal of consumption as a means of individuality (Andrejevic, 2003: 142). Such trends are directly linked to the exteriority of identity in postmodern consumer culture. The modern sense of self is constructed against a backdrop of interior spaces, feelings, emotions and desires (Elliot, 2001: 141). Conversely, the postmodern self of mobile commerce is defined through the externalization of authentic subjectivity. The following discussion of advertising and convergence technologies develops this observation.

Convergence technologies are radically transforming our experience of media entertainment. Wireless Application Protocol (WAP) enables 3G users to access mini browsers on their portable handsets. 3G mobile phones now offer speeds of up to 2Mbps, thus enabling users to watch short video clips and enhanced multimedia advertising. Live television streaming is generally considered to be the next big thing as network operators eagerly promote the mind-boggling capabilities of 4G (Webb, 2006). Elsewhere, Internet search engines are mutating into entertainment systems as providers continue apace to develop platforms which enable access to music, blogs, e-mails and downloads from wireless handheld devices. Telecoms companies are transforming into broadcasters as they diversify into video-on-demand. Network operators are converging with Internet providers to combine search engines and messaging services. Technology companies are transforming mobile handsets into mobile home entertainment systems. And broadcasters eagerly tout the virtues of multiple outlets capable of simultaneously distributing entertainment programmes over the Internet, on MP3 players, mobile phones and television.

Ultimately the flow of innovation is sweeping towards the integration of the television and personal computer, leading to the widespread adoption of HTML interactive television (Hellmund, 2001; Robinson, 2005). The versatility of set design is changing rapidly, making interactivity a more habitual part of television viewing (Dobres, 2004). Broadband Internet access already provides advertisers with a format which mimics TV. With download speeds ten times that of standard 56k modems, broadband enables the use of faster, and more complex visual advertising formats (Swinfen-Green, 2002). Broadband also enables the combined use of audio and visual advertising formats. While narrowband environments are able to transmit video imagery, this is often tediously slow and of poor quality. Conversely broadband enables the transmission of high definition audio and video advertisements. Faster download speeds also enable the delivery of large transitional advertisements (e.g., interstitial), that have duration of several seconds before the main page opens (ibid.: 43). The use of complex formats in narrowband advertising relies on the need for consumers to expend time laboriously downloading software, broadband access provides for an environment, which facilitates the quick and less cumbersome use of plug-ins (e.g., RealPlayer) in the production of visually stimulating advertisements (ibid.: 43).

Convergence technologies offer advertising its potential of operating at the epicentre of our media-saturated economy of signs. Multi-media advertising is the material realization of capitalism's insatiable appetite for time/space efficiency in the expropriation of 'more for less'. In the logic of post-Fordist production, the efficiency of the medium depends entirely on the extent it can be tailored to its audience. The impact of personalization in mobile commerce has meant that advertisers need not rely upon mass communication to push their contents onto consumers at pre-scheduled points in time. Data-driven mobile commerce is based on the real-time monitoring of consumers, thus enabling the spatial customization of advertising content. Similar economies of scale are apparent in Internet advertising. The interactivity, speed and flexibility of information exchange on-line 'provides considerable opportunity for tailoring an advertisement message to a particular prospective consumer' (Drèze and Zufrydeni, 2000: 27) (Figure 7.4). The Internet has the added advantage of enabling the continuous circulation of signs. Radio and television advertising, using analogue (as opposed to digital), requires that the broadcaster interrupt the linear flow of transmission to broadcast the advertisement. Consequently, the whole of the available bandwidth is allocated to either programme content or advertising. Conversely, the Internet enables content providers to embed advertisements within the real-time flow of their broadcasts. This process is described

Figure 7.4 *'Waste time faster', Siemens S45, 2006*

Source: Reproduced by permission of BenQ Mobile UK.

as 'spatial multiplexing' as it requires that content providers allocate only a fraction of their bandwidth to the advertisement (ibid.: 34).

Multi-media advertising is light years away from the asynchronous diffusion of signs discussed in Part 1 of this book. The advent of corporate advertising in the nineteenth century relied upon the mechanical dissemination of advertising content across vast distances. In this era of steam-powered travel and chronometric telegraphy, the circulation of signs extended over vast horizons of time. Human reaction to signs was similarly 'delayed for considerable periods of time' (McLuhan, 1997: 4). Advertising in this mechanistic era depended on the 'content' of other medium to communicate its message (ibid.: 8). Thus, the circulation of newspaper advertising depended on the printed press and likewise radio advertising relied upon the advent of wireless telegraphy to channel its message. According to McLuhan, this 'merely underlines the point that "the medium is the message" because it is the medium that shapes and controls the scale and form of human association and action' (ibid.: 9). In this sense each innovation in advertising communication involves an 'extension of man' (ibid.: 4). And each 'extension, whether of skin, hand, or foot, affects the whole psychic and social complex' (ibid.: 4). Reason-why advertising (1920s) traded upon the rational capabilities of consumers. Motivational psychology (1960s) had as its focus the psyche and the psychodynamic properties of the self. And the narrational properties of the commodity-sign require the existence of a 'remembering subject' (Williamson, 2000: 158). In the postmodern era, the digital convergence of advertising channels introduces into human development 'a greater degree of immediate participation, an incessant response, a total plasticity' (Baudrillard, 1983: 119). In the high-tech environment of postmodern advertising, the receiver is expected not only to decipher and decode signs but also to be a participant in the production of signs.

Mobile commerce and the Internet are emblematic of high-involvement advertising media which require both the extension of the body in time/space and also 'the creative process of knowing' (McLuhan, 1997: 3). As Drèze and Zufrydeni put it, 'ads from standard media come to prospective customers whereas prospective customers on the Internet medium come to ads' (2000: 29). Thus, the technological stimulation of postmodern advertising is 'an era of tactile communication' in which the 'message becomes "massage", tentacular solicitation' (Baudrillard, 1983: 123–4). For example, Internet content providers can send instructions to consumers to retrieve product/service promotions directly from the advertiser (Drèze and Zufrydeni, 2000: 26). According to marketing rhetoric, this enables 'a closing of the marketing-response loop which permits the potential development of appropriate advertising and marketing strategies that will best influence a prospective consumer's purchase behavior' (ibid.: 35). But this also suggests a field of 'tactile simulation' (Baudrillard, 1983: 124) in which the receiver becomes both consumer and producer.

In marketing theory, 'interactivity' is defined as the 'extent to which users can participate in modifying the form and content of a mediated environment in real time' (Steuer, 1992, quoted in Fiore et al., 2005: 39). Interactivity is an extension of postmodern time/space compression. The digitalized messages of interactive advertising are all signs of instantaneity in our quotidian experience of time/space. Digital convergence in advertising channels heightens our experience of time/space compression as signs enter into endless 'games of duplication and reduplication of the object in detail' (Baudrillard, 1983: 144). Advance forms of integrated digital media promotions can provide the consumer with a panorama of signs, synchronously transmitted from TV, iTV, the Internet, e-mail, mobile phones and PDAs (Johnson, 2002: 38). These scattered fragments of signs 'short-circuit' the modernist 'dialectic of signifier and signified' (Baudrillard, 1983: 122). Multi-media advertising radically disrupts our experiences of spatial and temporal contiguity so that identities have become 'eminently contingent and continually reproduced in specific discursive contexts' (Tribe, 1993: 4).

While it is evident that in postmodern consumer culture identity assumes indeterminacy, traces of continuity and regulation are also apparent. This is because the circuits of sign production retain their historical function as the outputs of human labour time. The PDAs and PCs of multi-media advertising incorporate into the market-response loop human labour time which serves to accomplish specified applications (e.g., activate RealPlayer). As Spencer observes, the micro-processing units, which enable multi-media program applications, depend on humans to interpret 'a variety of internal states ... in terms of information and even function in relation to the task at hand' (1996: 64). In Chapter 3 it was argued that advertising operates to reproduce the expropriation of human labour time as part of capitalist accumulation. The profusion of digitality in advertising media involves consumers in continual procedures of coding and decoding digital command structures. The 'real-time' interaction systems built into digital advertising media have the effect of simplifying stimuli 'into successive sequences', for which 'there can be only instantaneous response, yes or no' (Baudrillard, 1983: 119). One consequence of this progression has been the transformation of the potentially complex syntactical decoding of digital signs into a 'binary sign system of question/answer' (ibid.: 117). Baudrillard describes these binary responses as 'the limit of an abbreviated reaction' (ibid.: 119). Thus, it is necessary to recognize that the digital convergence of advertising channels ultimately relies upon the participation of human subjects in dematerialized productive activity. In the third order of simulacra, the circulation of signs is inextricably contingent on the expropriation of human labour time, which is itself an effect of the sign system.

Conclusion

The de-centred subject of postmodern advertising unsettles representational conceptions of time and space. In the writings of Baudrillard, advertising hyper-spaces are an allegory for depthless selves. 'Textual spaces' invite a form of liminality in which durable selfhood is replaced by 'a kind of supermarket identity – an assemblage of scraps, random desires, chance encounters, the accidental and the fleeting' (Elliot, 2001: 131). In postmodernity, self-determination is the outcome of the direct and often physical involvement of human subjects in 'technologies and images (signs) which continually replicate and circulate' within a self-referential system of floating signifiers (Rodaway, 1996: 251).

Conclusion

Globalization and the future of advertising

There is little doubt that global electronic communication makes possible a new kind of relationship between advertising and capitalist production. In the 'software universe' of modern communication, space can be traversed literally in 'no time' (Bauman, 2001: 117). Advertising has responded enthusiastically to the wealth of opportunities presented by global electronic communication. According to the media agency ZenithOptimedia, global advertising accounted for 0.96 per cent of world GDP in 2005 and this is predicted to rise to 0.99 per cent by 2008 (2006: 2). Global trends in digital convergence and communication integration have fortuitously reshaped the infrastructure of advertising. Traditional agency practice involved co-ordinating planning decisions across vertical communication channels comprising telephony, visual communication and data (Ancarani and Shankar, 2003: 57). Global electronic communication has precipitated a new digital convergent industry, which has revolutionized the logic of traditional advertising. In this new multimedia industry content production converges horizontally with transmission, packaging and reception (ibid.: 57). Consequently, there has been a transition from information distribution 'dependent on content, specific technology and dedicated hardware' towards an 'independent content system distributed through a shared infrastructure' (ibid.: 57). Advertisers can now supply a more homogeneous service in a more synergistic way. In the brand new world of digital convergence, commercials and programme content are delivered synchronously through layered multi-media channels at any place and time of day. Nevertheless, these innovations suggest that advertising's past continues to shape its future especially in its ability to provide post-Fordist production systems with a mechanism for adapting to the new sign economy.

Part I of this book traced the advent of modern advertising to the aftermath of the Great Depression (1875–1890s), which engulfed the whole of the capitalist world. During this era production exceeded the capacities of existing markets and Western economies experienced the deleterious effects of the 'first unambiguous crisis of capitalist overaccumulation' (Harvey, 2001: 134). Capitalism needed a mechanism of matching the rhythms of capitalist production with surplus labour time and advertising provided the solution. Time discipline was the driving force of the Industrial Revolution. Although the workers of pre-capitalist economies laboured hard for a living, their work routines were in principle self-determined. Conversely, the factory worker was compelled to adopt the mechanistic work rhythms of the clock. The vice of 'wasting time' was severely castigated, thus generating tensions between capital and labour. Capitalism required mechanisms for popularizing time-keeping and inculcating a subservient attitude to the tyranny of time. Chapter 1 examined the historical emergence of corporate advertising in the nineteenth century. The chapter established significant links between the conditions of emergence of corporate advertising and capitalism's need to make the punctilious regulation of space an obligation of commercial practice. Similar motives bolstered the marketing activities of the insurance industry during this era. Insurance companies allied with advertising in a concerted effort to relinquish their dubious links with speculative gambling. English culture, at this time, was very much influenced by the Victorian work-ethic, 'which led to "spare time" ... being regarded as a reward for hard work' (Whitrow, 1989: 163). Victorian morality was also highly unsympathetic to the plight of the poor and chastised this group as a burdensome responsibility. Capitalism required a mechanism to address the rapacious effects of the market economy. Insurance provided an efficacious fit between this need and the attendant need to inculcate subjects into a financially self-disciplined relation to the future. Advertising was a primary force in the fortuitous re-branding of the insurance industry in the mid-nineteenth century. Bartels claims that 'interest in advertising increased around 1900 ... as buyers' markets began to replace sellers' markets' (1986: 192). This appears to have been the turning point for marketing and advertising although it was not until the second decade of the century that basic concepts in marketing 'emerged and were crystallised' (ibid.: 193).

Industrial production brought linear synchronicity to the assembly lines of Fordist factories. Fordism used assembly-line production to enhance the control of the labour process and to furnish the expropriation of surplus labour time. These imperatives required a level of technical, organizational and cultural restructuring defined as a regime of accumulation. The Fordist regime of accumulation is premised on large-scale production carried out by vertically integrated organizations geared toward meeting the 'needs' of mass consumer markets. Ford explicitly recognized that 'mass production meant mass consumption', which required 'a new aesthetics and psychology, in short, a new kind of modernist, and populist democratic society' (Harvey, 1990: 125–6). Advertising provided the necessary link between Fordism's mechanistic production systems and the timing of consumer demand. Ford's famous declaration that 'you can have any color as long as it's black' reflected the fact that simply buying a car was sufficiently distinctive not to have to be bothered about its colour. Chapter 3 examined Fordist conceptions of consumer behaviour. These early models assumed marketing to be exclusively 'economic exchange' and therefore not about other kinds of human behaviour and emphasized the power of the marketer to influence or control consumer behaviour (Sheth and Gardner, 1986: 212). Axiomatic to this concept of economic exchange is a notion of transactions as 'one-time exchanges of values between two parties who have no prior or subsequent interaction' (Easton and Araujo, 1994: 74). The identities of parties are of limited significance as 'transactions are assumed to be perfectly replaceable across parties with similar utility functions' (ibid.: 74). This conception of consumer subjectivity directly attended to Fordism's intention to link labour time, culture and identity more closely to commercial objectives.

Part III of this book examined time and postmodern commodity culture. The project of modernity was founded on instrumental rationality, a progressive history and the suppression of *difference*. Its representational linear time is premised on the rational ordering and control of space and time, the denial of *differance*, 'a refusal to accept limits and the insistence on continually reaching out ... [to] a destiny that is always beyond; beyond morality, beyond tragedy, beyond culture' (Bell, 1976: 50). But despite its hegemony, representational time is struggling to contain radical challenges to the sovereignty of its Cartesian subject, its rational ordering of time and space and its subversion of *differance*. Indeed, the postmodern world of simulacra and 'hyper-reality' is a world without 'fixed' references of meaning.

Postmodern consumer culture is a fragmented and indiscriminate world. It radically displaces any totalizing ordering of time and space. There is no longer a single general equivalence against which our experience of time can be compared. In the 'techno-luminous' spaces of postmodern culture, our experience of duration is 'made out of myriads of stimuli' with many in 'distinctive opposition' (Baudrillard, 1983: 139). This also means the collapse of representational time into a 'hyper-realism' of free-floating, self-determining signifiers. Such degrees of ephemerality present capitalism with a formidable enterprise in its endeavour to sustain a system of production in an unstable market (Venkatesh, 1999). Capitalism ameliorates this potential danger through deregulation, 'flexibility' (new forms of production), diversification of commodities, mobile capital and the continuous development of new information technologies (Herman and McChesney, 1998: 111).

Flexible technologies and economies of scale enable firms to 'respond to the growth of flexible markets' (Amin, 1995: 15). The flexibly organized space of post-Fordist inter-firm networks invokes changes in the temporality of production systems. While vertically integrated geographical dispersed production operated according to objective linear time, outsourcing 'makes possible the just-in-time delivery of intermediate goods and materials' (Lash and Urry, 1994: 56). Just-in-time operations incorporate flexibility into the productive process and enable short production cycles 'in which the core product remains the same but is differentiated on the basis of some intangible benefits and incorporating the sign system' (Venkatesh, 1999: 14). This is certainly the impression evident in the Regulation School which highlights the transition from Fordism to flexible accumulation to have precipitated an intense phase of time/space compression. Advertising is linked with several modalities of this contraction of time/space. Of particular relevance is the use of corporate branding as a mode of regulating consumption and identity at work. In contrast with Fordist corporate branding, the marketing of post-Fordist corporations is designed to harness the mental capabilities and communicative skills of everyone involved in the organisation (Rifkin, 1996). This is because language has gained a key role in every facet of the production process (Gorz, 1999: 41). In the rhetoric and hyperbole of marketing gurus, it is the worker's personality and attitude that now represent key components of the brand. 'Selling oneself and particularly selling "the whole of oneself" is the very essence of the subjugation of labour to capital (ibid.: 43)'. Chapter 5 argued that the 'sale of the self' (ibid.: 43) takes the regulation of work and leisure time to new insidious levels of expropriation. This is effectively because every-where and anytime are transformed into raw material to be continually 'struc-tured, manufactured and shaped' in the 'personality market' of post-Fordist corporate branding.

Multinational corporations have been equally keen to attach the brand to an organizational culture which is both 'bold and innovative internally' and 'strong externally' (Kunde, 2000: 30). Evidently the international corpora-tions which prosper are those in which the management 'knows how the company's profile and position varies from market to market' (ibid.: 33). Multinationals faulter 'because they let their decentralized subsidiaries con-trol development' (ibid.: 34). Conversely, multinationals which manage their companies and markets in the same way as their brands gain 'protec-tion against the complexity of new products and the speed of market change' (ibid.: 30). Unparalleled advances in information technology have enabled multinationals to maximize knowledge-based productivity (Lury, 2004). In the writings of Castells, capital accumulation proceeds and profit is generated, 'increasingly in the global financial markets enacted by infor-mation networks in the timeless space of financial flows' (2000: 472). Castells identifies a revolution in information technology and a dramatic restructuring of world capitalism to have brought into being 'a new social structure, the network society' (ibid.: 336). Axiomatic to this revolution of informationalism has been the digital convergence of advertising channels. Corporations traditionally communicated with their clients a-synchronously across vast expanses of time and space. This required scheduling advertising content to coincide with local information communication technologies. In the high-tech environment of digital convergence, advertising involves 'not just one type of media, but all types combined into one' (Harper, 2000: 31). Unlike Fordist advertising with its a-synchronous flows of content circulat-ing on a national scale, post-Fordist advertising maps onto the global net-works of capital. Global electronic communications has given rise to a new kind of mobile advertising system capable of bypassing nation–states and dematerializing geography. Flows of capital, information, images and symbols challenge the rational ordering of time and space by 'disordering the sequence of events and making them simultaneous, thus installing society in eternal ephemerality' (Castells, 2000: 467).

Postmodern advertising imagery is devoid of 'a referential being or a sub-stance' against which some ideal of reality can be equated (Baudrillard, 1983: 3). It subverts the metaphysics that posit differences between real and imaginary (ibid.: 5). In so doing, it confounds the quest for control and domination in which modernist marketing epistemologies appear to be grounded. In this new episteme, creatives can no longer claim the 'dialectical capacity' of advertising imagery to provide an 'intelligible mediation' of desire (ibid.: 10). Postmodern advertising confounds the principle of equivalence linking 'the sign and the real' (ibid.: 11). Signs circulate irrespective of a figurative code of appearance driven only by the self-referential seffervescence of difference.

Bibliography

Adam, B. (1990) *Time and Social Theory*. Cambridge: Polity Press.

Adam, B. (1992) 'Modern times: the technology connection and its implications for social theory', *Time and Society*, 1(2): 175–91.

Adam, B. (1993) 'Within and beyond the time economy of employment relations; conceptual issues pertinent to research on time and work', *Social Science Information*, 32: 163–184.

Adam, B. (1995) *Timewatch*. Cambridge: Polity Press.

Advertising Archive (2006) *On Archive*. http://www.advertisingarchives.co.uk.

Ahola, H. (2000) 'internet marketing – literature review and research agenda', http://www.tekniikka.oamk.fi/netties/2000/papers/InternetMarketing.

Allport, H. (1924) *Social Psychology*. Boston: Houghton Mifflin.

Amin, A. (1995) *Post-Fordism: A Reader*. Oxford: Blackwell.

Ancarani, F. and Shankar, V. (2003) 'Symbian: customer interaction through collaboration and competition in a convergent industry', *Journal of Interactive Marketing.*, 17(1): 56–76.

Andrejevic, M. (2003) 'Monitored mobility in the era of mass customization', *Space and Culture*. 6(2): 132–150.

Andrew Irving Associates (1992) *Women Research Report*. Marketing research study by Andrew Irving Associates, commissioned by the Halifax.

Appadurai, A. (1996) *Modernity at Large: Cultural Dimensions of Globalization*. Minneapolis, MN: University of Minnesota Press.

Auerbach, J. (2002) 'Art, advertising and the legacy of empire', *Journal of Popular Culture*, 35: 1–23.

Barnes, S. (2002) 'Under the skin: short-range embedded wireless technology', *International Journal of Information Management*, 22: 165–179.

Bartels, R. (1986) *The History of Marketing Thought*. Columbus, OH: Horizons.

Barthes, R. (1977) *Image, Music, Text*. Trans. S. Heath, London: Fontana.

Baudrillard, J., (1968/1996) *The System of Objects*, trans. J. Benedict. London: Verso.

Baudrillard, J. (1975) *The Mirror of Production*. St Louis, MO: Telos Press.

Baudrillard, J. (1981) *For a Critique of the Political Economy of the Sign*, trans. C. Levin, St Louis, MO: Telos.

Baudrillard, J. (1983*) Simulations*. Trans. P. Foss, P. Patton, and P. Beitchman. New York: Semiotext(e).

Baudrillard, J. (1985) 'The ecstasy of communication', in H. Foster, (ed.), *Postmodern Culture*. Wiltshire: Pluto pp. 126–35.

Baudrillard, J. (1990) *Seduction*. Trans. B. Singer New York: St Martin's Press.

Baudrillard, J. (2001) *Jean Baudrillard; Selected Writings*. Ed. M. Poster. Oxford: Polity Press.

Baudrillard, J. (2003) *The Consumer Society: Myths and Structures*. London: Sage.

Bauman, Z. (1988) *Freedom*. Milton Keynes: Open University Press.

Bauman, Z. (1992) *Intimations of Postmodernity*. London: Routledge.

Bauman, Z. (2001) *Liquid Modernity*. Cambridge: Polity.

BBC.co.uk (2005) 'L'Oréal slammed over cream claims', 17 August 2005,http://news.bbc.co.uk/1/hi/health/4158648.stm.

Becker, G. (1965) 'A theory of the allocation of time', *Economic Journal*, 75: 493–517.

Bell, D. (1976) *The Cultural Contradictions of Capitalism*. London: Heinemann.

Benjamin, W. (1999) *Illuminations*. Trans. Harry Zorn. London: Pimlico.

Bernstein, R. (1980) 'Philosophy in the conversation of mankind', *Review of Metaphysics*, 32(4): 762.

Best, S. and Kellner, D. (1991) *Postmodern Theory: Critical Interrogations*. Basingstoke: Macmillan.

Bettman, J. (1979) *An Information Processing Theory of Consumer Choice.* Reading, MA: Addison-Wesley.

Blair, M. (2003) 'Turning viral marketing into a main stream proposition', http://www.ogilvy.com/viewpoint/pdf/v4_blair.pdf.

Blau, P. and Schoenherr, R. (1971) *The Structure of Organizations.* London: Basic Books.

Bloomfield, M. (1915) 'The new profession of handling men', *Annals of the American Academy of Political and Social Science.*, LXI (September).

Boorstin, D. (1964) *The Image: A Guide to Pseudo Events in America.* New York.

Bordo, S. (1986) 'The Cartesian masculinisation of thought', *Signs: Journal of Women in Culture and Society*, 2(3): 439–457.

Bourke, L. (1991) *Women and Money.* London: Thorsons.

Bowlby, R. (1993) *Shopping with Freud.* London: Routledge.

Brandon, R. (2002) *How the Car Changed Life: Automobile.* London: Macmillan.

Braun, K.A. Ellis, R. and Loftus, E.P. (2002) 'Make my memory: how advertising can change our memories of the past', *Psychology and Marketing*, 19(1): 1–23.

Braverman, H. (1974) *Labor and Monopoly Capital: The Degradation of Work in the Twentieth Century.* London: Monthly Review Press.

Brierley, S. (2002) *The Advertising Handbosok.* London: Routledge.

Bruttini, A. (1982) 'Advertising and socio-economic transformations in England 1720–1760', *Journal of Advertising History*, 5: 8–26.

Burchell, G. Gordon, C. and Miller, P. (1991) *The Foucault Effect: Studies in Governmentality.* Hemel Hempstead: Harvester.

Burrill, D. (2005) 'Out of the Box: Performance. Drama and Interactive Software', *Modern Drama*, 48(3): 492–512.

Business Insights (2005) 'Turning information into knowledge'. Business Insights.http://www.bizinsights.com.

Calkins, E. (1930) 'The new consumption engineer and the artist', in J.G. Frederick (ed.), *A Philosophy of Production.* New York: The Business Bourse.

Campbell C. (1995) 'When the meaning is not the message: a critique of the consumption as communication thesis', in M. Nava (ed.), *Buy This Book.* London: Routledge.

Castells, M. (1998) *The Information Age: Economy, Society and Culture. Vol. II: End of Millennium.* Malden, MA: Blackwell.

Castells, M. (2000) *The Rise of the Network Society.* Oxford: Blackwell.

Church, R. (1993) 'Mass marketing motor cars in Britain before 1950', in R. Church (ed.), *The Rise and Fall of Mass Marketing.* London: Routledge.

Clammer, J. (1992) 'Aesthetics of the self: shopping and social being in contemporary urban Japan', in R. Shields (ed.), *Lifestyle Shopping: The Subject of Consumption.* London: Routledge.

Clark, G. (1999) *Betting on Lives: The Culture of Life Insurance in England, 1695–1775.* Manchester: Manchester University Press.

Clark, G. (2002) 'Embracing fatality through life insurance in eighteenth-century England', in T. Baskar and J. Simon (eds), *Embracing Risk: The Changing Culture of Insurance and Responsibility.* Chicago: The University of Chicago Press.

Clarke, D. (2000) 'Space, knowledge and consumption', in P. Daniels, J. Bryson et al., (eds), *Knowledge, Space and Economy.* London: Routledge pp. 209–26.

Clarke, J. and Critcher, C. (1985) *The Devil Makes Work: Leisure in Capitalist Britain.* Basingstoke: Macmillan.

Cohen, G.A. (1978) *Karl Marx's Theory of History: A Defence*, Oxford: Clarendon Press.

Cooper, R. and Law, J. (1995) 'Organisation: distal and proximal views', in S. Bocharach, P. Gaghardi, and B. Mundell (eds), *Research in the Sociology of Organisations,*. Greenwich, CT: JAI Press.

Corrigan, P. (1997) *The Sociology of Consumption.* London: Sage.

Cousins, M. and Hussain, A. (1984) *Michel Foucault.* Basingstoke: Macmillan.

Dalla Costa, M. and James, S. (1975) *The Power of Women and the Subversion of the Community.* Bristol: Falling Wall Press,

Daniel, B. (1976) *The Cultural Contradictions of Capitalism*. London: Heinemann.

Daston, L. (1995) *Classical Probability in the Enlightenment*. Princeton, NJ: Princeton University Press.

Datamonitor, (2004) *Skincare and Suncare in the UK to 2008*. London: Datamonitor.

Davidoff, L. (1979) 'The rationalization of housework', in D. Barker and S. Allen (eds), *Dependence and Exploitation in Work and Marriage*. London: Longman.

Davies, K. (1990) *Women and Time: Weaving the Strands of Everyday Life*. Aldershot: Avebury.

Davis, J. and Elliot, J. (2006) 'This is the girl band you can buy', *The Sunday Times.*, 9 April, p. 4.

Defert, D. (1991) 'Popular life and insurance technology', in J. Burchell, C. Gordon and P. Miller (eds), *The Foucault Effect: Studies in Governmentality*. Hemel Hempstead: Harvester, pp. 211–33.

Derrida, J. (1978) *Writing and Difference*, trans. A. Bass. Chicago: University of Chicago Press.

Derrida, J. (1982) *Margins of Philosophy*, trans. A. Bass. Chicago: University of Chicago Press.

Descartes, R. (1952) *Descartes: Philosophical Writings*, ed. and trans. N.K. Smith. London: Macmillan.

Dichter, E. (1964) *Handbook of Consumer Motivation*. New York: McGraw-Hill.

Dicks, B. (2003) *Culture on Display: The Production of Contemporary Visibility*. Maidenhead: Open University Press.

Diggins, J. (1978) *The Bard of Savagery: Thorstein Veblen and Modern Social Theory*. Sussex: Harvester Press Ltd.

Dill Scott, W. (1908) *The Psychology of Advertising: A Simple Exposition of the Principles of Psychology in their Relation to Successful Advertising*. Boston: Small Maynard.

Dirks, T. (2006) *The Manchurian Candidate*. (1962) http://www.filmsite.org/manc.html.

Dobres, C. (2004) Towards an Interactive World, *Admap*, October, pp. 95–6.

Douglas, J. D. (1970) Understanding Everyday Life, London: Routledge and Kegan Paul.

Douglas, M. and Isherwood, B. (1978) *The World of Goods: Towards an Anthropology of Consumption*. London: Allen Lane.

Dreyfus, H. and Rabinow, P. (1982) *Beyond Structuralism and Hermeneutics*. London: Harvester Wheatsheaf.

Drèze, X and Zufrydeni, F. (2000) 'Internet advertising: the medium is the difference', *Consumption Markets and Culture*, 4(1): 23–37.

Du Gay, P. (1996) *Consumption and Identity at Wsork*. London: Sage.

Dunbar, D. (1979) 'The agency commission system in Britain: a first sketch of its history to 1941', *Journal of Advertising History*, Jan.: 19–28.

Dunlop, C. (1994) *The Culture Vulture: A Guide to Style Period and Ism*. Washington, DC: The Preservation Press.

Dyer, G. (1993) *Advertising as Communication*. London: Routledge.

Dymock, E. (1993) *Rover: The First Ninety Years. One of Britain's Fine Cars 1904–1994*. London: G.T. Foulis & Co (Haynes Group).

Easton, G. and Araujo, L. (1994) 'Market exchange, social structures and time', *European Journal of Marketing*, 28(3): 72–84.

Eby, C. (1998) 'Veblen's assault on time', *Journal of Economic Issues.*, 32(3): 680–707.

Elliot, A. (2001) *Concepts of the Self*. Cambridge: Polity.

Elliot, R. (1999) 'Symbolic meaning and postmodern consumer culture', in D. Brownlie. et al. (eds), *Rethinking Marketing: Towards Critical Marketing Accountings*. London: Sage.

Eliot, T.S. (1979) *Four Quartets*. London: Faber & Faber.

Elliott, B. (1962) *A History of English Advertising*. London: Business Publications Ltd in association with B.T. Batsford Limited.

Engels, F. (1968) 'The origin of the family, private property and the state', in *Marx and Engels: Selected Works*. London: Lawrence and Wishart.

Equitable Life (2006) *Today and History*. http://www.equitable.co.uk/content/content_7.htm.

Ermarth, E. (1992) *Sequel to History: Postmodernism and the Crisis of Representational Time*. Princeton, NJ: Princeton University Press.

Ewald, F. (1991) 'Insurance and risk', in J. Burchell, C. Gordon and P. Miller, *The Foucault Effect: Studies in Governmentality*. Hemel Hempstead: Harvester.

Ewen, S. (1977) *Captains of Consciousness: Advertising and the Social Roots of the Consumer Culture*. Maidenhead: McGraw-Hill.

Ezzy, D. (1997) 'Subjectivity and the labour process: conceptualising "good work"', *Sociology*, 31(3): 427–44.

Fabian, J. (1983) *Time and the Other: How Anthropology Makes its Object*. New York: Columbia University Press.

Featherstone, M. (1991) *Consumer Culture and Postmodernism*. London: Sage.

Fiore, A. Kim, J. and Lee, H. (2005) 'Effects of image interactivity technology on consumer responses toward online retailers', *Journal of Interactive Marketing*, 19(3): 38–53.

Firat, F. (1994) 'Gender and consumption: transcending the feminine?' in J.A. Costa (ed.), *Gender Issues and Consumer Behaviour*. London: Sage.

Firat, A. and Venkatesh, A. (1993) 'Postmodernity: the age of marketing', *International Journal of Research in Marketing*, (10)3: 227–50.

Flower, R. and Wynn Jones, M. (1987) *Lloyd's of London: An Illustrated History*. Essex: Lloyds of London Press.

Ford, H. (1910) *My Life and Work*. Chicago.

Forman, A. (1978) *Femininity as Alienation: Women and the Family in Marxism and Psychoanalysis*. London: Pluto Press.

Forman, F. (1989) 'Feminizing time: an introduction', in F. Forman and C. Sowton (eds), *Taking Our Time: Feminist Perspectives of Temporality*. Oxford: Pergamon Press.

Foucault, M. (1970) *The Order of Things: An Archaeology of the Human Sciences*. London: Tavistock Publications.

Foucault, M. (1977) *Discipline and Punish*. Trans. A. Sheridan., London: Penguin.

Foucault, M. (1979) *History of Sexuality*, vol. 1. London: Allen Lane.

Foucault, M. (1980) *Power/Knowledge: Selected Interviews and Other Writings, 1972–1977*, ed. C. Gordon, Hemel Hempstead: Harvester.

Foucault, M. (1982a) 'The subject and power', in H.L. Dreyfus and R. Rabinow (eds), *Michel Foucault: Beyond Structuralism and Hermeneutics*. Chicago: University of Chicago Press.

Foucault, M. (1982b) 'Truth, power, self: an interview', in L. Martin et al. (eds), *Technologies of the Self*. Amherst, MA: University of Massachusetts Press.

Foxall, G. Goldsmith, R. and Brown, S. (1998) *Consumer Psychology for Marketing*. London: International Thomson Business Press.

Frank, T. (1997) *The Conquest of Cool: Business Culture, Counterculture and the Rise of Hip Consumerism*. Chicago: University of Chicago Press.

Fraser, N. (2003) 'From discipline to flexibilization? Rereading Foucault in the shadow of globalization', *Constellations*, 10(2): 160–71.

Freeman, J. (1977) 'The publicity of the Empire Marketing Board 1926–1933', *Journal of Advertising History*, 1: 12–14.

Frow, J. (1997) *Time and Commodity Culture: Essays in Cultural Theory and Postmodernity*. Oxford: Clarendon Press.

Gabriel, Y. and Lang, T. (1995) *The Unmanageable Consumer: Contemporary Consumption and its Fragmentation*. London: Sage.

Game, A. (1991) *Undoing the Social: Towards a Deconstructive Sociology*. Maidenhead: Open University Press.

Gardiner, J. (1976) 'The political economy of domestic labour in capitalist society', in D. Barker and S. Allen (eds), *Dependence and Exploitation in Work and Marriage*. Harlow: Longman.

Geddes, B. (1934) *Horizons*. London: John Lane.

Gibson, O. (2005) L'Oréal pulls TV ads after ruling. *Guardian Unlimited*. http://www. guardian. co.uk/uk_news/story/0.1550401.00.html.

Giddens, A. (1979) 'Central problems in social theory', In *Action, Structure and Contradiction in Social Analysis*. Basingstoke: Macmillan.

Giddens A. (1993) *Modernity and Self Identity*. Cambridge: Polity Press.

Giddens, A. (1994) 'Living in a post-traditional society', in U. Beck, A. Giddens and S. Lash (eds), *Reflexive Modernisation: Politics, Tradition and Aesthetics in the Modern Social Order*, Cambridge: Polity Press, pp. 56–109.

Gigerenzer, G. Swijtink, Z. Porter, T. Daston, L. Beatty, J. and Kruger, L. (1989) *The Empire of Chance: How Probability Changed Science and Everyday Life.* Cambridge: Cambridge University Press.

Girard, L. and Mulard, C. (2004) 'Fighting the battle against age', *Guardian Weekly.* 10 September http://www.guardian.co.uk/guardianweekly/story/0.1301015.00.html.

Gitlin, T. (1989) 'Postmodernism: Roots and Politics', in I. Angus and S. Jhally (eds), *Cultural Politics in Contemporary America.* New York: Routledge.

Gittins, D. (1994) *The Family in Question: Changing Households and Familiar Ideologies.* Basingstoke: Macmillan.

Gleick, J. (1998) *Chaos: the Amazing Science of the Unpredictable.* London: Vintage.

Goldman, R. (1983–1984) 'Capitalist development and the development of leisure', *Social Text,* 8: 84–103.

Goldman, R. (1987) *Social Text.,* 'Marketing fragrances: advertising and the production of commodity signs', *Theory, Culture & Society,* 4(4): 691–726.

Goldman, R. (1994) 'Contradictions in a political economy of sign value', *Current Perspectives in Social Theory,* 14: 183–211.

Goldman, R. (1995) *Reading Ads Socially.* London: Routledge.

Goldman, R. (2003) 'A theoretical sketch of the history of commodity-signs', http://www.lclark.edu/~goldman/contradictions/poleconsv4.html.

Gordon, C. (1980) 'Michel Foucault: power/knowledge', in *Selected Interviews and Other Writings 1972–1977.* Hemel Hempstead: Harvester Press.

Gorz, A. (1976) *Division of Labour: The Labour Process and Class Struggle in Modern Capitalism.* Hassocks: Harvester.

Gorz, A. (1980) *Ecology Politics.* London: Pluto Press.

Gorz., A. (1983) *Ecology Politics.* London: Pluto Press.

Gorz, A. (1989) *Critique of Economic Reason.* London: Verso.

Gorz, A. (1994) *Capitalism, Socialism, Ecology.* London: Verso.

Gorz, A. (1999) *Reclaiming Work: Beyond the Wage-Based Society.* Cambridge: Polity Press.

Goss, J. (1995) 'We know who you are and we know where you live: the instrumental rationality of geodemographics', *Economic Geography,* 71: 171–98.

Graham, P. (2000) 'Hypercapitalism: a political economy of informational idealism', *New Media and Society,* 12: 131–56.

Gregson, N. (1997) 'On duality and dualism: the case of structuration and time geography', in C. Bryant and D. Jary (eds), *Giddens' Theory of Structuration: A Critical Appreciation.* London: Routledge.

Grimshaw, J. (1993) *Philosophy and Feminist Thinking.* Minneapolis, MN: University of Minnesota Press.

Gunter, B. and Furnham, A. (1992) *Consumer Profiles: An Introduction to Psychographics.* London: Routledge.

Hacking, I. (1990) *The Taming of Chance.* Cambridge: Cambridge University Press.

Hackley, C. (2002) 'The panoptic role of advertising agencies in the production of consumer culture', *Consumption Markets and Cultures,* 5(3): 211–29.

Hall, S. and Jacques, H. (1989) *New Times.* London: Lawrence and Wishart.

Harper, J. (2000) '"Rich Media" mixes news, ads and entertainment', *Insights,* 7 August, p. 31.

Harvey, D. (1990) *The Condition of Postmodernity: An Inquiry into the Origins of Cultural Change.* Oxford: Basil Blackwell.

Harvey, D. (2001) 'Time–space compression and the rise of modernism as a cultural force', in F. Lechner and J. Boli (eds), *The Globalization Reader.* Oxford: Blackwell.

Hassard, J. (1990) *The Sociology of Time.* Basingstoke: Macmillan.

Hassard, J. (2001) 'Commodification, construction and compression: a review of time metaphors in organizational analysis', *International Journal of Management Reviews,* 3(2): 131–40.

Haug, W. (1986) *Critique of Commodity Aesthetics: Appearance, Sexuality, and Advertising in Capitalist Society.* Trans. R. Bock. Minneapolis: University of Minnesota Press.

Hawking, S. and Mlodinow, L. (2005) *A Briefer History of Time.* London: Bantam Press.

Heidegger, M. (1962) *Being and Time*, trans. J. Macquarrie and E. Robinson. Oxford: Blackwell.

Hekman, S. (1990) *Gender and Knowledge: Elements of a Postmodern Feminism*. Cambridge: Polity Press.

Hellmund, M. (2001) 'Convergence: WebTV versus interactive digital TV or Internet, TV and humans', www.mitbiz.de/gallery/publications/convergence.doc.

Hemingway, J. (1996) 'Emancipating leisure: the recovery of freedom in leisure', *Journal of Leisure Research.*, 28(1): 27–43.

Hendra, C. (2003) 'The next new new thing: brand storytelling 24x7x365', http://www.ogilvy.com/viewpoint/pdf/v5_hendra.pdf.

Henley Centre (2001) 'Tired of feeling pushed for time?' London: Henley Centre.

Hepburn, A. and Daiches, D. (1959) *Robert Burns: Poems and Selected Letters*. Glasgow: Collins.

Herman, E. and McChesney, R. (1997) *The Global Media: The New Missionaries of Global Capitalism*. London: Cassell.

Hernes, H. (1987) *Welfare State and Woman Power: Essays in State Feminism*. Oslo: Norwegian University Press.

Heydebrand, W. (2003) 'The time dimension in Marxian social theory', *Time and Society*, 12(2/3): 147–89.

Hindley, D. and Hindley, G. (1972) *Advertising in Victorian England, 1837–1901*. London: Wayland Publishers.

Hirschman, E. (1987) 'Theoretical perspectives of time use: implications for consumer behaviour research', *Research in Consumer Behaviour*, 2: 55–81.

Holloway, J. (1992) 'Crisis, fetishism, class composition', in W. Bonefeld, R. Gunn, and K. Psychopedis (eds), *Open Marxism*. London: Pluto.

Holstein, J. and Gubrium, J. (2000) *The Self We Live By: Narrative Identity in a Postmodern World*. Oxford: Oxford University Press.

Howard, D.T. (1932) *The Psychology of Advertising by Walter Dill Scott*. London: Sir Isaac Pitman and Sons Ltd.

Howard, J. and J. Sheth (1969) *The Theory of Buyer Behaviour*. New York: John Wiley and Sons.

Hume, D. ([1739]1967) *A Treatise of Human Nature*; ed. L.A. Selby-Bigge. Oxford: Clarendon Press.

Husserl, E. (1928) *The Phenomenology of Internal Time-Consciousness*, (ed.) M. Heidegger, trans. J. Churchill. Bloomington, IN: Indiana University Press.

Ingold, T. (1993) 'The temporality of landscape', *World Archaeology*, 25: 152–74.

Jackson P. and Thrift, N. (1995) 'Geographies of consumption', in D. Miller (ed.), *Acknowledging Consumption: A Review of New Studies*. London: Routledge.

Jacobs, M. (1998) *Sigmund Freud*. London: Sage.

Jameson, F. (1985) 'Postmodernism and consumer society', in H. Foster (ed.), *Postmodern Culture*. Wiltshire: Pluto, pp. 111–26.

Jameson, F. (1992) *Postmodernism; or the Cultural Logic of Late Capitalism*. London: Verso.

Jenkins, A. (1994) 'Just-in-time "regimes" and reductionism', *Sociology*, 28(1): 21–30.

Jhally, S. (1987) *The Codes of Advertising*. London: Routledge.

Johnson, I. (2002) 'Interactive TV advertising: a worldwide perspective', *Admap*, June: 36–8.

Kannan, P., Chang, A., and Whinston, A., (2001) 'Wireless commerce: marketing issues and possibilities', in *Proceedings of the 34th Hawaii International Conference on System Sciences*.

Kates, S. and Shaw-Garlock, G. (1999) 'The ever entangling web: a study of ideologies and discourses in advertising to women', *Journal of Advertising*, 28(2): 33–49.

King, A. (1998) 'A critique of Baudrillard's hyperreality: towards a sociology of postmodernism', *Philosophy and Social Criticism*, 24(6): 47–66.

King, M. (2000) 'Make love, not work: new management theory and the social self', *Radical History Review*, 76: 15–24.

Kline & Company (2004) *Global Cosmetics and Toiletries*. Kline. http://www.klinegroup.com/reports/y559.asp.

Kline, S. and Leiss, W. (1978) 'Advertising needs and commodity fetishism', *Canadian Journal of Political and Social Theory*, 2: 5–21.

Knights, D. (1997) 'Governmentality and financial services welfare crisis and the financial self-disciplined subject', in G. Morgan and D. Knights (eds), *Deregulation and Regulation in European Financial Services.* London: Palgrave.

Knights, D. and Odih, P., (2002) '"Big Brother is watching you!": call centre surveillance and the time disciplined subject', G. Crow and S. Heath (eds), *Social Conceptions of Time: Structure and Process in Work and Everyday Life.* London: Palgrave Macmillan.

Knights, D. with assistance of Tinker, T., (1988) Risk, Financial Self-discipline and Commodity Relations: An Analysis of the Growth and Development of Life Insurance in Contemporary Capitalism', *Advances in Public Interest Accounting,* 2: 47–69.

Knights, D. and Vurdubakis, T. (1993) 'Calculations of risk: towards an understanding of insurance as a moral and political technology", *Accounting Organisation and Society,* 19(718): 729–64.

Krishnan, S. and Trappey, C. (1999) 'Nonconscious memory processes in marketing: a historical perspective and future directions', *Psychology and Marketing,* 16(6): 451–7.

Krugman, H. (1966–1967) 'The measurement of advertising involvement', *The Public Opinion Quarterly,* 30(4): 583–96.

Kunde, J. (2000) *Corporate Religion: Building a Strong Company Through Personality and Corporate Soul.* London: Prentice Hall.

Lane, R. (2000) *Jean Baudrillard.* London: Routledge.

Larrain, J., (1989) *Theories of Development: Capitalism, Colonialism and Dependency.* Cambridge: Polity Press.

Lash, S. and Urry, J. (1987) *The End of Organized Capitalism.* Cambridge: Polity Press.

Lash, S. and Urry, J. (1994) *Economies of Signs and space.* London: Sage.

Lee, M. (1993) *Consumer Culture Reborn: The Cultural Politics of Consumption.* London: Routledge.

Lefebvre, H. (1991) *The Production of Space,* trans. D.Nicholson-Smith. Oxford: Basil Blackwell.

Lee, M. (1993) *Consumer Culture Roborn: The Cultural Politics of Consumption.* London: Routledge.

Leiss, W. Kline, S. and Jhally, S. (1990) *Social Communication in Advertising.* London: Routledge.

Leslie, D. (1998) 'Consumer subjectivity, space and advertising research', *Environment and Planning,* 31: 1443–57.

Litchford, T. (2001) '"Mobile commerce helps retailers move ahead", Microsoft (2000); SAP and Microsoft join forces to bring business solutions to pocket PCs', http://www. microsoft. com/presspass/press/2000/Apr00/SAPppcPR.mspx.

Lubove, R. (1981) Book review of Zelizer, V. (1979) *Morals and Markets: The Development of Life Insurance in the United States. Journal of American History,* 67(4): 938.

Lury, C. (2004) *Brands: The Logos of the Global Economy.* New York: Routledge.

Luxembury, R. (1971) *The Accumulation of Captial.* London: Routledge and Kegan Paul Ltd.

Lyon, D. (2002) 'Surveillance in cyberspace: the Internet, personal data and social control', *Queen's Quarterly,* 109(3): 345–57.

Macaulay, T.B. (1830) 'Mr Montgomery's Poems and the Modern Practice of Puffing', *Edinburgh Review,* April, 51: 193–210.

MacCannell, D. (1999) *The Tourist: A New Theory of the Leisure Class,* 2nd edn. Berkeley, CA: University of California Press.

Macpherson, C.B. (1962) *The Political Theory of Possessive Individualism.* Oxford: Clarendon Press.

Maddison, A. (1987) 'Growth and slowdown in advanced capitalist economics: techniques of quantitative assessment', *Journal of Economic Literature,* 35: 650.

MapInfo (2001) *Getting Started with MapInfo.* Berkshire: MapInfo Corporation.

MapInfo (2005a) *MapInfo Retail: Harness the Power of Predictive Analytics.* Berkshire: MapInfo Corporation.

MapInfo (2005b) *TargetPro: The Geo-Demographic Analysis Solution for Better Business Intelligence.* Berkshire: MapInfo Corporation.

MapInfo (2006) *MapInfo Corporation* www.mapinfo.co.uk/products/geo.cfm.

Marchand, R. (1985) *Advertising the American Dream*. Berkeley, CA: University of California Press.

Marx, K. (1967) *Essential Writings of Karl Marx*, ed. D. Caute. London: Panther.

Marx, K. (1971) *Critique of Political Economy*. Chicago: Charles Kerr Publishing.

Marx, K. (1973) *Grundrisse: Introduction to the Culture of the Critique of Political Economy*. Harmondsworth: Penguin Books.

Marx, K. (1983) *Capital Vol. 1*. London: Lawrence and Wishart.

Mason, R. (1995) 'Interpersonal effects on consumer demand in economic theory and marketing thought, 1890–1950', *Journal of Economic Issues*, 24(3): 871–81.

Mathew, I. (2005) *Review of 2005 Trends Presentations*. http://www.in-cosmetics.com/page.cfm/link=25.

McCracken, G. (1990) 'Culture and consumer behaviour', *Journal of the Market Research Society*, 32(1): 3–11.

McFall, L. (2002) 'What about the old cultural intermediaries? An historical review of advertising producers', *Cultural Studies*, 16(4): 532–52.

McIntyre, R. (1992) 'Consumption in contemporary capitalism: beyond Marx and Veblen', *Review of Social Economy*, 50(1): 40–60.

McLuhan, M. (1997) *Understanding Media: The Extension of Man*. London: Routledge.

Meek, R. (1979) *Studies in the Labour Theory of Value*. London: Lawrence and Wishart.

Michael, R.T. and Becker, G.S. (1973) 'On the new theory of consumer behavior', *Swedish Journal of Economics*, 75: 378–96.

Michman, R. (1991) *Lifestyle Market Segmentation*. New York: Praeger.

Miller, G. (1962) *Psychology: The Science of Mental Life*. Middlesex: Penguin.

Miller, P. and Rose, N. (1997) 'Mobilizing the consumer: assembling the subject of consumption', *Theory, Culture & Society*, 14(1): 1–36.

Mintel (2005) *Women's Bodycare Products – UK – April 2005*. London: Mintel International Group Ltd Market Research and Consumer Intelligence.

Mintel (2004) *Skincare UK*. London: Mintel International Group Ltd Market Research and Consumer Intelligence.

Mitchell, A. (2002) *Right Side Up: Building Brands in the Age of the Organized Consumer*. London: HarperCollins.

Montgomery, J. (1968) *1900: The End of an Era*. London: George Allen and Unwin Ltd.

Morley, D. and K.Robins (1995) *Spaces of Identity: Global Media, Electronic Landscapes and Cultural Boundaries*. London: Routledge.

Morse, M. (1990) 'An ontology of everyday distraction: the freeway, the mall and television', P. Mellencamp (ed.), *Logics of Television: Essays in Cultural Criticism*. London: BFI Publishing.

Mort, F. (1988) 'Boys Own? Masculinity, style and popular culture', in R. Chapman and J. Rutherford (eds) *Male Order: Unwrapping Masculinity*. London: Lawrence and Wishart.

Mumford, L. (1955) 'The monastery and the clock', in *The Human Prospect*, Boston: Beacon Press.

Murray, A. (1998) *Who's Who in Mythology*. Middlesex: Senate Press.

Nevett, T. (1982) *Advertising in Britain: A History*. London: Heinemann.

Nickel, D. (1998) 'Director's Foreword', in *Picturing Modernity*. San Francisco: The San Francisco Museum of Modern Art.

Nowotny, H. (1976) 'Time structuring and time measurement: on the interrelation between time keepers and social time', in J. T. Fraser and N. Lawrence (eds), *The Study of Time 2*. New York: Springer Verlag.

O'Barr, W.M. (1994) *Culture and the Ad: Exploring Otherness in the World of Advertising*. Boulder, CO: Westview Press.

O'Connell, S. (1998) *The Car in British Society: Class, Gender and Motoring, 1896–1939*. Manchester: Manchester University Press.

O'Connor, J. (1974) *The Corporations and the State: Essays in the Theory of Capitalism and Imperialism*. New York: Harper & Row.

Odih, P. (1998) 'Gendered time and financial services consumption', PhD thesis, UMIST, Manchester. United Kingdom.

Odih, P. (1999a) 'The women's market: marketing fact or apparition?', *Consumption, Markets and Culture*, 3(2): 165–93.

Odih, P. (1999b) 'Gendered time in the age of deconstruction', *Time and Society*, 8(1): 9–39.

O'Farrell, C. (1989) *Foucault: Historian or Philosopher?* Hampshire: Macmillan.

Offe, C. and Ronge, V. (1984) 'Theses on the theory of the state', in C. Offe (ed.), *Contradictions of the Welfare State*. London: Hutchinson.

Ogilvy, D. (1965) *Confessions of an Advertising Man*. London: Longmans.

O'Malley, P. (2002) 'Imagining insurance: risk, thrift and life insurance in britain', in T. Baker and J. Simon (eds), *Embracing Risk: The Changing Culture of Insurance and Responsibility*. Chicago: The University of Chicago Press.

Ovid (1904) *Metamorphoses*, Book XV, trans. A. Golding. Carbondale, IL: University of Southern Illinois.

Parker, M. and Slaughter, J. (1988) *Choosing Sides: Unions and the Team Concept: A Labor Notes Book*. Boston: South End Press.

Pawley, M. Winstone, D. and Bentley, P. (1991) *UK Financial Institutions and Markets*. Hampshire: Macmillan.

Peirce, C.S. ([1892] 1937) *The Doctrine of Necessity Examined. The Monist*, 2(3): 321–37.

Pietrykowski, B. (1999) 'Beyond the Fordist/post-Fordist dichotomy: working through the Second Industrial Divide', *Review of Social Economy*, 57(2): 177–98.

Piore, M. and Sable, C. (1984) *The Second Industrial Divide: Possibilities for Prosperity*. New York: Basic Books.

Pollard, S. (1965) 'The adaptation of the labour force', in S. Pollard (ed.), *The Genesis of Modern Management*. London: Edward Arnold.

Poole, R. (1985) 'Morality, masculinity and the market', *Radical Philosophy*, No. 39, Princeton, NJ: Princeton University Press.

Pope, D. (1983) *The Making of Modern Advertising*. New York: Basic Books.

Postma, P. (1999) *The New Marketing Era: Marketing to the Imagination in a Technology-Driven World*. New York: McGraw-Hill.

Poster, M. (1995) *The Second Media Age*. Cambridge: Cambridge University Press.

Poster, M. (1998) *Jean Baudrillard: Selected Writings*. Cambridge: Polity.

Preston, G. (1971) *Advertising*. London: Batsford.

Proctor, S. Proctor, T. and Papasolomou-Doukakis, I. (2002) 'A post-modern perspective on advertisements and their analysis', *Journal of Marketing Communications*, 8: 31–44.

Quinones, R. (1972) *The Renaissance Discovery of Time*. Cambridge, MA: Harvard University Press.

Raney, A. Arpan, L. Pashupati, K. and Brill, D. (2003) 'At the movies, on the Web; an investigation of the effects of entertaining and interactive Web content on site and brand evaluations', *Journal of Interactive Marketing*, 17(4): 38–53.

Richardson, D. (1993) *Women, Motherhood and Child Rearing*. Basingstoke: Macmillan.

Richardson, T. (1991) *The Commodity Culture of Victorian England: Advertising and Spectacle, 1851–1914*. London: Verso.

Rifkin, J. (1996) *The End of Work: The Decline of the Global Labour Force and the Dawn of the Post-Market Era*. New York: Tarcher Putman.

Riffaterre, M. (1990) 'Compulsory reader response: the intertextual drive', in M. Worton and J. Still (eds), *Intertextuality: Theories and Practice*. Manchester: Manchester University Press, pp. 58–78.

Roberts, K. (1976) *Contemporary Society and the Growth of Leisure*. London: Longman.

Roberts, P. (1976) *Any Colour As Long as It's Black*. London: David & Charles.

Robins, K. and Webster, F. (1999) *Times of the Technoculture: From the Information Society to the Virtual Life*. London: Routledge.

Robinson, J. (2005) 'Time heals all dotcom wounds', *The Observer*. http://media.guardian.co.uk/newmedia/story/0..1604501.00.html.

Rodaway, P. (1996) 'Exploring the subject in hyper-reality', in S. Pile and N. Thrift (eds), *Mapping the Subject*. London: Routledge.

Rosaldo, R. (1989) *Culture and Truth*. Boston: Beacon Press.

Rose, M. (1975) *Industrial Behaviour: Theoretical Development Science*. Middlesex: Taylor and Francis.

Sampson, H. (1874) *A History of Advertising: From the Earliest Times*. London: Chatto and Windus.

Sarup, M. (1998) *Identity Culture and the Postmodern World*. Edinburgh: Edinburgh University Press.

Sayer, D. (1989) *Readings from Karl Marx*. London: Routledge.

Seccombe, W. (1973) 'The housewife and her labour under capitalism', *New Left Review*, 83(January–February): 3–24; http://www.newleftreview.net/Issue182.asp?Article=01.

Sheppard, D. (1983) *Bias to the Poor*. London: Hodder and Stoughton.

Sherman, C. and Price, G. (2001) *The Invisible Web; Uncovering Information Sources Search Engines Can't See*. Medford, NJ: Information Today, Inc.

Sheth, J. and Gardner, M. (1986) 'History of marketing thought: an update', in J. Sheth and D. Garrett (eds), *Marketing Theory: Classic and Contemporary Readings*. Cincinnati, OH: South-Western Publishing Co.

Shields, R. (1992) *Lifestyle Shopping: The Subject of Consumption*. London: Routledge.

Slater, D. (1998) 'Work/leisure', in C. Jenks (ed.), *Core Sociological Dichotomies*. London: Sage.

SMART (2005) 'Market segmentation. Strategic Marketing and Research Techniques'; www.S-M-A-R-T.com.

Somers, M. (1992) 'Narrativity, narrative identity and social action: rethinking English working-class formation', *Social Science History*, 16(4): 591–630.

Spencer, G. (1996) 'Microcybernetics as the meta-technology of pure control', in Z. Sardar and J. Ravetz (eds), *Cyberfutures*. London: Pluto, pp. 42–61.

Stalson, J. (1942) *Marketing Life Insurance: Its History in America*. Cambridge, MA: Harvard University Press.

Stern, J. and Stern, M. (1978) *Auto Ads*. New York: Random House.

Steuer, J. (1992) 'Defining virtual reality: dimensions determining telepresence', *Journal of Communications*, 42(4): 73–93.

Stuart, R. (1889) 'Letters from the Lake Poets to Daniel Stuart', London. *The History of the Times*, vol., 1 n.d.

Swinfen-Green, J. (2002) 'Broadband: the advertising opportunity', *Admap*, March: 43–46.

Taylor, F. (1911) *The Principles of Scientific Management*. New York: Harper and Brothers.

Thomas, J. (1997) *Time, Culture and Identity: An Interpretive Archaeology*. London: Routledge.

Thompson, E.P. (1967) 'Time work discipline and industrial capitalism', *Past and Present*, 38: 56–97.

Tribe, M. (1993) *Postmodern Time*. http://mural.uv.es/alulla/defin.html.

Turner, E. (1952) *The Shocking History of Advertising*. London: Michael Joseph.

Urry, J. (1990) *The Tourist Gaze*. London: Sage.

Urry, J. (1995) *Consuming Places*. London: Routledge.

Urry, J. (2005) 'The complexities of the global', *Theory, Culture & Society*, 22(5): 235–54.

VEBLEN, T. ([1899] 1994) *The Theory of the Leisure Class*. New York: Modern Library.

Venkatesh, A. (1999) 'Postmodern perspectives for macromarketing: an inquiry into the global information and sign economy', *Journal of Macromarketing*, 19(12): 1–28.

Venkatesh, A., Meamber, L. and Firat, F. (1998) 'Cyberspace as the next marketing frontier(?): Questions and issues', in S. Brown and D. Turley (eds), *Consumer Research: Postcards from the Edge*. London: Routledge.

Wearing, B and Wearing, S. (1992) 'Identity and the commodification of leisure', *Leisure Studies*, 11: 3–18.

Webb, T. (2006) 'The blurred vision of 3G', *The Independent on Sunday*, 12 February, pp. 6–7.

Weedon, C. (1992) *Feminist Practice and Post-Structuralist Theory*. Oxford: Blackwell.

Wheale, N. (1995) *The Postmodern Arts: An Introductory Reader*. London: Routledge.

Whitrow, G.J. (1989) *Time in History*. Oxford: Oxford University Press.

Williams, R. (1980) 'Advertising: the magic system', in *Problems in Materialism and Culture*. London: Verso.

Williamson, A. (1993) 'Forms of simultaneity in The Waste Land and Burnt Norton', in R. Bush (ed.), *T.S. Eliot: The Modernist in History*. Cambridge: Cambridge University Press.

Williamson, J. ([1978] 2000) *Decoding Advertisements*. London: Marion Boyars Publishers.

Willis, P. (2000) *The Ethnographic Imagination*. Cambridge: Cambridge University Press.

Winship, J. (1980) 'Sexuality for sale', in S. Hall et al. (eds), *Culture, Media and Language*. London: Hutchinson & Co.

Wolf, W. (1996) *Car Mania: A Critical History of Transport*. London: Pluto.

Wright. L. (2000) 'Wireless Application Protocol, WAP', *Interactive Marketing*, 2(2): 148–57.

Yuan, S. and Tsao, Y. (2003) 'A recommendation mechanism for contextualised mobile advertising', *Expert Systems with Applications* 24: 399–414.

Zaretsky, E. (1976) *Capitalism, the Family and Personal Life*. London: Pluto Press.

Zelizer, V. (1983) *Morals and Markets: The Development of Life Insurance in the United States*. New Brunswick, NJ: Transactions Books.

ZenithOptimedia (2005) 'Ad growth stable with healthy hotspots', http://www.zenithoptimedia.com/gff/pdf/Adspend%20December%2005.pdf.

ZenithOptimedia (2006) Press Release: World Cup to boost adspend growth in 2006. http://www.zenithoptimedia.com.

Index

Entries in *italics* denote publications, films and foreign-language terms.

ABAA *see* Association of British Advertising Agencies
abreaction 99
absolute surplus value 83, 145
abstract art 45–6
abstract labour 79–80
abstraction 137, 138, 146
abundance culture 40–1
academic articles 32–3
actuarial tables 182
Adam, B. 15
Addis advertisements 123
Adventurer 32, 34
Advertiser's Review 36
advertising discourse 12–14
advertising psychology *see* psychology
Advertising Regulation Act 1907 31
Advertising Standards Authority (ASA) 131
advertising stations 24, 29
aesthetics 148, 155–9, 164–9
AGA cooker advertisement 91
ageing 130–9
agencies 37–8, 48–9
agriculture 24, 83
alienation 82
Allport, Henry Floyd 93
altruism 64, 66
America *see* United States
Amicable insurance company 68
Andrejevic, M. 9, 172–3, 202
Andrew Irving Associates 181
anti-ageing products 130–9
Armstrong-Siddeley Sapphire 156–7
art
    abstractionism 45–6
    photography as 114
    see also aesthetics
art nouveau 154–5
ASA *see* Advertising Standards Authority
assembly-line production *see* Fordism
Association of British Advertising Agencies (ABAA) 37, 49
Audit Bureau of Circulations 37

automation 102
    see also Fordism
AXA PPP healthcare 183–4

Barnes, S. 201
Barratt, T.J. 40
Bartels, R. 208
Baudrillard, J. 5–6, 112, 128–9, 187–8, 196–200, 206
Bauman, Z. 15–16, 159, 164
behavioural theories 11, 92, 95, 127–8
billboard advertising 24, 27–31
biological discourses 133
Blair, M. 168
book advertising 33
Boorstin, D. 42–3
brands 160–4, 199, 209–10
Braverman, H. 150
Brierley, Sean 127–8
British Empire *see* imperialism
broadband Internet 203
brokers, insurance 67
Burns, Robert 192
business communities 85–7, 90
Business Insights Inc. 171
buyers *see* consumers

Canon advertisements 107
capitalism 1–4, 207–10
    commodity-form 77–92
    desire creation 128–30
    domestic labour time 116–22
    insurance 70–2
    leisure time 145–70
    monopoly 26–40
    objects 112–13, 196
    'other' non-Western spaces 40–8
    postmodernity 6, 15–16
    selling-spaces 48
    time consciousness 58
cars *see* motor cars
Cartesian subject 199
    see also Descartes, René

case studies
  cosmetics industry 130–9
  women's market 181–6
Castells, M. 15, 210
cathexis 99–100
censorship 30, 35
chance 52–61
Chanel advertisements 132
chaos theory 17
charity relief 63, 72
childhood 134
chronology 193
Chrysler advertisements 146–7
Church, R. 154
cinema 124–5
circulation
  capital 88–9
  newspapers 31–2, 34–5, 36–7
class 121
  see also middle classes; working classes
Classical era 190, 192–3
cleanliness 121–2
Clinique advertisements 135
clock-time 16, 79, 84, 101
'closure' 100, 139
cluster analysis 175
collage 197
colonialism see imperialism
column rules, newspapers 27, 39–40
commercialism 122–6
commodity culture 21, 41–2
commodity fetishism 77, 81–2
commodity-form 14, 17, 77–104,
    113, 149
commodity relations 51, 72–3
commodity-signs
  exchange-value 5
  gender 130–9
  leisure 148, 154–9
  modernity 75
  postmodernity 205
  time 13–14, 17, 105–42
competitive capitalism 87, 158
Conant, Sir Nathaniel 57
consciousness 95–6, 98
conspicuous consumption 103–4
constructivism 190
consumers
  brand culture 163
  demand theories 148
  Fordism 102
  mass media 122–6
  motivations 94–101, 103
  post-Fordism 4–5
  social/symbolic 126–30

consumers cont.
  subjectivity 8–12, 106, 110, 112, 150,
    189–206, 209
  surveillance 171–86
  time discipline 87–101
  value-for-time 167–9
consumption, definitions 90, 108–10, 112
contractual products 181–2
controls
  display advertising 37–40
  markets 87
  newspaper circulation 36–7
  see also social control
convenience 168
convergent technologies 201–4, 207, 210
copyrighting 39
corporate branding 17–18, 113, 209–10
corporate economy 87–8, 89–90, 208
corporate religion 161–4
cosmetics industry 130–9
counter cultures 164–6
critical theory 145, 148, 154, 170, 172
cultural economy of time 1–19
cultural intermediaries 109, 180–1
cyberspace 201–2

Daily Advertiser 31–2
Dalla Costa, M. 116–19, 121
DamienChrysler advertisements 146–7
Dasein 139
Daston, L. 70
database marketing 172–3, 186
decision-making models 92
decoding symbolic meaning 108
Defoe, Daniel 57, 58
demand theories 148
de-massification 175
derivation 191, 193–4
Descartes, René 45, 59
  see also Cartesian subject
desire creation 92–3, 128–30, 168
determinism 16–17, 59–60
dialectics of advertising 7–10, 75–142
Dichter, Ernest 94, 96, 98–101, 103, 132
differentiation 45, 110, 209
digital media 205–7, 210
Dill Scott, Walter 8, 92, 95–6, 98
Dior advertisements 135
disaccumulation 113
discipline 84–101, 152, 173–86, 207–8
discontinuity 180
displacement 48, 158
display advertising 24, 37–40
disruptions 143, 187–206
dividends, lotteries 54

Dodson, James 69
domestic appliances 9–10, 121–3, 201
domestic labour time 116–23
Douglas, M. 108, 110
Drèze, X. 205

eclecticism 190, 197
economic depression 2, 27, 207
economic exchange 150, 152, 208
economic growth 41, 61, 87–8, 207
economic rationality 153
economies of scale 25, 48, 209
editorial controls 37–40
efficiency, rationality of 66
ego 94–5, 100
eighteenth century
    determinism 59–60
    insurance 51, 55–6, 67–70, 72
    newspaper advertising 31–5
    representation 43–5
Einstein, Albert 16
electronic media 6, 12–14, 19, 207, 210
Eliot, T.S. 1
Empire Marketing Board 45–7
emulation 104
encoding symbolic meaning 108
Enlightenment 43–5, 59, 71–2
environmentalism 173
Equitable Life Assurance Society
    (UK) 69–70
Equitable Life Insurance Company (US) 61
'events' 43, 107–8, 110
everyday life 125–6, 180–1, 188–9
Ewald, F. 51, 73
Ewen, S. 84–5, 87, 89–90, 93
exchange-value
    commodity-form 77–8, 81, 83, 103
    commodity-signs 5, 105, 107–8, 113
    cosmetics advertising 136–7
    Fordism 208–9
    hyper-reality 196
    leisure time 145–6, 170
    social/symbolic consumer 128
    see also economic exchange

Family Goldmine journal 25–6
family unit 9–10, 116–22
Farini's Earthmen 43, 44
'farming' 37–8
Father Time 193
FCUK advertisements 191, 194
femininity 121–2, 133–5
    see also women
feminism 116–22, 193–4
fetishism 77, 81–2

feudalism 79
Fielding, John 33
film 124–5
financial services 181–6
Firat, A. 197
fixed capital 2
'fixing' impressions 98–9
flexibility 17, 164, 209
'fly-by-night' operators 38–9
fly postering 29
Ford advertisements 13, 150–2
Ford, Henry 102, 149
Fordism 3–5, 9, 208–9
    commodity-form 102
    leisure time 149–53, 156, 158–60, 170
    linear time 15–16
    subjectivity 10, 150, 209
    see also post-Fordism
Foucault, Michel 18, 43–4, 140, 172–4,
    177, 179–80
Frank, Thomas 165–6
'free floating' signs 149, 159
freedom 146
Freud, Sigmund 10–11, 94–5, 134

gambling 51–3, 56–8, 60–1, 67–8
Gambling Act 1774 51, 52, 68
GDP growth 88–9, 207
gender 118–19, 123, 130–9, 182–3, 194–5
    see also women
geodemographics 172, 176–7, 179–80
geographic expansion 48
    see also imperialism
Geographic Information Systems (GIS)
    172, 177–80
geography literature 110
Giddens, A. 110, 140, 188
Gilded Age of insurance 51, 61–6, 71
GIS see Geographic Information Systems
Gittins, Diana 121
globalization 15–16, 207–11
Goldman, R. 14, 128, 131, 138
Gorz, A. 153, 161
Goss, J. 172, 179–80
government censorship 35
government lotteries 53, 56
Great Depression 2, 207
Greek mythology 193
guaranteed newspaper circulations 36–7
guilds 63

Halifax Building Society 181
Harvey, D. 4, 158
Harvey Nichols advertisements 198
health insurance 51, 182–4

Heidegger, M. 139
Hemingway, J. 148
Hendra, Carla 167–9
Henley Centre 167
hermeneutics 190
Hernes, H. 183
hoardings, bill-posting 29–30
Hodges, William 43
home as advertising site 9
  see also domestic...
housework *see* domestic labour time
Howard, D.T. 98–9
human management 85
Hume, David 59–60
hyper-reality 5–6, 187–9, 196–200,
  206, 209

id 95, 96
identity
  brands 160–2
  consumption 110, 112
  modernity 188–9
  recognition 129
  women 116, 121–2
  see also 'self'
illustrated advertisements 36, 39–40, 105
Illustrated London News 36
imperialism 24–5, 40–8
Incorporated Society of Advertising
  Agencies (ISAA) 49
Indecent Advertisement Act 1889 30
individualism 70–2, 185
industrial capitalism 1–2
  domestic labour 117–18
  insurance 70
  labour time 58, 83
  representation 196
  time discipline 85–7
  see also capitalism
industrialization 23–6, 34–5, 48, 79,
  145, 208
informationalism 210
'ingenious' technique 98
Institute of Motivational Research 94
insurance 50–73, 208
  chance 52–61
  lotteries 53–61
  prudence 61–70
  women's market 182–4
interactivity 200–6
Internet 168–9, 177, 200–6
'intertext' 193
ISAA *see* Incorporated Society of
  Advertising Agencies
Isherwood, B. 108, 110

James, S. 116–19, 121
Jameson, F. 194, 196, 197
Johnson, Mr 33–4
Joint Censorship Committee 30
Joyce, James 124
'judicial' technique 98–9
just-in-time systems 159–60,
  168, 209

kaizen 17
Kannan, P. 202
knowledge 34–5, 43–4
Kunde, Jesper 18, 160–4

labour/labour time
  domestic 9–10, 116–23
  Fordism 4
  industrial capitalism 58, 83
  interactivity 206
  postmodernity 15–16
  subjectivity 164–9
  value 2–3, 12, 77–84, 101, 104,
    119–21, 135–6
  see also work time
labour power
  definition 80
  reproduction of 120
  social/symbolic consumer 130
Lambert, Daneau 57
Lancôme advertisements 136
Land Rover advertisements 165, 166
landscape 44–5
language 160–1, 210
Laplace, P.S. 17
lean production 17, 102, 159, 160
legislation
  gambling 60, 68
  insurance 51–2, 55–6
  street advertising 29–31
  television advertising 125
  see also regulation
leisure/leisure time 17–18
  commodity-signs 154–9
  post-Fordism 159–69
  transformations 145–70
liberalism 71–2
life insurance 51, 52–3, 64–71, 73
lifestyle research 12–14, 127–8, 182–3
linear time 15–16
Lloyd's 53, 68
location-based advertising 168–9, 201
Lombard merchants 23
London 25–6, 31–2, 49, 55
London Bill-Posters Association 30
L'Oréal case study 131–8

lottery insurance 53–61
Lyon, D. 173

Macaulay, Thomas Babington 33
MacCannell, D. 45
McFall, L. 33
McLuhan, M. 124–6, 205
magazines 114
    see also media advertising
The Manchurian Candidate (film) 101
manufacturers 26, 89–90, 113–14
MapInfo 172, 177–9
mapping subjects 171–86
maps 196
Marchand, Roland 94
maritime insurance 52, 67
market economies 88
    see also markets
marketing 18–19
    consumer surveillance 172–86
    Fordism 152–3
    insurance 64–7
    interactivity 205
    need creation 152, 167–8
    subjectivity 188
    twentieth century 126–8
    women's market 181–6
marketing mix 4, 126–7
markets
    commodity fetishism 82
    control 87
    creation 90
    leisure time 145, 153
    nineteenth century 26
    saturation 88–9
    segmentation 175–6, 179–80
Marx, Karl/Marxism
    commodity-form 77–82, 84,
        87–8, 101–3
    commodity-signs 116–22
    labour time 2, 12
    leisure time 148
    postmodernity 172, 196
masculinity 133–5
mass intellectuality 161
mass media 122–6
mass production 23–4
    aesthetics 155–6, 158
    domestic appliances 121–3
    gender segregation 118–19
    leisure 149–54
    time-disciplined consumers 87–101
    see also Fordism
materialism 73, 81
    see also objects

mathematical insurance calculations 69–70
meaning systems 108–9, 112–13, 128
meaning transfer 57, 180, 185–6, 189
'mechanical' technique 98
media advertising 122–6, 127–8, 199
    see also newspapers; radio
        advertising; television
Medieval era see Middle Ages
medium as message 200–6
memory 98–9, 138
men see gender; masculinity
message, medium as 200–6
Metropolitan Paving Acts 29–30
Microsoft 202
Middle Ages 23, 193
middle classes 60, 67, 68, 155
Millais, Sir John Everett 39–40
mimesis 190, 194
Mitchell, Alan 167, 168, 173
mobile commerce 18, 172–3, 201–3,
        205, 210
modernity
    dialectics 7–10, 75–142
    emergence of advertising 21–74
    identity 188–9
    perceptions 51
    power 171
    subjectivity 199, 200
    time 3, 6–7, 14–16, 18, 209
    transformations 145–70
'moments of truth' 167–9
monopoly capitalism 26–40, 83–4, 145
morality 60, 65–8, 70
Morse, M. 187
Mort, F. 110
mortality tables 69–70
Mortimar, Thomas 55
motherhood 106, 183–5
    see also women
motivation research 94–101, 103,
        179, 205
motor cars 1, 146–70
multi-media culture 189–90, 198, 203–7
multinational corporations 210
Mumford, L. 58
music 199–200
mutual aid 64
Mutual Life Insurance Company of
        New York 65

narratives 14, 124, 139–40, 188
national markets 89–91
National Society... see Society...
nature 192–3
needs/need creation 34, 92, 152, 167–8

neo-classical theories 148, 150, 153
network society 15, 173
Nevett, T. 26, 36, 113
New York Insurance Company 61
newspapers 24, 205
  agency relations 48–9
  editorial controls 37–40
  guaranteed circulations 36–7
  restrictions 27
  Stamp Duty 31–5
Newton, Isaac 16, 57
Nike 5, 197
nineteenth century
  car advertising 154–5
  domestic labour 121–2
  expansion 70–2
  imperialism 25
  industrialization 25–6
  insurance 51–2, 61–70, 73
  newspaper advertising 33, 35–7, 39–40
  street advertising 27–31
  tableau vivant 94
  see also Victorian Britain
NIVEA advertisements 135–6
No 7 advertisements 136
non-Western spaces 40–8
normalization 179
North British and Mercantile Insurance
  Company Ltd 71
Northampton Mercury 35
nostalgia 44–5, 194–6
nuclear family 117

objectification of leisure time 146, 148,
  154, 170
objects
  desire creation 128–9
  positioning 138–9
  psychology of 94–101
  seduction 200
  as signs 196
  symbolic meaning 108–9, 112–13
  see also materialism
Ocean Railway and General Accident
  Assurance Co. Ltd. 30
Oedipus complex 134
Offe, C. 72
Ogilvy, David 14
Olay advertisements 131
Olympus advertisements 115
oligopolies 9
on-line advertising 19
Orwell, George 172, 186
'other' non-Western spaces 40–8
Ovid 192–3

package tours 42–3
panoptic systems 172, 186
Parliamentary reports 55–7
parody 190–4
parsimony culture 90
pastiche 194–6
Patek Philippe advertisements 108–9
pawnbrokers 23
Pears Soap 39–40
pecuniary emulation 104
Peirce, C.S. 59
perfectionism 122
Permanent Health Insurance (PHI)
  182–3, 185
personality traits 10–11
personalization 203
persuasion 33–4
PHI *see* Permanent Health Insurance
photography 114–16, 125
Piore, M. 4
Pope, Alexander 60
Pope, D. 9, 63
popular music 199–200
population growth 24, 25
post-Fordism 4–5, 16–18
  globalization 209–10
  leisure time 148–9, 159–69
  multi-media culture 203, 207
  see also Fordism
posters 45–7
  see also billboard advertising
postmodernity 210–11
  consumer culture 5
  disruptions 187–206
  subjectivity 189–206
  technology 171–86
  time 6, 14–19, 143–206, 209
  transformations 145–70
poverty 63, 70–2
power 171, 174–86
The Primitive Methodist 36
private/public sphere separation
  118–19, 198–9
privatization of domestic labour 116–17
probability calculus 69–70, 73
product life-cycles 102
productive labour 116, 119–20
productivity rates 88–9
Protestant work ethic 83
providentialism 58–9, 64
provincial merchants 25–6
provincial newspapers 34–5, 48–9
prudence 61–70
Prudential PLC advertisements 50, 62
pseudo-events 43

psyche energy 99–100
psychoanalytic theory 99–100, 133–4
psychodynamic discourse 10–12, 96–8,
    100–1, 103
psychographics 95, 127–8
psychology 8, 10–12
    commodity-form 92–4, 103–4
    commodity-signs 127
    of objects 94–101
    postmodern disruptions 205
    public/private sphere separation
        118–19, 198–9
public transport 157
'puffery' 29, 33, 38–9, 53–61

Quantum theory 16

racial differentiation 45
radio advertising 128, 203, 205
Range Rover advertisements 164–7
rationalism 8–9, 12
    decision-making models 92
    insurance 66
    leisure time 169–70
    'other' non-Western spaces 40–8
    probability calculus 69
    utility 90, 148, 149–54
    see also reason-why advertising
real-time advertising 168–9
reality 196–7
    see also hyper-reality
reason-why advertising 8–10, 12, 205
    commodity-form 90–3, 96, 102
    commodity-signs 109–10, 129
recognition of identity 129
recruitment advertisements 61
regulation of advertising 24, 209
    see also legislation
reification 137–8
relative surplus value 83, 84, 145
relativism 15
Renaissance time perceptions 86, 193
representation
    hyper-reality 196–7, 199
    'other' non-Western spaces 43–5
    parody 191, 194
    photography 114–15
repression 96
research methods 125–6, 127–8
retailers 26, 113–14
Riffaterre, M. 193
Rifkin, J. 88
risk analysis 67, 69, 73
risk sharing 52
RoC advertisements 135, 138

Ronge, V. 72
Rosaldo, R. 44–5
Rover advertisements 2
Royal Agricultural Hall World's Fair 41

Saatchi & Saatchi UK 199
Sable, C. 4
Sampson, H. 54–5
saturation of markets 88–9
Saussurean signs 112, 196
SCAPA see Society for Checking the
    Abuses of Public Advertising
schools 86
scientific determinism see determinism
scientific management 149–50
Scott, Walter Dill see Dill Scott, Walter
Screen Advertising Association 124
Seccombe, W. 119–21
Second World War 113, 158
security 63–4, 185
seduction 198–200
segmentation of markets 175–6, 179–80
SEIKO advertisements 111
'self'
    Allport 93
    Enlightenment 59
    narratives 140
    postmodernity 199, 202
    psychology 94–6, 100
    time-space events 110
    see also identity
self-interest 71–3
self-referentialism 194–5, 197, 206, 211
selling
    spaces 23–49
    time 50–73
semiotics 5, 139, 156
    see also signs
sexuality 134–5
Sheila's Wheels 194–5
shopping precincts 187
short-term risk analysis 67
Siemens advertisements 204
sign-values 14, 105–6, 112–13, 129–30
signboards 23
signs 5–6, 43–4
    Classical era 192
    'free floating' 149, 159
    multi-media culture 198, 203–6
    objects as 196
    self-referentialism 194–5, 197, 206, 211
    television advertising 126
    see also commodity-signs;
        semiotics; symbolism
simulacra, orders of 196–8, 200, 206

SMART 175–6
Smith, Adam 72
social commentators 33–4
social consumers 126–30
social control 85–7, 90, 153
social meaning 108
social relations 137
social sciences 86–7
'social time' concept 107, 174–5
Society for Checking the Abuses of Public
    Advertising (SCAPA) 30–1, 49
socio-biological discourse 133
space
    Classical era 192
    commodity-signs 107–8, 110
    determinism 59
    displacement 48, 158
    disruptions 143
    interactivity 200–2
    modernity 3, 6–7, 14–16, 18
    postmodernity 6, 14–19, 145–70, 187
    reason-why advertising 8–9
    selling 23–49
    see also time
spatial multiplexing 204
Spencer, G. 206
spiritual management 162
Stalson, J. 62–3
Stamp Duty 24, 31–5, 36
State see government...
Steel Roll Manufacturing Company 122
streamlining 155–6, 159, 167
street advertising 27–31
    see also billboard advertising
style 75, 116
subconscious 95–6, 98
subjectivity 6, 8–9, 100–1, 104
    commodity-signs 106–8, 110, 112
    Fordism 10, 150, 209
    labour 164–9
    mapping the subject 171–86
    mobilization of 10–12
    modernity 188
    post-Fordism 17–18
    postmodernity 189–206
    reification 137–8
subliminal messages 101
superego 95
suppression 96
Surf advertisements 105–6
surplus value/labour time 78–81, 83–4,
    117–18, 120, 145
    see also labour/labour time
surveillance 171–86
Surveyors of the Pavement 30

symbolic consumers 126–30
symbolic work 189
symbolism 13–14
    car advertising 156–8
    commodity-signs 105, 107–9, 112–13
    cosmetics advertising 136
    everyday life 188–9
    motherhood 183, 185
    style 116
    see also signs
synchronicity 141, 168
synopticism 25

tableau vivant 94
taste 115–16
taxation see Stamp Duty
Taylor, Frederick Winslow 85, 149–50
technical knowledge circulation 34–5
technology
    convergence 201–4, 207, 210
    postmodernity 171–86
telecommunications 202–3
telematics 169
television 13–14, 124–8, 202–3, 206
Television Act 1954 125
temporal... see time
'tension to closure' 100
text, parody 190, 193
textual spaces 206
Thompson, E.P. 58, 83, 85–6, 153
time
    capturing 141
    Classical era 192–3
    commodity-form 77–104
    commodity-signs 14, 105–42
    consciousness 58
    cultural economy of 1–19
    discipline 84–101, 152, 207–8
    displacement 48, 158
    disruptions 143
    gender 130–9
    media advertising 127–8
    modernity 3, 6–7, 14–16, 18, 21–74,
        188, 209
    photographic manipulation 114
    postmodernity 6, 14–19,
        143–206, 209
    psychology 92–4
    reason-why advertising 8–9, 12
    selling 50–73
    utility 91, 101–2
    value of labour 3
    see also labour/labour time
Toshiba advertisements 143
tourism 42–3, 45

towns 24
  see also urbanization
trait factor theory 10
transformations 145–70
'travellers' 43
twentieth century
  car advertising 146, 149, 155
  commodity-signs 105
  domestic labour 122
  economic growth 87–8
  manufacturers 113–14
  marketing 126–8
  'other' non-Western spaces 46–8
  psychodynamic discourse 96–7
twenty-first century consumption 112

unconscious 95, 100
underwriting insurance 67
United Kingdom Bill-Posters Association
  29, 30
United States (US) 61–6, 84–5, 88, 97,
  102, 149
Universal Chronicle 32, 33–4
unproductive labour 116, 119–20
urbanization 25, 26
  see also towns
US *see* United States
use-value 5, 13–14, 77–81, 103,
  119–20, 196
  see also utility
'useful' labour 79–80
utility 75
  advertising discourse 13
  car advertising 146–7
  commodity-signs 105
  rationalism 90, 148, 149–54
  reason-why advertising 12
  time 91, 101–2
  see also use-value

value
  labour time 2–3, 12, 77–84, 101, 104,
    119–21, 135–6
  see also exchange-value; sign-values;
    surplus value...; use-value
value-for-time revolution 167–9
Veblen, Thorstein 103, 104, 148
Venkatesh, A. 197
Victorian Britain 21, 40–8, 208
  see also nineteenth century
virtual worlds 143, 187
vitamin cult 132
Vogue 114

wage labour 120, 153
  see also labour...
Web *see* Internet
Wedgwood, Josiah 86
West, Benjamin 43
Whirlpool advertisements 75
Williams, R. 105
Williamson, J. 138, 139–41
wireless communication 201–2
women
  cosmetics industry 133–5
  domestic labour time 116–22
  marketing case study 181–6
  pastiche 194–5
work time 17, 51, 145–70,
  182, 189
  see also labour/labour time
working classes 84–7

Yeoman, Thomas 35

Zelizer, Viviana Rotman 63–6
Zufrydeni, F. 205

Printed in the United Kingdom
by Lightning Source UK Ltd.
127819UK00001B/163-231/A